THE ACHIEVEMENT OF WALLACE STEVENS

· HARRIET MONROE · MARIANNE MOORE ·
· LLEWELYN POWYS · PAUL ROSENFELD ·
· GORHAM B. MUNSON · MORTON DAUWEN
ZABEL · R. P. BLACKMUR · HOWARD BAKER ·
HI SIMONS · JULIAN SYMONS · J. V. CUNNINGHAM
· MARIUS BEWLEY · DONALD DAVIE · RANDALL
JARRELL · SAMUEL FRENCH MORSE ·
· LOUIS L. MARTZ · MICHEL BENAMOU ·
· GEOFFREY MOORE ·

the ACHIEVEMENT of
WALLACE STEVENS

edited by ASHLEY BROWN

and ROBERT S. HALLER

GORDIAN PRESS
NEW YORK
1973

Originally Published 1962
Reprinted 1973

Acknowledgment is made to Alfred A. Knopf, Inc., for permission to reproduce all quotations from the works of Wallace Stevens, including: *The Collected Poems of Wallace Stevens* (1954); *The Necessary Angel* (1951); and *Opus Posthumous* (1957). Acknowledgment is also made to Alfred A. Knopf, Inc., for permission to quote the passage from Thomas Mann's *Joseph in Egypt* (1938) which appears on page 86 of Howard Baker's essay.

Brown, Ashley, 1923–   ed.
  The achievement of Wallace Stevens.

  Bibliography: p.
  1. Stevens, Wallace, 1879–1955. I. Haller,
Robert S., 1933–   joint ed. II. Title.
[PS3537.T4753Z62 1973]   811'.5'2 [B]   73–5858
ISBN 0–87752–161–1

9-6-73

CONTENTS

THE ACHIEVEMENT OF WALLACE STEVENS

INTRODUCTION

Poetic schools have long been a part of the literary scene. They establish their credo, adopt their new style, vilify the poets of the previous generation, and set to work in hope that their energy will produce the work appropriate to their own time and, paradoxically, more in touch with the true tradition of poetic expression. The reading public is provided with new terms to account for the characteristics of the new poetry. The poets who are identified with these schools can be conveniently classified and analyzed, and frequently, a few years later, conveniently forgotten. Of course, the better poets transcend their critical vocabulary, and thereby grow in stature over the years, requiring new critics to reinterpret them to later generations who are no longer impressed with old concerns. The act of classifying a poet whose continuing worth demonstrates the inadequacy of the labels formerly applied to him is embarrassing and frustrating. If his work is still being read, if his style is exercising an influence on younger poets, if there seem to be new meanings coming from him for later generations, then it is clear that his essence has not been exhausted by the critical "tools" previously available.

The poetic movement known as Imagism has already been neatly classified in literary histories, and the Americans who came under its influence are, for the most part, of purely antiquarian interest. Amy Lowell, Maxwell Bodenheim, John Gould Fletcher, and even H. D. no longer command much of an audience or much critical interest. (Ezra Pound and William Carlos Williams represent something more complex than Imagism.) But Wallace Stevens, contemporary with the Imagists and indeed sometimes associated with them by critics, is being read more and more. The number of books and articles on his work published in the last few years is probably greater than the total which appeared during his lifetime. He had attained a place of importance in twentieth-century literature even before he died, and he continues to serve as a model for younger poets, and to acquire a larger and more appreciative reading public. At the same time, he remains somewhat of an enigma. He has the reputation of being a difficult poet, or a critic's poet.

This book is a project to gather under one cover examples of the attempt to read the enigma, to explicate the difficulty. In one sense, it chronicles Stevens' emergence from the group of poets with whom he was originally associated, and the development of a larger point of view among his critics. It tells the history of a reputation, to borrow the phrase from the title of the essay Hi Simons wrote in the Stevens issue of *The Harvard Advocate* some twenty years ago. It is secondarily a survey of changing critical attitudes, and reflects the poetic climates of the last four decades. But most important, the essays here collected, many of them out of print and hard to come by, are the work of some of our best critical minds. To see a poem in different perspectives is, one hopes, to come closer to a total view of it. Some of these essays treat the same poems, notably "Sunday Morning" and "The Comedian as the Letter C," and so have played upon each other to the point where the reader will feel much more confident of his understanding of these poems. The essays, of course, offer a variety of interpretations of the total *œuvre*, and so by a dialectical and cumulative process finally arrive at what seem like sensible and perceptive estimates, dropping along the way enough insights into particular poems to enrich anyone's reading.

A collection of this sort, however, would be of little use if it did not suggest possibilities for further investigation. For one thing, the trend of the essays over the years has been to move away from a consideration of Stevens' principal theme—the relation of the imagination to reality. Most of the recent essays have taken into account the poems from the later volumes, but have often treated them as further footnotes to *Harmonium*, the volume which still receives the greatest attention. There has been very scant treatment given to the later poems in themselves, and doubtless readers will continue to think of Stevens as the "gaudy" poet of his first volume until the last poems have become familiar enough to talk about comfortably. And finally, in the continuing modification of our ideas about Stevens, the beginnings get lost; one value of this collection is to revive older opinions which are perhaps valid in their own terms, and perhaps need to be reinterpreted for the newer generation. There is a certain amount of truth in the theory that all of the responses of sensitive readers are a part of the meaning of poetry, and so it is part of the job of synthesis to take into account what is essentially true about explications which now seem dated.

Each of these essays, therefore, contains at least a partial truth, and to feel that they no longer apply to the poetry is to deny certain of its effects which were once alive. And so Harriet Monroe's tentative, but admiring, remarks, with which this book begins, are of especial interest. She knew Stevens, and it was during her editorship of *Poetry* that he received his first recognition, winning the 1916 *Poetry* award for a group of poems entitled "Sur Ma Guzzla Gracile." His plays also come from around this time, and, although he was not very happy about them, it is apparent from Miss Monroe's remarks that she and her friends considered them significant events. If Stevens at this point had received equally sympathetic, and perhaps more penetrating, criticism, it might not have been so long after the first *Harmonium* before he ventured once again into the publication of poems.

Unfortunately, though, most of the early criticism stems from an attempt to account for the luxuriance of the surface of the poems, and words like "preciosity" and "dandyism" were to be the terms of Stevens criticism for a decade, drawing attention away from other more important matters. Stevens became the center of a controversy between two poets in *The New Republic* in 1919, and this argument would scarcely have improved his standing in the literary world. When Louis Untermeyer attacked Stevens for his preciosity, Conrad Aiken defended him by defending preciosity, a strategy hardly calculated to establish Stevens as a significant poet. Aiken apparently did not have his heart in his defense, however, for he recorded—in *Skepticisms*, published in the same year—a rather different attitude:

> Whether or not narrative poetry is doomed to decay, we must hope for two sorts of development in the lyric. In one

direction we get the sort of thing Mr. Maxwell Bodenheim, Mr. John Gould Fletcher, and Mr. Wallace Stevens
tentatively indicate for us, a kind of superficially detached
colorism, or what corresponds to absolute music; and in
the other direction, we should get a development of the
dramatic lyric, the lyric presenting an emotion not singly
but in its matrix, beginning with the situation which gives
rise to it and concluding with the situation to which it has
led. Indications of this method are to be found in the
work of Mr. Masefield, Mr. Frost, and Mr. Eliot. . . . If
the lyric is to compete with narrative poetry, or to sup-
plant it, it must certainly develop in the latter of these two
manners. If it is merely to evolve further on its own base—
and it is hard to see any excuse for its continuance as a
mere bonbon for the lazy-mindedly sentimental—it must
choose the former.[1]

This controversy serves as a background for the next essays we
have included in this collection. Llewelyn Powys' article in *The
Dial* takes up the theme of preciosity, and though he is not so harsh
as Aiken or Untermeyer, he still finds the poetry "corrupt" and
"artificial" in its language, and seems to feel that the poetry would
have been much better if it were separated from the language which
composes it. Gorham Munson's "The Dandyism of Wallace Stevens" came shortly thereafter and, despite its title, tried to establish
a rationale for Stevens' peculiar rhetoric which would make it poetically viable. He shows that it is an American phenomenon, arising
in reaction to the almost total lack of "elegance" in the tradition
of American literature. It is therefore not a frivolous escape from
real conditions, but rather an attempt to remedy a deprivation in
American life. Paul Rosenfeld's observations are more appreciative
than systematic; he describes, but does not justify, the pleasure he
has received from Stevens' work. They are perhaps unconsciously
proof of Gorham Munson's assertion that Stevens' poetry came to
fulfill the need in America for a tradition of poetry which would
appeal to sensibilities created by European dandyism.

If the critics of the 'twenties were inhibited by their inability to

[1] Conrad Aiken, *Skepticisms* (New York, 1919), pp. 176-77.

take seriously the idea that a dilettantish sensibility, which produced frivolous poetry, could produce what was also important poetry, at least some other poets saw his language in terms which we can still appreciate—as a unique and powerful medium, adaptable to important modern themes. Hart Crane, who is not often thought of in connection with Stevens, remarked in his letters the effect the older poet's language had on him, and it is not hard to find echoes of Stevens in certain of Crane's poems. (The influence of Stevens' rhetoric on Crane is a subject which needs investigation.) Likewise, Marianne Moore in her fine review of *Harmonium* gave Stevens his due as a craftsman rather than as a sensibility. She very early saw that the question of preciosity was a bit irrelevant.

It was the essays by Morton Zabel and R. P. Blackmur, however, which finally shifted the terms of criticism. We have included Blackmur's essay, despite its availability elsewhere, because so much of the subsequent criticism takes off from the remarks it contains. Blackmur first of all eliminated the objection to preciosity by showing that Stevens' unusual language is deliberate and integral to a poem's total meaning and effect. He then analyzed at length "The Comedian as the Letter C" and thereby showed that the most important theme running through *Harmonium*—the relationship between imagination and reality—was given a sophisticated and important treatment in this long poem. Since this essay, it has been impossible for critics to say that Stevens' subject is trivial or nonexistent, no matter what cavils they might have with his ideas on the subject or his manner of treating them. Howard Baker's essay examines the nature of Stevens' imagery as a psychological manifestation. He makes many valuable comparisons between Stevens and Jung, and shows that the strange objects which inhabit the poems are perhaps not as playful and arbitrary as had once been thought. Hi Simons' long explication of the "Comedian" is a part of the study he once projected of the poet. He refines Blackmur's general statements, and suggests a wealth of related ideas, concerning the "mental weather" of the poet, and the manner in which it forces him into certain philosophical and poetic postures. Both Baker's and Simons' essays are sympathetic and exploratory.

Stevens was not always received with unreserved praise during the decade of depression and social concern. If some of the amateurs of the 'twenties had regarded his presumed dandyism with favor, few Marxist men and women of letters were likely to have anything but scorn for this pose. Stevens himself seems to have been amused by the indignation of some of these critics, having written a mocking poem to Stanley Burnshaw, who had said in a review in *The New Masses* of *Ideas of Order:* "It is the kind of verse that people concerned with the murderous world collapse can hardly swallow today except in tiny doses." [2] Even Theodore Roethke, who doubtless had a stronger stomach than Burnshaw, felt it a pity "that such a rich and special sensibility should be content with the order of words and music, and not project itself more vigorously upon the present-day world." We can no longer accept such a rigorous attitude, but this is not to say that all Marxist criticism of the time was invalid. Dorothy Van Ghent, although she took Stevens more as a symptom than a poet, noted in him "an increasing sadness and even anguish, an increasing sense that the facts of our present society are the doom of imagination, an increasing fear, loneliness . . . and preoccupation with the concept of decadence." Although Stevens, insofar as he might admit to the description, would not believe that Marxism was the answer to it, her observation does have the merit of giving dignity to his poetry, if it needed it, in the world of social ideas.

It was F. O. Matthiessen, whose Marxism never destroyed his critical sense, who saw much better than the others that Stevens' poetry did refer to the political history of the day, insofar as it reproduced the forms of life and thought that are the natural subjects of poetry. He observed that "Sad Strains of a Gay Waltz" "notes the emptiness that has crept into conventional forms of thought and feeling, and the stirring of the immense suppressed energies beyond these forms." Very few more lucid statements have been made of this continuing theme in Stevens, and it is no wonder that Matthiessen concludes this review of *Ideas of Order* with the statement that "this is the nearest approach to major poetry being made in this country today."

[2] Recently Mr. Burnshaw has carefully explained his part in this episode. See *The Sewanee Review* for Summer, 1961.

After *Ideas of Order*, every critic, adverse or favorable, has had to treat Stevens with respect. Even Yvor Winters, who, from a non-Marxist point of view, lamented the hedonism of Stevens' poetry, had to admit that "Sunday Morning" was one of the great poems of the century. In *Primitivism and Decadence* he associates Stevens with the latter term, and proceeds to show how the hedonism which is both the poet's subject and his technique has in it the possibility of its own destruction, since the style will necessarily fall into formlessness without the discipline of something more rigid than hedonism.[3] If Stevens' continued production of poetry after the 'thirties seems to deny this thesis, very few critics so far accorded the later poems a stature equal to the more famous poems in *Harmonium*.

But by the 'forties, with the publication of the Stevens issue of *The Harvard Advocate*, with tributes from many eminent men of letters, the question of Stevens' importance and seriousness of purpose was not relevant. This issue celebrated many phases of Stevens' work, and treated various themes that were to be developed more fully by later critics. Stevens' imagery connected with places, his Platonism, and his connection with the spirit of contemporary paintings were all explored. This was the moment when Stevens was first noticed by critics in England. Julian Symons' essay, reprinted here, attempts to describe the character of Stevens' work for the British public. Drawing on earlier American critiques, Symons composes his own evaluation of Stevens' production up to 1940, with special reference to *The Man With the Blue Guitar*. He balances Stevens' faults and virtues judiciously, perhaps so judiciously that he fails to give a public not familiar with Stevens' work a sense of its excitement. Marius Bewley, who has done so much to enlighten Americans as well as Englishmen about American literature, does a fine job of elucidation in his essay. The technique he uses, the tracing back of themes in Stevens' later books to their manifestation in *Harmonium*, is so rewarding that one is surprised that it has not been tried more often. Bewley's perceptive remarks reveal how

[3] Winters' essay, "Wallace Stevens, or the Hedonist's Progress," collected in his *In Defense of Reason* (New York, 1947), is the best sustained attack on some aspects of Stevens' work.

much, despite his change in style, Stevens remained the same poet throughout his productive life.

Although it is true that Stevens has remained comparatively unknown in England up to the last few years, it is not for lack of admirers across the Atlantic. (A volume of Stevens' poetry was first published in England in 1953; this was the *Selected Poems* [Faber and Faber] chosen by the poet himself.) We have reprinted two very recent English readings of Stevens, one by the poet Donald Davie, the other a general appreciation by Geoffrey Moore. Davie's close reading of the title poem of *Auroras of Autumn* is one of the few extended treatments of individual poems from the later volumes. And the implications of his reading of this poem and its proposed solution to the problem of evil apply to a great many of the other later poems. In addition, he has established criteria by which Stevens' poems can be judged. Geoffrey Moore's lecture, which does not claim to be more than an introduction to Stevens directed at the common reader, nevertheless contains so many good general ideas (especially on the American literary tradition), and so many perceptive comments on individual poems, that it is a worthy conclusion to this symposium.

In America, what distinguishes the criticism of the 'forties and 'fifties is the broadening of perspectives, what with the new "evidence" which the later volumes of poetry have added, and the discovery, or rather the exploitation of themes other than the important one of imagination versus reality. From the 'forties we have reprinted an essay by J. V. Cunningham, which has recently been revised. Cunningham picks up where Yvor Winters left off, and, using the evidence of the later poems, applies the moral categories of Winters with considerable subtlety to the changes which Stevens has gone through over the years; and his references to Wordsworth are valuable clues which future critics might pick up. Marianne Moore, an important member of Stevens' generation, has written several appreciations of his poetry over many years; we reprint her review of *The Auroras of Autumn*. Randall Jarrell's review of the *Collected Poems*, the judgment of a poet of a later generation, indicates the importance which Stevens' late poems in *The Rock* should have for many readers. Michel Benamou traces the connection, only briefly noted before, between Stevens' technique and the work of certain painters who have trained his eye to see certain combinations of form and color. His observations about the relationship between Stevens' poems and the techniques and aesthetics of painting suggest a great deal about the inspiration and purpose of Stevens' way of writing. Samuel French Morse, a poet himself and Stevens' official biographer, places Stevens against his American background, and discusses the prose essays and epigrams of his later years. And Louis L. Martz, an eminent student of Renaissance poetry, makes out an interesting connection between Stevens' late poems and the tradition Mr. Martz calls "the poetry of meditation."

There are, of course, many first-rate critiques of Stevens which the limitations of this collection have forced us to exclude; most of them date from the last decade. There are now four books on his poetry, to which we refer the reader who wishes to explore the subject further. We especially recommend the chapter on Stevens in Sister M. Bernetta Quinn's book, *The Metamorphic Tradition in Modern Poetry,* for her approach brings out facets of Stevens' poetry neglected in most other approaches. We have also included only one of the four essays which the late Hi Simons, an early admirer of the poet, wrote; all of them are perceptive works of explication.

Those essays which we have collected, however, we feel give a balanced view of Stevens, and a sense that as his work has become increasingly familiar, it has also been more deeply understood. A reader who has found Stevens forbidding before should be able, after reading these essays, to see a great deal that is familiar and enjoyable. And the reader who has long savored his work should see something that he has not noticed before. It would also be our hope that this book will encourage further study. Stevens deliberately excludes the appeal to traditional poetic subjects, as though he felt that such an appeal would obscure the serious intentions of his poetry. Criticism is fulfilling its function when the poet is celebrated through the stating of those ideas which make clearest the essential aim of his poetry, and we can expect that readers will continue to offer such an homage to Wallace Stevens.

ASHLEY BROWN
ROBERT S. HALLER

HARRIET MONROE

From MR. YEATS AND THE
POETIC DRAMA

1920

Mr. [W. B.] Yeats, in his brief address [at a banquet given in his honor by *Poetry*, March 3, 1920], took the Poetic Drama for his subject, and told of the little theater and the small audience which he and other poets are conspiring for in Dublin; the aristocratic theater in which from a dozen to fifty of the elect shall see plays worthy of spirits highly attuned and keyed, and shall pass them on authoritatively to the next age; a theater modeled on the Noh drama of Japan, whose playwrights and players were always blissfully absorbed in their art and royally unconscious of the crowd.

Without venturing to question this aesthetic authority of the elect in our unimperial age, I was reminded of a dramatic exhibition which I had attended in New York two or three weeks before, one which fulfilled Mr. Yeats's conditions as closely as any little-theater enterprise is like to do in our time and country. The distinguished Irish poet, unfortunately, was not there, and it is only too probable that less important engagements kept him away during the entire week or two that the Provincetown Players were giving "Three

.   .   .   .

Miss Monroe's comments on Wallace Stevens' verse play, "Three Travellers Watch a Sunset," form part of an essay first published in *Poetry: A Magazine of Verse*, XVI, April, 1920, and reprinted here by permission of Mr. H. S. Monroe on behalf of Miss Monroe's heirs.

Travellers Watch a Sunrise"; so that we are forever prevented from knowing whether the performance was in line with his desire. But there was the small audience (over fifty, perhaps, but under one hundred) of the presumably elect—for who but the elect would venture down past Washington Square through slushy snowdrifts too mountainous for taxis? There also was the small stage, almost as informal as a drawing room, upon which artists had thought out a not too elaborate setting. And there, in Wallace Stevens' play, was the Poetic Drama.

I had almost forgotten how beautiful this brief play is; even though I had read it twenty times, more or less, in manuscript and proof, when it took *Poetry*'s play-contest prize and appeared in the July, 1916, issue of the magazine. But the "three travellers"—were they from Provincetown or China?—appearing with their candle in the dark wood and vesting themselves in gorgeous robes for the ritual of the sunrise, took me back to those "windless pavilions" of Mr. Stevens' magic country, and asserted with unimpeachable validity the high audacity of the poet's imagination.

The girl was not so adequate. It is her province to enforce the tragedy by bringing the three dreamers face to face with the grim realities of agony and death. With hardly a dozen lines to speak, she would need be a Duse to give them their due effect. As she seemed merely a high-school amateur, the elect audience had to imagine nobly during the tragic climax of the play; the more because the sunrise, instead of approaching slowly, with gradual revelation of the dead figure among the branches, appeared with the sudden flare of an electric light. However, for at least one auditor, the three travellers, uttering their beautiful lines, had woven a spell which no later inadequacy could destroy: the brief tragedy was complete and wonderful, as perfect as a Greek vase in its assertion of beauty. . . .

MARIANNE MOORE

WELL MOUSED, LION

1924

It is not too much to say that some writers are entirely without imagination—without that associative kind of imagination certainly, of which the final tests are said to be simplicity, harmony, and truth. In Mr. Stevens' work, however, imagination precludes banality and order prevails. In his book, he calls imagination "the will of things," "the magnificent cause of being," and demonstrates how imagination may evade "the world without imagination"; effecting an escape which, in certain manifestations of "bravura," is uneasy rather than bold. One feels, however, an achieved remoteness as in Tu Muh's lyric criticism: "Powerful is the painting . . . and high is it hung on the spotless wall in the lofty hall of your mansion." There is the love of magnificence and the effect of it in these sharp, solemn, rhapsodic elegant pieces of eloquence; one assents to the view taken by the author, of Crispin whose

> mind was free
> And more than free, elate, intent, profound.

The riot of gorgeousness in which Mr. Stevens' imagination takes refuge recalls Balzac's reputed attitude to money, to which he was indifferent unless he could have it "in heaps or by the ton." It is "a flourishing tropic he requires"; so wakeful is he in his appetite

·   ·   ·   ·   ·   ·   ·   ·

A review of the 1923 edition of *Harmonium*, first published in *The Dial*, LXXVI, January, 1924, and reprinted by permission of the author.

for color and in perceiving what is needed to meet the requirements of a new tone key, that Oscar Wilde, Frank Alvah Parsons, Tappé, and John Murray Anderson seem children asleep in comparison with him. One is met in these poems by some such clash of pigment as where in a showman's display of orchids or gladiolas, one receives the effect of vials of picracarmine, magenta, gamboge, and violet mingled each at the highest point of intensity:

> In Yucatan, the Maya sonneteers
> Of the Caribbean amphitheatre,
> In spite of hawk and falcon, green toucan
> And jay, still to the night-bird made their plea,
> As if raspberry tanagers in palms,
> High up in orange air, were barbarous.

One is excited by the sense of proximity to Java peacocks, golden pheasants, South American macaw feather capes, Chilcat blankets, hair seal needlework, Singhalese masks, and Rousseau's paintings of banana leaves and alligators. We have the hydrangeas and dogwood, the "blue, gold, pink, and green" of the temperate zone, the hibiscus, "red as red," of the tropics.

> . . . moonlight on the thick, cadaverous bloom
> That yuccas breed . . .

> . . . with serpent-kin encoiled
> Among the purple tufts, the scarlet crowns,

and as in a shot-spun fabric, the infinitude of variation of the colors of the ocean:

> . . . the blue
> And the colored purple of the lazy sea,

the emerald, indigos, and mauves of disturbed water, the azure and basalt of lakes; we have Venus "the centre of sea-green pomp" and America "polar purple." Mr. Stevens' exact demand, moreover, projects itself from nature to human nature. It is the eye of no "maidenly greenhorn" which has differentiated Crispin's daughters; which characterizes "the ordinary women" as "gaunt guitarists" and issues the junior-to-senior mandate in "Floral Decorations for Bananas":

> Pile the bananas on planks.
> The women will be all shanks
> And bangles and slatted eyes.

He is a student of "the flambeaued manner,"

> . . . not indifferent to smart detail . . .

> . . . hang of coat, degree
> Of buttons . . .

One resents the temper of certain of these poems. Mr. Stevens is never inadvertently crude; one is conscious, however, of a deliberate bearishness—a shadow of acrimonious, unprovoked contumely. Despite the sweet-Clementine-will-you-be-mine nonchalance of the "Apostrophe to Vincentine," one feels oneself to be in danger of unearthing the ogre and in "Last Looks at the Lilacs," a pride in unserviceableness is suggested which makes it a microcosm of cannibalism.

Occasionally the possession of one good is remedy for not possessing another, as when Mr. Stevens speaks of "the young emerald, evening star," "tranquillizing . . . the torments of confusion." "Sunday Morning" on the other hand—a poem so suggestive of a masterly equipoise—gives ultimately the effect of the mind disturbed by the intangible; of a mind oppressed by the properties of the world which it is expert in manipulating. And proportionately; aware as one is of the author's susceptibility to the fever of actuality, one notes the accurate gusto with which he discovers the Negro, that veritable "medicine of cherries" to the badgered analyst. In their resilience and certitude, the "Hymn From a Watermelon Pavilion" and the commemorating of a Negress who

> Took seven white dogs
> To ride in a cab,

are proud harmonies.

One's humor is based upon the most serious part of one's nature. "Le Monocle de Mon Oncle"; "A Nice Shady Home"; and "Daughters With Curls": the capacity for self-mockery in these titles illustrates the author's disgust with mere vocativeness.

Instinct for words is well determined by the nature of the liberties taken with them, some writers giving the effect merely of presumptuous egotism—an unavoided outlandishness; others, not: Shakespeare arresting one continually with nutritious permutations as when he apostrophizes the lion in A *Midsummer Night's Dream*—"Well Moused, Lion." Mr. Stevens' "Junipers Shagged With Ice" is properly courageous as are certain of his adjectives which have the force of verbs: "the spick torrent," "tidal skies," "loquacious columns"; there is the immunity to fear, of the good artist, in "the blather that the water made." His precise diction and verve are grateful as contrasts to the current vulgarizations of "gesture," "dimensions," and "intrigue." He is able not only to express an idea with mere perspicuity; he is able to do it by implication, as in "Thirteen Ways of Looking at a Blackbird" in which the glass coach evolved from icicles; the shadow, from birds; it becomes a kind of aristocratic cipher. "The Emperor of Ice-Cream," moreover, despite its not especially original theme of poverty enriched by death, is a triumph of explicit ambiguity. He gets a special effect with those adjectives which often weaken as in the lines:

> . . . That all beasts should . . .
> be beautiful
> As large, ferocious tigers are

and in the phrase, "the eye of the young alligator," the adjective, as it is perhaps superfluous to point out, makes for activity. There is a certain bellicose sensitiveness in

> I do not know which to prefer . . .
> The blackbird whistling
> Or just after

and in the characterization of the snow man who

> . . . nothing himself, beholds
> The nothing that is not there and the nothing that is.

In its nimbleness *con brio* with seriousness, moreover, "Nomad Exquisite" is a piece of that ferocity for which one values Mr. Stevens most:

> As the immense dew of Florida
> Brings forth

The big-finned palm
And green vine angering for life.

Poetic virtuosities are allied—especially those of diction, imagery, and cadence. In no writer's work are metaphors less "winter starved." In "Architecture" Mr. Stevens asks:

How shall we hew the sun, . . .
How carve the violet moon
To set in nicks?

Pierce, too, with buttresses of coral air
And purple timbers,
Various argentines

and "The Comedian as the Letter C," as the account of the craftsman's un"simple jaunt," is an expanded metaphor which becomes, as one contemplates it, hypnotically incandescent like the rose-tinged fringe of the night-blooming cereus. One applauds those analogies derived from an enthusiasm for the sea:

She scuds the glitters,
Noiselessly, like one more wave.

The salt hung on his spirit like a frost,
The dead brine melted in him like a dew.

In his positiveness, aplomb, and verbal security, he has the mind and the method of China; in such conversational effects as:

Of what was it I was thinking?
So the meaning escapes,

and certainly in dogged craftsmanship. Infinitely conscious in his processes, he says

Speak even as if I did not hear you speaking
But spoke for you perfectly in my thoughts.

One is not subject, in reading him, to the disillusionment experienced in reading novices and charlatans who achieve flashes of beauty and immediately contradict the pleasure afforded by offending in precisely those respects in which they have pleased—showing that they are deficient in conscious artistry.

Imagination implies energy and imagination of the finest type

MARIANNE MOORE · 25

involves an energy which results in order "as the motion of a snake's body goes through all parts at once, and its volition acts at the same instant in coils that go contrary ways." There is the sense of the architectural diagram in the disjoined titles of poems with related themes. Refraining for fear of impairing its litheness of contour, from overelaborating felicities inherent in a subject, Mr. Stevens uses only such elements as the theme demands; for example, his delineation of the peacock in "Domination of Black" is austerely restricted, splendor being achieved cumulatively in "Bantams in Pine-Woods," "The Load of Sugar-Cane," "The Palace of the Babies," and "The Bird With the Coppery, Keen Claws."

That "there have been many most excellent poets that never versified, and now swarm many versifiers that need never answer to the name of poets," needs no demonstration. The following lines, as poetry independent of rhyme, beg the question as to whether rhyme is indispensably contributory to poetic enjoyment:

> There is not nothing, no, no, never nothing,
> Like the clashed edges of two words that kill

and

> The clambering wings of birds of black revolved,
> Making harsh torment of the solitude.

It is of course evident that, subsidiary to beauty of thought, rhyme is powerful in so far as it never appears to be invented for its own sake. In this matter of apparent naturalness, Mr. Stevens is faultless —as in correctness of assonance:

> Chieftain Iffucan of Azcan in caftan
> Of tan with henna hackles, halt!

The better the artist, moreover, the more determined he will be to set down words in such a way as to admit of no interpretation of the accent but the one intended, his ultimate power appearing in a self-sufficing, willowy, firmly contrived cadence such as we have in "Peter Quince at the Clavier" and in "Cortège for Rosenbloom":

> That tread
> The wooden ascents
> Of the ascending of the dead.

One has the effect of poised uninterrupted harmony, a simple-appearing, complicated phase of symmetry of movements as in figure skating, tightrope dancing, in the kaleidoscopically centrifugal circular motion of certain medieval dances. It recalls the snake in *Far Away and Long Ago*, "moving like quicksilver in a ropelike stream" or the conflict at sea when, after a storm, the wind shifts and waves are formed counter to those still running. These expertnesses of concept with their nicely luted edges and effect of flowing continuity of motion, are indeed

> . . . pomps
> Of speech which are like music so profound
> They seem an exaltation without sound.

One further notes accomplishment in the use of reiteration—that pitfall of half-poets:

> Death is absolute and without memorial,
> As in a season of autumn,
> When the wind stops,
>
> When the wind stops . . .

In brilliance gained by accelerated tempo in accordance with a fixed melodic sign, the precise patterns of many of these poems are interesting.

> It was snowing
> And it was going to snow

and the parallelism in "Domination of Black" suggests the Hebrew idea of something added, although there is, one admits, more the suggestion of mannerism than in Hebrew poetry. Tea takes precedence of other experiments with which one is familiar, in emotional shorthand of this unwestern type, and in "Earthy Anecdote" and the "Invective Against Swans," symmetry of design is brought to a high degree of perfection.

It is rude perhaps, after attributing conscious artistry and a severely intentional method of procedure to an artist, to cite work that he has been careful to omit from his collected work. One regrets, however, the omission by Mr. Stevens of "The Indigo Glass in the Grass," "The Man Whose Pharynx Was Bad," "La Mort du Soldat Est Près des Choses Naturelles (5 Mars)" and "Comme Dieu Dispense de Grâces":

> Here I keep thinking of the primitives—
> The sensitive and conscientious themes
> Of mountain pallors ebbing into air.

However, in this collection one has eloquence. "The author's violence is for aggrandizement and not for stupor"; one consents, therefore, to the suggestion that when the book of moonlight is written, we leave room for Crispin. In the event of moonlight and a veil to be made gory, he would, one feels, be appropriate in this legitimately sensational act of a ferocious jungle animal.

LLEWELYN POWYS

THE THIRTEENTH WAY

1924

Just as in the 'nineties, golden quill in hand, Aubrey Beardsley, seated under a crucifix, traced with degenerate wax-white fingers pictures that revealed a new world, a world exact, precise, and convincing, squeezed out, so to speak, between the attenuated crevices of a hypersensitive imagination, so in his poetry Mr. Wallace Stevens chips apertures in the commonplace and deftly constructs on the other side of the ramparts of the world, tier upon tier, pinnacle upon pinnacle, his own supersophisticated superterrestrial township of the mind.

And it may well be that his eccentric verse does actually reveal more of the insecure fluctuating secrets of the universe than are to be found in other more sedate, more decorous artistic creations. Wavering, uncertain, bereft of ancient consolations, the human race comes more and more to realize that it has won to consciousness in a world in which all is relative and undulating. In such a world it is indeed possible that intimations of some incalculable absolute are more nearly to be come at under the influence of cloud-shadows floating beneath a violet moon than under that of the splashes of actual sunshine lying so confidently on grass, and brick, and stone, and metal.

.   .   .   .

First published in *The Dial*, LXXVII, July, 1924, and reprinted by permission of Llewelyn Powys' literary executrix, Miss Alyse Gregory.

From king to beggar we are aware of our manifold delusions, aware that nothing is as false as the face value of things. We have, alas! grown only too cognizant of the essential mendacity of the physical aspects of a universe that has no bottom. And this being so, it is perhaps in suggestions, in mere phantasms, that we come nearest to the evocations of the fourth-dimensional consciousness which may well be farthest removed from illusion. If the surface of the visible world then is nothing, who can tell but that the shadows of the surface of the visible world may be everything? And no poet, not Baudelaire, not Edgar Allan Poe even, has revealed with a surer touch, a surer ambiguity, the very shades and tinctures of this indefinable borderland than has this ultramodern supersubtle lawyer from the confines of Hartford, Connecticut.

It is impossible for us to read Mr. Stevens' poetry without feeling that we are being initiated into the quintessential tapering expression of a unique personality—a personality as original and authentic as it is fastidious and calculating. He stands quite alone amongst the poets of the more modern schools in that each unexpected verbal manipulation conceals some obscure harmony of sense and sound which not only provokes intellectual appreciation, but in the strangest possible way troubles the imagination. Listening to his poetry is like listening to the humming cadences of an inspired daddy longlegs akimbo in sunset light against the colored panes of a sanct window above a cathedral altar.

Mr. Wallace Stevens' poetry is beyond good and evil, beyond hope and despair, beyond thought of any kind, one might almost say.

> The soul, O ganders, flies beyond the parks
> And far beyond the discords of the wind.

And yet he is not so far removed from the palpable foundations of existence as to be altogether oblivious to the passing of the seasons. Like other poets before him, his spirit feels the impact of the spring and finds for its emotions unabashed punctilious expression.

> Timeless mother,
> How is it that your aspic nipples
> For once vent honey?

Very curious, very corrupt, very artificial are the seascape vignettes, the landscape vignettes of his demi-world, artificial and yet pointed and penetrating in their decorative integrity.

> In the sea, Biscayne, there prinks
> The young emerald, evening star. . . .

> By this light the salty fishes
> Arch in the sea like tree-branches,
> Going in many directions
> Up and down.

> Her terrace was the sand
> And the palms and the twilight. . . .

> And thus she roamed
> In the roamings of her fan,

> Partaking of the sea,
> And of the evening,
> As they flowed around
> And uttered their subsiding sound.

Indeed, as in the last quotation, one continually comes upon passages that seem to suggest a curious sensuality such as one might fancifully associate with certain of the stranger apparitions seen in the circus ring, a bizarre niggling sensuality in accord with some dainty physical disability: the sensuality of a crotchety detached mind which itself is removed from the object of its adoration by convoluted covert laws of super-refined cerebrations.

> To what good, in the alleys of the lilacs,
> O caliper, do you scratch your buttocks
> And tell the divine ingénue, your companion,
> That. . . .

> Poor buffo! Look at the lavender
> And look your last and look still steadily,
> And say how it comes that you see
> Nothing but trash and that you no longer feel
> Her body quivering in the Floréal

> Toward the cool night and its fantastic star,
> Prime paramour and belted paragon,
> Well-booted, rugged, arrogantly male,
> Patron and imager of the gold Don John,
> Who will embrace her before summer comes.

LLEWELYN POWYS · 31

It may be, however, that what I wish to convey will be still better illustrated by a quotation from that enchanting poem entitled "Cy Est Pourtraicte, Madame Ste Ursule, et Les Unze Mille Vierges," in which God himself is portrayed as being subject to the most unexpected emotion in realizing, with delicious perverse satisfaction, that the young girl's sacrifice of "radishes and flowers" in no way interests him.

> The good Lord in His garden sought
> New leaf and shadowy tinct,
> And they were all His thought.
> He heard her low accord,
> Half prayer and half ditty,
> And He felt a subtle quiver,
> That was not heavenly love,
> Or pity.

Or does one approach more closely to a clear understanding of Wallace Stevens' hermetic art and finicky preoccupations in contemplating the glazed halls and nocturnal palaces that his eclectic fantasy has set dangling for us in mid-space? There is something terrible about these suspended edifices. They are made of the same stuff, of the same unreal reality, obscure and yet objective, that might disturb the painted dreams of a praying mantis asleep in all its scaly emerald beauty on a linen-laid tropical table.

> Then from their poverty they rose,
> From dry catarrhs, and to guitars
> They flitted
> Through the palace walls.
>
> They flung monotony behind,
> Turned from their want, and, nonchalant,
> They crowded
> The nocturnal halls. . . .
>
> How explicit the coiffures became,
> The diamond point, the sapphire point,
> The sequins
> Of the civil fans!

The construction of such dagobas is no easy matter.

> How shall we hew the sun,
> Split it and make blocks,
> To build a ruddy palace?
> How carve the violet moon
> To set in nicks?
> Let us fix portals, east and west,
> Abhorring green-blue north and blue-green south.

And none knows better than the poet himself that it is no wise thing to let one's glance wander from these charmed interiors.

> Out of the window
> I saw how the planets gathered
> Like the leaves themselves
> Turning in the wind.
> I saw how the night came,
> Came striding like the color of the heavy hemlocks.
> I felt afraid.
> And I remembered the cry of the peacocks.

Surely this "Socrates of snails, musician of pears . . . lutanist of fleas" can make us aware of the ghastly lot of our kind with a most exquisite and convincing dexterity.

> If her horny feet protrude, they come
> To show how cold she is and dumb.

Clearly enough we are made to feel the ultimate fate of that company who, "gaudy as tulips," mount the stairways of those "wickless halls." The worms speak at Heaven's gate:

> Out of the tomb, we bring Badroulbadour,
> Within our bellies, we her chariot.
> Here is an eye. And here are, one by one,
> The lashes of that eye and its white lid.

But possibly the most perfect example of Mr. Stevens' genius is to be found in the poem called "The Cortège of Rosenbloom" [sic]. It defies completely all rational explanations, and yet at the same time tingles with vague imaginative evocations. What strange subterfugitive symphonies of infinitesimal tomtoms titillate the listener's ears as the cadaver of the wry, wizened one "of the color of horn" is carried to his burial place up in the sky! What sly bemused

LLEWELYN POWYS · 33

tambourine cacophony beats upon the eardrum with the reiterated "tread, tread" of the mourners.

> It is turbans they wear
> And boots of fur.

One of Mr. Stevens' most impertinent and precocious productions is entitled "Thirteen Ways of Looking at a Blackbird." The sixth of the thirteen ways is described as follows:

> Icicles filled the long window
> With barbaric glass.
> The shadow of the blackbird
> Crossed it, to and fro.
> The mood
> Traced in the shadow
> An indecipherable cause,

the eleventh way after this manner:

> He rode over Connecticut
> In a glass coach.
> Once, a fear pierced him,
> In that he mistook
> The shadow of his equipage
> For blackbirds.

May we not be perhaps permitted to regard Mr. Stevens' own poetry as the thirteenth way of looking upon life—the thirteenth way of Mr. Wallace Stevens, this "tiptoe cozener":

> This connoisseur of elemental Fate
> Aware of exquisite thought.

PAUL ROSENFELD

WALLACE STEVENS

1925

The playing of a Chinese orchestra. On a gong a bonze creates a copper din. The most amazing cacophony amid dissolving labials and silkiest sibilants. Quirks, booms, whistles, quavers. Lord, what instruments has he there? Small muffled drums? Plucked wires? The falsetto of an ecstatic eunuch? Upon deliberate examination it appears Stevens' matter is the perfectly grammatical arrangement of an English vocabulary not too abstract, Elizabethan, legal, with accidentals of alien terms and purely imitative sounds. But so novel and fantastic is the tintinnabulation of unusual words, and words unusually rhymed and arranged, that you nearly overlook the significations, and hear outlandish sharp and melting musics. While the motley collection prances past, a horn winds its golden cantilene; funeral tam-tams pulse; a violin modulates sharply through quarter-tones and metal particles chunk and chink. Irregular and occasional interior rhymes furnish curious accords. And mixed with the instrumental tones, the fowl persuasion utters its proper squawky staccato: clucking of strutting bantams—

> Chieftain Iffucan of Azcan in caftan
> Of tan with henna hackles, halt!

•   •   •   •   •   •   •   •

Reprinted from *Men Seen*, by Paul Rosenfeld (New York, The Dial Press, 1925), by permission of Mrs. Arthur Schwab, executrix for the estate of Paul Rosenfeld.

parleyings of cockatoos in tropic woods—

> He is not paradise of parakeets
> Of his gold ether, gold alguazil.

Together with new auditory sensations, the poems of Wallace Stevens release new intensities of visual ones. Music remains the prime element of this diverting art; with Alfred Kreymborg the author represents the musical imagist; nevertheless he lets us perceive sea water

> dissolved in shifting diaphanes
> Of blue and green,

as well as hear it swish 'longside the boat; and brings with the whisper of the surf upon Florida beaches the nuances of balmy summer twilights. And the visual imagery alternates extremely refined with biting forceful impressions no less suavely and deliciously than does the auditory. Stevens is precise among the shyest, most elusive of movements and shadings. He sees distinctly by way of delicacy the undulations of the pigeon sinking downward, the darkening of a calm among water-lights, the variations of the deep-blue tones in dusky landscapes. Quite as regularly as the colors themselves, it is their shades of difference that are registered by him:

> green sides
> And gold sides of green sides;

> raspberry tanagers in palms
> High up in orange air;

> sea-shades and sky-shades
> Like umbrellas in Java;

Yet this fastidious, aristocratic nature possesses a blunt power of utterance, a concentrated violence, that is almost naturalistic. Stevens recognizes the cruel, the combative principles of life as well as the soft and yielding; sees hanging by the side of the "golden gourds" he loves to contemplate, some "warty squashes, streaked and rayed"; knows that together with purple tufts and scarlet crowns the tropics hold "the green vine angering for life." We discover him momentarily piling gristling images, the fine roughnesses of color and acrid turns of language upon each other, hacking with

36 · WALLACE STEVENS

lines of poetry and banging harsh rhyme upon rhyme. "Last Looks at the Lilacs" and "Floral Decorations for Bananas," for all their levity of manner, approach the pitch of crude and ferocious language.

But sensation alone is liberated to new intensities by Stevens' forms. Emotion, on the contrary, is curiously constrained by them within a small range of experience and small volumes of expression. The title *Harmonium*, given by the author to his unique collection, makes to declare this littleness the effect entirely of deliberate simplification, and the conscious accommodation of matter to the range of an intimate instrument. But *Harmonium* seems to us something of a misnomer. Stevens appears to us not so much with the aspect of the austere artist as with that of the artist mysteriously, disconcertingly faithful to the technique of an instrument long transcended by the requirements of his nature and incapable of drawing out of himself in all their power his latent emotions. He resembles one born, say, for the grand piano who, while lovingly touching the keys as only the born pianist can, nevertheless persists in using certain processes appropriate to the reed organ, and consequently produces a strange and hybrid music, half Stravinsky and half hymn tune. That chamber orchestra of his, with its range of novel and delightful sounds—he has a genuine feeling for it. He loves its odd and piercing timbres, and toys bewitchingly with them. And still, we get no indication of its real limits. We are never given to know quite the fullness of its dynamics; it is too exclusively engaged in *chinoiseries*. Stevens' rhythms are chiefly secondary rhythms. Scarcely ever is his attack a direct and simple one. Generally, it is oblique, patronizing, and twisted with self-intended mockery. The measure is sometimes languid, sometimes mincing, almost invariably buffoon-like. It trips, pirouettes, executes an hundred little foppish turns and graces. It rocks complacently like a preening waterfowl upon its perch; waltzes in grotesque fury; keens like a comic rabbi; begins a movement and lets it end in air. Besides, the humor is consistently personal in reference. The poet is perceived leaning in evident boredom against the corner of a mantelpiece, or adjusting his monocle with a look of martyrdom.

Another Pierrot. The white clown will not from the pages [*sic*].

PAUL ROSENFELD · 37

For as defined by Laforgue and his following he stands the spiritual type for all correct young men in mourning, like Wallace Stevens, for an "I-the-Magnificent." You recalled it was too evident Destiny intended that Lord Pierrot play a princely tragic role. She gave him noble melancholy, contempt for the vulgar, proud port and gesture; poured into his mold the very stuff of Hamlets. Unfortunately, Pierrot glanced down along his body; and as he did so, it seemed to him that he was clad in loose flopping ridiculous raiment. And the sentiment of the preposterousness of his person follows the white clown more faithfully than a shadow, and lays fingers of ice on every living moment. Uncomfortably self-aware, the pitiable gentleman can never quite spend himself in living, and remains emotionally naïve, O Horrors! as a romantic poet. To be sure, little in his mask betrays him. Pierrot is sophisticated, worldly, lettered, read in philosophical authors Greek and Germanic. He is excessively correct, partly from natural elegance and partly in protest against romantic dishevelment; and functions suavely as reader to an empress, teller of a London bank, or lawyer in Hartford, Connecticut. Nevertheless, his unprojected energies and nobilities and grandiosities are perpetually assuming shapes of self-pity, yearning for enveloping love, and woman-worship; and although Pierrot is entirely too aware to mistake them for cosmic pains or enchantments of the heart, his sentimentalities threaten shamelessly to overcome him, and add immeasurably to his embarrassment. Hence his ideal self, the cruelly murdered "I-the-Magnificent," incapable of revealing itself in all its princeliness, gains satisfaction in the shape of revenge. It takes the exaltations of the subject emotional self, and very archly turns them into parody. Of melancholy soliloquy and philosophical dudgeon it makes a silvery music signifying nothing. Amid the tinkling ice of exquisite perceptions it lightly ridicules the objects of sentimental effusion, diverts the emotional current toward slightly grotesque ones, or comes

> as belle design
> Of foppish line;

thus simultaneously ceding to the pressure of inferior emotion and attesting amid extravagant waltzes and verbal fireworks its own ineffable superiorities.

Nor is Wallace Stevens the sole distinguished American poet of distinct Laforguian cut. Lord Pierrot is called T. S. Eliot, too, and sports other and smaller names as well. The series is a perfectly natural one. American life has hitherto tended to excite the painful tension between the two portions of the self, so determining a factor in the Laforguian expression; the curiously Yankee flavor of the parodistic manner of the "Watteau of the café-concerts," and of his ironic usage of journalistic and demotic idiom, has been remarked by not a few critics. Certainly, each of the new western additions to the company, poorer in general virtuosity than their great archetype although they are, have enriched the tradition with a perfectly individual color, and enlarged its scope. Stevens, for example, is full of a jazzy American sensuousness; and the polyglot American towns have made him peculiarly sensitive to the unusual and remote sounds of the English language. Nevertheless, the expression which he brings amid flowers, frost and "good fat guzzly fruit," remains to a degree characteristic of the school. His music is a music signaled as vain, an exaltation, not so much "without sound" as without object, a bland, curiously philosophical movement of the soul without signification. What he has to say appears too useless for him to say it out. The words, deliciously Elizabethan and comically abstract, remain "musical" merely, morsels rolled upon an epicure's palate. And world-weariness becomes an "Invective Against Swans," woman-worship a burlesque hymn to "Heavenly Vincentine," and exaltation takes idly to tracing the processional of clouds across the sky. The senses dance, but they achieve only a sort of titillation, a vague naughtiness; intelligence sits coldly in the center of the ring and directs their gyrations. The disillusionments troop across: the story of the wildcat which always bars the center of the road and falls asleep only in death; Florida nights which yield nothing more than a caress of fingertips; love turned stale at forty; vain dreams erected "upon the basis of the common drudge." The lengthy narrative poem "The Comedian as the Letter C" contains the history of a poetic career, the feeling of the war, the hope of a national expression, the tragedy of environment; but it secretes them behind a shimmer of language and archness piled upon archness; and takes

PAUL ROSENFELD · 39

for its protagonist—Crispin.

In spite of its perfect things, "Nuances of a Theme by Williams" and the others, *Harmonium* does not, therefore, entirely represent the day. Little reveals the movement which has occurred in the American mind of late more simply than the fact that we should willingly feel its qualities of evasiveness, of archness and comic pudicity as slightly timed. The characteristic note of 1890 was not outworn for us ten years ago; and yet, today, even though nothing in the basic character of life appears transformed, and Plymouth Rock in the bosom of all has not offered to melt, or freemen's arms grown lighter, we have transcended it. We are somewhat less self-aware; and irritated by what tends to recall us to the old bad consciousness. And it is precisely embarrassment, shyness, and holy shame which do the wicked work; we find the attitude of the Venus de' Medici suggestive. An impulse in us bids authors be more simple and direct, and give completely what they feel; above all to advance from behind the curtain of language. Tragical disabilities are the very ordinary stuff of life, and what today requires most is impersonality, perspective, objectivity. No need subtracting from James Joyce. —And yet, *Harmonium* remains one of the jewel boxes of contemporary verse. If certain of its elements appear a trifle outworn, others very definitely thrust the art of poetry toward unknown boundaries. As a musician, Stevens is revealed an almost impeccable craftsman. Not only is his idiom new and delicious; his surface is almost invariably complete. Experimental rhymes have an inevitability under his hands, and his rhythms do not break. He produces his material as conceived by him with exquisite tact, giving the just amount, and not re-covering traversed ground. The terminations and cadences of his pieces are usually quite unpredictable; only very rarely, as in "Six Significant Landscapes," do the final surprising extensions of the idea grow mechanical. We have a number of artists working in the medium of poetry; Pound, Eliot and others have produced work both delicate and hard. Yet the arrival of a volume of verse on each of its one hundred and twenty-odd pages very patently the pretty booklet *arida modo pumice expolitum* is an event not hitherto seen by our generation. And for the moment Wallace Stevens remains eminently the artist in his field.

40 · WALLACE STEVENS

GORHAM B. MUNSON

THE DANDYISM OF
WALLACE STEVENS

1925

The impeccability of the dandy resolves itself into two elements: correctness and elegance. Both elements transcend merely good taste, for correctness implies a knowledge of the rules governing the modes of expression, feeling, thinking, conduct; and elegance is, of course, good taste that has been polished.

Until the advent of Wallace Stevens, American literature has lacked a dandy. Of swaggering macaronis there have been aplenty, but the grace and ceremony, the appropriate nimbleness of the dandy, have been lacking. Certainly, as a craftsman, he has absorbed the teachings of the academy; at any rate he can trust himself to the musical risks of poetry—making use of alliteration, assonance, free rhymes, irregular stanzaic forms, and *vers libre*—and can be counted on to overcome them. The effective use of exclamation in poetry is exceedingly difficult, because the accent must be carefully prepared for and must coincide with a real rise in the material. He has many times run the risk of overexclamation, always winning, and perhaps most handsomely in "Bantams in Pine-Woods":

• • • • • • • •

First published in *The Dial*, LXXIX, November, 1925, and later collected in *Destinations*, by Gorham B. Munson (New York, J. H. Sears & Co., Inc., 1928); reprinted by permission of the author.

Chieftain Iffucan of Azcan in caftan
Of tan with henna hackles, halt!

Damned universal cock, as if the sun
Was blackamoor to bear your blazing tail.

Fat! Fat! Fat! Fat! I am the personal.
Your world is you. I am my world.

You ten-foot poet among inchlings. Fat!
Begone! An inchling bristles in these pines,

Bristles, and points their Appalachian tangs,
And fears not portly Azcan nor his hoos.

Elegance he attains in his fastidious vocabulary—in the surprising aplomb and blandness of his images. He will say "harmonium" instead of "small organ," "lacustrine" instead of "lakeside," "sequin" instead of "spangle"; he will speak of "hibiscus," "panache," "fabliau," and "poor buffo." The whole tendency of his vocabulary is, in fact, toward the lightness and coolness and transparency of French. As for his images, they are frequently surprising in themselves, yet they always produce the effect of naturalness—an effect which is cool, bland, transparent, natural, and gracefully mobile.

In the dandy of letters, impeccability is primarily achieved by adding elegance to correctness. Yet life is disturbing and horrifying as well as interesting and delightful: one is inevitably tossed by the "torments of confusion"; and the dandy, if he would maintain his urbane demeanor, must adopt protective measures. The safeguards employed by Mr. Stevens against "the torments of confusion" are three: wit, speculation, and reticence. As an antidote to love-sick quandary, to the fear of decrepitude, to the disturbing vastness of the ocean, there is wit—that self-mockery which we have in "Le Monocle de Mon Oncle," and "The Comedian as the Letter C." Doubt of reality must be admitted as a purely speculative doubt, "as a calm darkens among water-lights." Let speculative doubt play gently across the surface of a steadfast materialism. And finally, let us be reticent, for reticence is becoming in its implication that one is aware of enigmatic miseries, and yet too proud to wear one's heart upon one's sleeve.

Mr. Stevens possesses an imagination that is ordered. "Imagination," he says, "is the will of things." It is "the magnificent cause of being . . . the one reality in this imagined world." By its aid, at least, one may invent a literary cosmos, moving according to calculations, subject to its own laws and hierarchies, consistent with itself, a minute but sustained harmony floating above the chaos of life. It is whole and understandable and therefore a refuge in a life that is fragmentary and perplexing. It, in being form, is a polite answer to the hugeness which we cannot form.

Upon what, may we ask, is this imaginative order of Wallace Stevens based? It is not humanism, for the humanist searches for unifying standards of general human experience. Needless to say, it is not religion, for the religious man strives for a knowledge of the absolute. It is discipline—the discipline of one who is a connoisseur of the senses and the emotions. Mr. Stevens' imagination comes to rest on them; it is at their service, it veils them in splendor. The integration achieved is one of feeling; in the final analysis, it is a temperate romanticism.

Wallace Stevens has a quality, however, which is rarely associated with romanticism, a quality that his illustrious predecessor, Baudelaire, lacked to complete his dandyism. Baudelaire's dandyism might be called a metallic shell secreted by a restless man against a despised shifting social order. It cannot be called a placid dandyism, whereas tranquillity enfolds Mr. Stevens. This same lack of tranquillity impairs the dandyism of T. S. Eliot in those respects in which he is a dandy—turning his promenade through the alleged barrenness of modern life into bitter melancholy. Mr. Stevens, however, appears to sit comfortably in the age, to enjoy a sense of security, to be conscious of no need of fighting the times. The world is a gay and bright phenomenon, and he gives the impression of feasting on it without misgiving. Here in "Gubbinal" is his answer to those who repine because the world is blasted and its people are miserable:

> That strange flower, the sun,
> Is just what you say.
> Have it your way.
>
> The world is ugly,
> And the people are sad.

GORHAM B. MUNSON · 43

That tuft of jungle feathers,
That animal eye,
Is just what you say.

That savage of fire,
That seed,
Have it your way.

The world is ugly,
And the people are sad.

Because of this tranquillity, this well-fed and well-booted dandy-ism of contentment, Mr. Stevens has been called Chinese. Undeniably, he has been influenced by Chinese verse, as he has been by French verse, but one must not force the comparison. For Chinese poetry as a whole rests upon great humanistic and religious traditions: its quiet strength and peace are often simply by-products of a profound understanding; its epicureanism is less an end, more a function, than the tranquillity—may I say—the decidedly American tranquillity of Wallace Stevens.

The American nation drives passionately toward comfort. The aim of the frenzied practical life in which it engages is to attain material ease, and the symbols of its paradise are significant. They are wide, accurately barbered lawns, white yachts with bright awnings, the silvered motorcar, the small regiment of obsequious servants. Naturally, in paradise one would not wish to be annoyed by a suspicion that all was a brilliant fake, a magnificent evanescent dream, but rather, to refine upon one's luxurious means of existence. This is where in America the artistic intelligence may enter and play, elaborating, coloring, bedecking, adding splendor to the circumstances of one's comfort. Is there not fundamentally a kinship between the sensory discriminations and comfortable tranquillity of Wallace Stevens' poetry and the America that owns baronial estates?

Growing more reckless, we might say that if Dr. Jung is correct in asserting that in American psychology there is a unique alliance of wildness and restraint, then Wallace Stevens would seem in another respect to be at one with his country. I do not discover in him the ferocity that some critics have remarked upon, but there is at least a flair for bright savagery, for "that tuft of jungle feathers,

that animal eye, that savage of fire." In the case of certain roman-
ticists, such symbols would betray insatiable longing, the desire for
a nature that never existed. In his case, they are purely spectacular.
The Old World Romantic, restless amid the stratifications of his
culture, yearns for the untamed: the New World Romantic assumes
the easy posture of an audience.

American readers may well rejoice in this artist who is so gifted
in depicting sea-surfaces full of clouds. No American poet excels
him in the sensory delights that a spick-and-span craft can stimulate: none is more skillful in arranging his music, his figures, and
his design. None else, monocled and gloved, can cut so faultless a
figure standing in his box at the circus of life.

There are masters of art and art-masters. Seldom has an artist
been more canny and more definite in distinguishing between major and minor than Wallace Stevens. No one has more carefully
observed to the letter the restrictions of the art-master, or more
perfectly exemplified to us the virtue of impeccable form.

MORTON DAUWEN ZABEL

THE HARMONIUM OF
WALLACE STEVENS

1931

Precision of the instrument is too infrequent in modern poetry to earn its masters anything less than the high distinction which this new edition of *Harmonium* again shows Wallace Stevens to possess. Yet the properties of his work, externally considered, might easily discredit him in the intemperate judgment. They are devices whose facile manipulation has won for a great share of contemporary verse a just—if usually ill-reasoned—reproach. Since Stevens has passed now safely beyond the need of any comparison with his contemporaries, it is enough to note on this score that the "modern" devices which appear in these calmer days as the trickery of a topical vaudeville had behind them in his case the authority of instinctive symbolism and method; that they proceeded from an interior vision and necessity; and that for him this style was not a conjurer's garment but an expression for ideas of no given date, of which he remains in many cases our only exact recorder.

·   ·   ·   ·   ·   ·   ·   ·

A review of the 1931 edition of *Harmonium*, first published in *Poetry: A Magazine of Verse*, XXXIX, December, 1931, and reprinted by permission of the author, who has made slight revisions, for this occasion, in the original text. A fuller discussion of Wallace Stevens is contained in Mr. Zabel's essay in the special Stevens number of the *Harvard Advocate*, CXXVII, December, 1940.

The dimensions of this poetry are strict. Even with fourteen poems added to the collection of 1923—and allowing for the uncollected plays, "Carlos Among the Candles" and "Three Travellers Watch a Sunrise"—Mr. Stevens' frugality of output is notable. Notable, however, only by contrast with the extravagance of his materials and the sensuous capacities they imply. The baroque attenuation, the lavish movement, the riot among colors and flowers, the panoply of limbs and lusters and tropical boskage, the fragile laces that edge seas terrifying, "snarled and yelping," the pomp of fat living and indulgent grossness—these mounting festivals of the senses that might emphasize in Parisian art its ineptitude and in the Oriental its austerity are vestiges of a romantic imagination whose scope is usually widest and whose technical impatience least bridled. But Mr. Stevens faced his resources with the diffidence of a critical principle. For him the "barbaric glass," the "rosy chocolate/ And gilt umbrellas," "Bananas hacked and hunched . . . from Carib trees," "effulgent, azure lakes," "the marguerite and coquelicot,/ And roses," "the cry of the peacocks" and the "forest of the parakeets," the "flowers in last month's newspapers" and the "forms, flames, and the flakes of flames," were at once a luxury for the senses and an assault upon the mind and integrity that nerves them.

Beyond the sense's capacity for creating wealth in experience, and the mind's capacity for containing it, lies the terrifying consequence of these appetites—confusion, the consequence of intellectual gluttony and physical satiation. Conscious of this threat to sanity, Stevens' poetry established its polarity in richness and in simplicity: in "our bawdiness/ Unpurged by epitaph" on the one hand, and on the other in that crystalline clarity of vision and judgment which, schooled by the "imagination which is the will of things," "guards and preserves the spirit," sees eye to eye with the blackbird "among twenty snowy mountains/ The only moving thing," and

> apprehends the most which sees and names,
> As in your name, an image that is sure,
> Among the arrant spices of the sun.

The sensibility that retains the uses of richness without endangering the security of simplicity makes little use of ascetic discipline for its own sake. Nor, in attempting a compromise between "mildew of summer and the deepening snow," will the sensibility risk a neutralization of its powers, a mere "up and down between two elements," what Mr. Stevens calls "the malady of the quotidian." Rather it will seek a balance which values the counterweights that maintain its poise. In this sense,

> Crispin knew
> It was a flourishing tropic he required
> For his refreshment, an abundant zone,
> Prickly and obdurate, dense, harmonious,
> Yet with a harmony not rarefied
> Nor fined for the inhibited instruments
> Of over-civil stops.

This balance is the reward of intelligence. Its reality in the sphere of the senses becomes for Mr. Stevens a symbol of its necessity in the sphere of thought and conduct. Between indulgence and austerity lies a luxury finer than either, the luxury of the two harmonized: of bravado and terror disciplined in fortitude, and of chaos and rectitude reconciled in order:

> We live in an old chaos of the sun,
> Or old dependency of day and night,
> Or island solitude, unsponsored, free,
> Of that wide water, inescapable.

Yet threatened by imminent dissolution, and surfeited by "the dreadful sundry of this world," we may yet win the beatitude which warms the ordered life like the pure Sabbath sunlight of "Sunday Morning," wherein

> the dark
> Encroachment of that old catastrophe

is arrested, and

> Death is the mother of beauty; hence from her,
> Alone, shall come fulfilment to our dreams.

Here is the tranquillity pointed out by Mr. Munson (*The Dial*, November, 1925)—the antidote, conceived in wit, "to love-sick quandary, to the fear of decrepitude, to the disturbing vastness of the ocean"—which is his important contribution to the elucidation of Mr. Stevens' quality. This tranquillity, unfortunately, gains little by being made an appendage of "dandyism" or a synonym for "contentment" or a dubious corollary of the notion that "the American nation drives passionately toward comfort." Dandyism is style without significant motive or conviction; contentment is resigned will, not the stasis of energy whose delight lies in suspense between the two dangers that threaten it; and the American ideal of comfort has never had anything but a feeble conception of the tranquil.

Mr. Stevens never urged the idea of denying danger by opposing it, or of disguising reality by order. Order is ultimately, for him, the product of that "will of things,"

> The magnificent cause of being,
> The imagination, the one reality
> In this imagined world.

The imminence of ruin remains inescapable:

> Foam and cloud are one.
> Sultry moon-monsters
> Are dissolving.
> . . . .
> There will never be an end
> To this droning of the surf.

The recognition of evil is patient and stoic, but not oblivious in cynical submission:

> That strange flower, the sun,
> Is just what you say.
> Have it your way.
>
> The world is ugly,
> And the people are sad.

"Poetry is the supreme fiction," but still a fiction—"heavenly labials in a world of gutturals." And whatever its powers,

> The imagination, here, could not evade,
> In poems of plums, the strict austerity
> Of one vast, subjugating, final tone.

The sole anchorage is the private fortitude of conscience and personal will. Mere philosophical attack on mystery in the manner of "The Doctor of Geneva":

> A man so used to plumb
> The multifarious heavens felt no awe
> Before these visible, voluble delugings,
>
> Which yet found means to set his simmering mind
> Spinning and hissing with oracular
> Notations of the wild, the ruinous waste,

is as fruitless as the arbitrary morality of the elders against Susanna. These poems have a sterner counsel:

> Lend no part to any humanity that suffuses
> You in its own light.

Upon this disciplined individualism is built the moral form and order that "takes dominion everywhere," and the music which "in its immortality" "makes a constant sacrament of praise."

The poetic means whereby Mr. Stevens has sublimated this individualism has made his style in every detail the component of his convictions as they emerge from experience. This hairline correspondence is at once the clue to the sensuous logic of his style, and to the realism which saves his imagery from imaginative extravagance, his wit from verbal exercise, and his morality from the illusory intellectual casuistry which has betrayed most of his colleagues. As the most perverse of his conceits holds to its roots in sincerity, so the most circuitous of his deductions refers directly to the actual conflict or moral challenge that initially demanded its unraveling. Mr. Stevens' method—on a different scale of emotional adjustment and sympathies—is almost exactly like Miss Moore's, although he has sought a fundamentally simpler resolution of the disparity between perception and intellectual habit than Miss Moore has in poems like "A Grave," "A Fish," and "Marriage." His book's resources of exactitude in imagery and rhythm, its supple variety of measure, and its creative virtuosity are at length referable to a set of pure principles which make his work a unity as well as a model of severe intention. Imputed derivations from the methods of France, China, and Skeltonic English still leave intact a personality which shares its brilliance with only a few contemporaries. It is a personality whose lucid fitness of phrase and imagery clarifies today

—as it did in an earlier more excited decade—the discord and prolixity of literary experience.

> It is a good light, then, for those
> That know the ultimate Plato,
> Tranquillizing with this jewel
> The torments of confusion.

R. P. BLACKMUR

EXAMPLES OF WALLACE STEVENS

1932

The most striking if not the most important thing about Mr. Stevens' verse is its vocabulary—the collection of words, many of them uncommon in English poetry, which on a superficial reading seems characteristic of the poems. An air of preciousness bathes the mind of the casual reader when he finds such words as fubbed, girandoles, curlicues, catarrhs, gobbet, diaphanes, clopping, minuscule, pipping, pannicles, carked, ructive, rapey, cantilene, buffo, fiscs, phylactery, princox, and funest. And such phrases as "thrum with a proud douceur," or "A pool of pink, clippered with lilies scudding the bright chromes," hastily read, merely increase the feeling of preciousness. Hence Mr. Stevens has a bad reputation among those who dislike the finicky, and a high one, unfortunately, among those who value the ornamental sounds of words but who see no purpose in developing sound from sense.

Both classes of reader are wrong. Not a word listed above is used preciously; not one was chosen as an elegant substitute for a plain term; each, in its context, was a word definitely meant. The impor-

. . . .

tant thing about Mr. Stevens' vocabulary is not the apparent oddity of certain words, but the uses to which he puts those words with others. It is the way that Mr. Stevens combines kinds of words, unusual in a single context, to reveal the substance he had in mind, which is of real interest to the reader.

Good poets gain their excellence by writing an existing language *as if* it were their own invention; and as a rule success in the effect of originality is best secured by fidelity, in an extreme sense, to the individual words as they appear in the dictionary. If a poet knows precisely what his words represent, what he writes is much more likely to seem new and strange—and even difficult to understand— than if he uses his words ignorantly and at random. That is because when each word has definite character the combinations cannot avoid uniqueness. Even if a text is wholly quotation, the condition of quotation itself qualifies the text and makes it so far unique. Thus a quotation made from Marvell by Eliot has a force slightly different from what it had when Marvell wrote it. Though the combination of words is unique it is read, if the reader knows his words either by usage or dictionary, with a shock like that of recognition. The recognition is not limited, however, to what was already known in the words; there is a perception of something previously unknown, something new which is a result of the combination of the words, something which is literally an access of knowledge. Upon the poet's skill in combining words as much as upon his private feelings, depends the importance or the value of the knowledge.

In some notes on the language of E. E. Cummings I tried to show how that poet, by relying on his private feelings and using words as if their meanings were spontaneous with use, succeeded mainly in turning his words into empty shells. With very likely no better inspiration in the life around him, Mr. Stevens, by combining the insides of those words he found fit to his feelings, has turned his words into knowledge. Both Mr. Stevens and Cummings issue in ambiguity—as any good poet does; but the ambiguity of Cummings is that of the absence of known content, the ambiguity of a phantom which no words could give being; while Mr. Stevens' ambiguity is that of a substance so dense with being, that it resists paraphrase and can be truly perceived only in the form of words in which it was given. It is the difference between poetry which depends on the poet and poetry which depends on itself. Reading Cummings you either guess or supply the substance yourself. Reading Mr. Stevens you have only to know the meanings of the words and to submit to the conditions of the poems. There is a precision in such ambiguity all the more precise because it clings so closely to the stuff of the poem that separated it means nothing.

Take what would seem to be the least common word in the whole of *Harmonium* [1]—funest. The word means sad or calamitous or mournful and is derived from a French word meaning fatal, melancholy, baneful, and has to do with death and funerals. It comes ultimately from the Latin *funus* for funeral. Small dictionaries do not stock it. The poem in which it appears is called "Of the Manner of Addressing Clouds," which begins as follows:

> Gloomy grammarians in golden gowns,
> Meekly you keep the mortal rendezvous,
> Eliciting the still sustaining pomps
> Of speech which are like music so profound
> They seem an exaltation without sound.
> Funest philosophers and ponderers,
> Their evocations are the speech of clouds.
> So speech of your processionals returns
> In the casual evocations of your tread
> Across the stale, mysterious seasons. . . .

The sentence in which funest occurs is almost a parenthesis. It *seems* the statement of something thought of by the way, suggested by the clouds, which had better be said at once before it is forgotten. In such a casual, disarming way, resembling the way of understatement, Mr. Stevens often introduces the most important elements in his poems. The oddity of the word having led us to look it up we find that, once used, funest is better than any of its synonyms. It is the essence of the funeral in its sadness, not its sadness alone, that makes it the right word: the clouds are going to their death, as not only philosophers but less indoctrinated ponderers know; so

<hr>

[1] The references are to the new edition of *Harmonium* (New York, Alfred A. Knopf, 1931). This differs from the first edition in that three poems have been cut out and fourteen added.

what they say, what they evoke, in pondering, has that much in common with the clouds. Suddenly we realize that the effect of funest philosophers is due to the larger context of the lines preceding, and at the same time we become aware that the statement about their evocations is central to the poem and illuminates it. The word pomps, above, means ceremony and comes from a Greek word meaning procession, often, by association, a funeral, as in the phrase funeral pomps. So the pomps of the clouds suggests the funeral in funest.

The whole thing increases in ambiguity the more it is analyzed, but if the poem is read over after analysis, it will be seen that *in the poem* the language is perfectly precise. In its own words it is clear, and becomes vague in analysis only because the analysis is not the poem. We use analysis properly in order to discard it and return that much better equipped to the poem.

The use of such a word as funest suggests more abstract considerations, apart from the present instance. The question is whether or not and how much the poet is stretching his words when they are made to carry as much weight as funest carries above. Any use of a word stretches it slightly, because any use selects from among many meanings the right one, and then modifies that in the context. Beyond this necessary stretching, words cannot perhaps be stretched without coming to nullity—as the popular stretching of awful, grand, swell, has more or less nullified the original senses of those words. If Mr. Stevens stretches his words slightly, as a live poet should and must, it is in such a way as to make them seem more precisely themselves than ever. The context is so delicately illuminated, or adumbrated, that the word must be looked up, or at least thought carefully about, before the precision can be seen. This is the precision of the expert pun, and every word, to a degree, carries with it in any given sense the puns of all its senses.

But it may be a rule that only the common words of a language, words with several, even groups of meanings, can be stretched the small amount that is possible. The reader must have room for his research; and the more complex words are usually plays upon common words, and limited in their play. In the instance above the word funest is not so much itself stretched by its association with philosophers as the word philosophers—a common word with many senses—stretches funest. That is, because Mr. Stevens has used the word funest, it cannot easily be detached and used by others. The point is subtle. The meaning so doubles upon itself that it can be understood only in context. It is the context that is stretched by the insertion of the word funest; and it is that stretch, by its ambiguity, that adds to our knowledge.

A use of words almost directly contrary to that just discussed may be seen in a very different sort of poem—"The Ordinary Women." I quote the first stanza to give the tone:

> Then from their poverty they rose,
> From dry catarrhs, and to guitars
> They flitted
> Through the palace walls.

Then skipping a stanza, we have this, for atmosphere:

> The lacquered loges huddled there
> Mumbled zay-zay and a-zay, a-zay.
> The moonlight
> Fubbed the girandoles.

The loges huddled probably because it was dark or because they didn't like the ordinary women, and mumbled perhaps because of the moonlight, perhaps because of the catarrhs, or even to keep key to the guitars. Moonlight, for Mr. Stevens, is mental, fictive, related to the imagination and meaning of things; naturally it fubbed the girandoles (which is equivalent to cheated the chandeliers, was stronger than the artificial light, if any) . . . Perhaps and probably but no doubt something else. I am at loss, and quite happy there, to know anything literally about this poem. Internally, inside its own words, I know it quite well by simple perusal. The charm of the rhymes is enough to carry it over any stile. The strange phrase, "Fubbed the girandoles," has another charm, like that of the rhyme, and as inexplicable: the approach of language, through the magic of elegance, to nonsense. That the phrase is not nonsense, that on inspection it retrieves itself to sense, is its inner virtue. Somewhere between the realms of ornamental sound and representative statement, the words pause and balance, dissolve and resolve. This is the mood of Euphues, and presents a poem with fine parts controlled internally by little surds of feeling that save both the poem and its parts from preciousness. The ambiguity of this sort of writing consists in the double importance of both sound and sense where neither has direct connection with the other but where neither can stand alone. It is as if Mr. Stevens wrote two poems at once with the real poem somewhere between, unwritten but vivid.

A poem which exemplifies not the approach merely but actual entrance into nonsense is "Disillusionment of Ten O'Clock." This poem begins by saying that houses are haunted by white nightgowns, not nightgowns of various other colors, and ends with these lines:

> People are not going
> To dream of baboons and periwinkles.
> Only, here and there, an old sailor,
> Drunk and asleep in his boots,
> Catches tigers
> In red weather.

The language is simple and declarative. There is no doubt about the words or the separate statements. Every part of the poem makes literal sense. Yet the combination makes a nonsense, and a nonsense much more convincing than the separate sensible statements. The statement about catching tigers in red weather coming after the white nightgowns and baboons and periwinkles, has a persuasive force out of all relation to the sense of the words. Literally, there is nothing alarming in the statement, and nothing ambiguous, but by so putting the statement that it appears as nonsense, infinite possibilities are made terrifying and plain. The shock and virtue of nonsense is this: it compels us to scrutinize the words in such a way that we see the enormous ambiguity in the substance of every phrase, every image, every word. The simpler the words are the more impressive and certain is the ambiguity. Half our sleeping knowledge is in nonsense; and when put in a poem it wakes.

The edge between sense and nonsense is shadow thin, and in all our deepest convictions we hover in the shadow, uncertain whether we know what our words mean, nevertheless bound by the conviction to say them. I quote the second half of "The Death of a Soldier":

Death is absolute and without memorial,
As in a season of autumn,
When the wind stops,

When the wind stops and, over the heavens,
The clouds go, nevertheless,
In their direction.

To gloss such a poem is almost impertinent, but I wish to observe that in the passage just quoted, which is the important half of the poem, there is an abstract statement, "Death is absolute and without memorial," followed by the notation of a natural phenomenon. The connection between the two is not a matter of course; it is syntactical, poetic, human. The point is, by combining the two, Mr. Stevens has given his abstract statement a concrete, sensual force; he has turned a conviction, an idea, into a feeling which did not exist, even in his own mind, until he had put it down in words. The feeling is not exactly in the words, it is because of them. As in the body sensations are definite but momentary, while feelings are ambiguous (with reference to sensations) but lasting; so in this poem the words are definite but instant, while the feelings they raise are ambiguous (with reference to the words) and have importance. Used in this way, words, like sensations, are blind facts which put together produce a feeling no part of which was in the data. We cannot say, abstractly, in words, any better what we know, yet the knowledge has become positive and the conviction behind it indestructible, because it has been put into words. That is one business of poetry, to use words to give quality and feeling to the precious abstract notions, and so doing to put them beyond words and beyond the sense of words.

A similar result from a different mode of the use of words may be noticed in such a poem as "The Emperor of Ice-Cream":

Call the roller of big cigars,
The muscular one, and bid him whip
In kitchen cups concupiscent curds.
Let the wenches dawdle in such dress
As they are used to wear, and let the boys
Bring flowers in last month's newspapers.
Let be be finale of seem.
The only emperor is the emperor of ice-cream.

Take from the dresser of deal,
Lacking the three glass knobs, that sheet
On which she embroidered fantails once
And spread it so as to cover her face.
If her horny feet protrude, they come
To show how cold she is, and dumb.
Let the lamp affix its beam.
The only emperor is the emperor of ice-cream.

The poem might be called Directions for a Funeral, with Two Epitaphs. We have a corpse laid out in the bedroom and we have people in the kitchen. The corpse is dead; then let the boys bring flowers in last month's (who would use today's?) newspapers. The corpse is dead; but let the wenches wear their everyday clothes—or is it the clothes they are used to wear at funerals? The conjunction of a muscular man whipping desirable desserts in the kitchen and the corpse protruding horny feet, gains its effect because of its oddity —not of fact, but of expression: the light frivolous words and rapid meters. Once made the conjunction is irretrievable and in its own measure exact. Two ideas or images about death—the living and the dead—have been associated, and are now permanently fused. If the mind is a rag-bag, pull out two rags and sew them together. If the materials were contradictory, the very contradiction, made permanent, becomes a kind of unison. By associating ambiguities found in nature in a poem we reach a clarity, a kind of transfiguration even, whereby we learn *what* the ambiguity was.

The point is, that the oddity of association would not have its effect without the couplets which conclude each stanza with the pungency of good epitaphs. Without the couplets the association would sink from wit to low humor or simple description. What, then, do the couplets mean? Either, or both, of two things. In the more obvious sense, "Let be be finale of seem," in the first stanza, means, take whatever seems to be, as really being; and in the second stanza, "Let the lamp affix its beam," means let it be plain that this woman is dead, that these things, impossibly ambiguous as they may be, are as they are. In this case, "The only emperor is the emperor of ice-cream," implies in both stanzas that the only power worth heeding is the power of the moment, of what is passing, of the flux.[2]

The less obvious sense of the couplets is more difficult to set down because, in all its difference, it rises out of the first sense, and while contradicting and supplanting, yet guarantees it. The connotation is, perhaps, that ice-cream and what it represents is the only power *heeded*, not the only power there is to heed. The irony recoils on itself: what seems *shall* finally be; the lamp *shall* affix its beam. The only emperor is the emperor of ice-cream. The king is dead; long live the king.

The virtue of the poem is that it discusses and settles these matters without mentioning them. The wit of the couplets does the work.

Allied to the method of this poem is the method of much of "Le Monocle de Mon Oncle." The light word is used with a more serious effect than the familiar, heavy words commonly chosen in poems about the nature of love. I take these lines from the first stanza:

> The sea of spuming thought foists up again
> The radiant bubble that she was. And then
> A deep up-pouring from some saltier well
> Within me, bursts its watery syllable.

The words foist and bubble are in origin and have remained in usage both light. One comes from a word meaning to palm false dice, and the other is derived by imitation from a gesture of the mouth. Whether the history of the words was present in Mr. Stevens' mind when he chose them is immaterial; the pristine flavor is still active by tradition and is what gives the rare taste to the lines quoted. By employing them in connection with a sea of spuming thought and the notion of radiance whatever vulgarity was in the two words is purged. They gain force while they lend their own lightness to the context; and I think it is the lightness of these words that permits and conditions the second sentence in the quotation,

[2] Mr. Stevens wrote me that his daughter put a superlative value on ice-cream. Up daughters!

by making the contrast between the foisted bubble and the bursting syllable possible.

Stanza IV of the same poem has a serious trope in which apples and skulls, love and death, are closely associated in subtle and vivid language. An apple, Mr. Stevens says, is as good as any skull to read because, like the skull, it finally rots away in the ground. The stanza ends with these lines:

> But it excels in this, that as the fruit
> Of love, it is a book too mad to read
> Before one merely reads to pass the time.

The light elegance and conversational tone give the stanza the cumulative force of understatement, and make it seem to carry a susurrus of irony between the lines. The word excels has a good deal to do with the success of the passage; superficially a syntactical word as much as anything else, actually, by its literal sense it saves the lines from possible triviality.

We have been considering poems where the light tone increases the gravity of the substance, and where an atmosphere of wit and elegance assures poignancy of meaning. It is only a step or so further to that use of language where tone and atmosphere are very nearly equivalent to substance and meaning themselves. "Sea Surface Full of Clouds" has many lines and several images in its five sections which contribute by their own force to the sense of the poem, but it would be very difficult to attach special importance to any one of them. The burden of the poem is the color and tone of the whole. It is as near a tone-poem, in the musical sense, as language can come. The sense of single lines cannot profitably be abstracted from the context, and literal analysis does nothing but hinder understanding. We may say, if we like, that Mr. Stevens found himself in ecstasy—that he stood aside from himself emotionally—before the spectacle of endlessly varied appearances of California seas off Tehuantepec; and that he has tried to equal the complexity of what he saw in the technical intricacy of his poem. But that is all we can say. Neither the material of the poem nor what we get out of it is by nature susceptible of direct treatment in words. It might at first seem more a painter's subject than a poet's, because its interest is more obviously visual and formal than mental. Such an assumption would lead to apt criticism if Mr. Stevens had tried, in his words, to present a series of seascapes with a visual atmosphere to each picture. His intention was quite different and germane to poetry; he wanted to present the tone, in his mind, of five different aspects of the sea. The strictly visual form is in the background, merely indicated by the words; it is what the visual form gave off after it had been felt in the mind that concerned him. Only by the precise interweaving of association and suggestion, by the development of a delicate verbal pattern, could he secure the overtones that possessed him. A looser form would have captured nothing.

The choice of certain elements in the poem may seem arbitrary, but it is an arbitrariness without reference to their rightness and wrongness. That is, any choice would have been equally arbitrary, and, aesthetically, equally right. In the second stanza of each section, for example, one is reminded of different kinds of chocolate and different shades of green, thus: rosy chocolate and paradisal green; chop-house chocolate and sham-like green; porcelain chocolate and uncertain green; musky chocolate and too-fluent green; Chinese chocolate and motley green. And each section gives us umbrellas variously gilt, sham, pied, frail, and large. The ocean is successively a machine which is perplexed, tense, tranced, dry, and obese. The ocean produces sea-blooms, from the clouds, mortal massives of the blooms of water, silver petals of white blooms, figures of the clouds like blooms, and, finally, a wind of green blooms. These items, and many more, repeated and modified, at once impervious to and merging each in the other, make up the words of the poem. Directly they do nothing but rouse the small sensations and smaller feelings of atmosphere and tone. The poem itself, what it means, is somewhere in the background; we know it through the tone. The motley hue we see is crisped to "clearing opalescence."

> Then the sea
> And heaven rolled as one and from the two
> Came fresh transfigurings of freshest blue.

Here we have words used as a tone of feeling to secure the discursive evanescence of appearances; words bringing the senses into the mind which they created; the establishment of interior experience by the construction of its tone in words. In "Tattoo," we have the opposite effect, where the mind is intensified in a simple visual image. The tone existed beforehand, so to speak, in the nature of the subject.

> The light is like a spider.
> It crawls over the water.
> It crawls over the edges of the snow.
> It crawls under your eyelids
> And spreads its webs there—
> Its two webs.
>
> The webs of your eyes
> Are fastened
> To the flesh and bones of you
> As to rafters or grass.
>
> There are filaments of your eyes
> On the surface of the water
> And in the edges of the snow.

The problem of language here hardly existed: the words make the simplest of statements, and the poet had only to avoid dramatizing what was already drama in itself, the sensation of the eyes in contact with what they looked at. By attempting *not* to set up a tone the tone of truth is secured for statements literally false. Fairy tales and Mother Goose use the same language. Because there is no point where the statements stop being true, they leap the gap unnoticed between literal truth and imaginative truth. It is worth observing that the strong sensual quality of the poem is defined without the use of a single sensual word; and it is that ambiguity between the words and their subject which makes the poem valuable.

There is nothing which has been said so far about Mr. Stevens' uses of language which might not have been said, with different examples, of any good poet equally varied and equally erudite [3]—by

---

[3] See *Words and Idioms*, by Logan Pearsall Smith (Boston, Houghton Mifflin, 1926), page 121. "One of the great defects of our critical vocabulary is the lack of a neutral, non-derogatory name for these great artificers, these artists who derive their inspiration more from the formal than the emotional aspects of their art, and who are more interested in the masterly control of their material, than in the expression of their

which I mean intensely careful of effects. We have been dealing with words primarily, and words are not limited either to an author or a subject. Hence they form unique data and are to be understood and commented on by themselves. You can hardly more compare two poets' use of a word than you can compare, profitably, trees to cyclones. Synonyms are accidental, superficial, and never genuine. Comparison begins to be possible at the level of more complicated tropes than may occur in single words.

Let us compare then, for the sake of distinguishing the kinds of import, certain tropes taken from Ezra Pound, T. S. Eliot, and Mr. Stevens.

From Mr. Pound—the first and third from the *Cantos* and the second from "Hugh Selwyn Mauberley":

> In the gloom, the gold gathers the light against it.

> Tawn foreshores
> Washed in the cobalt of oblivion.

> A catalogue, his jewels of conversation.

From T. S. Eliot—one from "Prufrock," one from *The Waste Land*, and one from "Ash Wednesday":

> I should have been a pair of ragged claws
> Scuttling across the floors of silent seas.

> The awful daring of a moment's surrender
> Which an age of prudence can never retract.

> Struggling with the devil of the stairs who wears
> The deceitful face of hope and of despair.

The unequaled versatility of Ezra Pound (Eliot in a dedication addresses him as *Il miglior fabbro*) prevents assurance that the three lines quoted from him are typical of all his work. At least they are

---

own feelings, or the prophetic aspects of their calling." Mr. Smith then suggests the use of the words erudite and erudition and gives as reason their derivation "from *erudire* (E 'out of,' and *rudis*, 'rude,' 'rough' or 'raw'), a verb meaning in classical Latin to bring out of the rough, to form by means of art, to polish, to instruct." Mr. Stevens is such an *erudite*; though he is often more, when he deals with emotional matters as if they were matters for *erudition*.

characteristic of his later verse, and the kind of feeling they exhibit may be taken as Pound's own. Something like their effect may be expected in reading a good deal of his work.

The first thing to be noticed is that the first two tropes are visual images—not physical observation, but something to be seen in the mind's eye; and that as the images are so seen their meaning is exhausted. The third trope while not directly visual acts as if it were. What differentiates all three from physical observation is in each case the nonvisual associations of a single word—*gathers*, which in the active voice has an air of intention; *oblivion*, which has the purely mental sense of forgetfulness; and, less obviously, *conversation*, in the third trope, which while it helps *jewels* to give the line a visual quality it does not literally possess, also acts to condense in the line a great many nonvisual associations.

The lines quoted from T. S. Eliot are none of them in intention visual; they deal with a totally different realm of experience—the realm in which the mind dramatizes, at a given moment, its feelings toward a whole aspect of life. The emotion with which these lines charge the reader's mind is a quality of emotion which has so surmounted the senses as to require no longer the support of direct contact with them. Abstract words have reached the intensity of thought and feeling where the senses have been condensed into abstraction. The first distich is an impossible statement which in its context is terrifying. The language has sensual elements but as such they mean nothing: it is the act of abstract dramatization which counts. In the second and third distichs words such as *surrender* and *prudence, hope* and *despair*, assume, by their dramatization, a definite sensual force.

Both Eliot and Pound condense; their best verse is weighted— Pound's with sensual experience primarily, and Eliot's with beliefs. Where the mind's life is concerned the senses produce images, and beliefs produce dramatic cries. The condensation is important.

Mr. Stevens' tropes, in his best work and where he is most characteristic, are neither visual like Pound nor dramatic like Eliot. The scope and reach of his verse are no less but are different. His visual images never condense the matter of his poems; they either accent or elaborate it. His dramatic statements, likewise, tend rather to give another, perhaps more final, form to what has already been put in different language.

The best evidence of these differences is the fact that it is almost impossible to quote anything short of a stanza from Mr. Stevens without essential injustice to the meaning. His kind of condensation, too, is very different in character and degree from Eliot and Pound. Little details are left in the verse to show what it is he has condensed. And occasionally, in order to make the details fit into the poem, what has once been condensed is again elaborated. It is this habit of slight re-elaboration which gives the firm textural quality to the verse.

Another way of contrasting Mr. Stevens' kind of condensation with those of Eliot and Pound will emerge if we remember Mr. Stevens' *intentional* ambiguity. Any observation, as between the observer and what is observed, is the notation of an ambiguity. To Mr. Stevens the sky, "the basal slate," "the universal hue," which surrounds us and is always upon us is the great ambiguity. Mr. Stevens associates two or more such observations so as to accent their ambiguities. But what is ambiguous in the association is not the same as in the things associated; it is something new, and it has the air of something condensed. This is the quality that makes his poems grow, rise in the mind like a tide. The poems cannot be exhausted, because the words that make them, intentionally ambiguous at their crucial points, are themselves inexhaustible. Eliot obtains many of his effects by the sharpness of surprise, Pound his by visual definition; they tend to exhaust their words in the individual use, and they are successful because they know when to stop, they know when sharpness and definition lay most hold on their subjects, they know the maximal limit of their kinds of condensation. Mr. Stevens is just as precise in his kind; he brings ambiguity to the point of sharpness, of reality, without destroying, but rather preserving, clarified, the ambiguity. It is a difference in subject matter, and a difference in accent. Mr. Stevens makes you aware of how much is *already* condensed in any word.

The first stanza of "Sunday Morning" may be quoted. It should be remembered that the title is an integral part of the poem, directly affecting the meaning of many lines and generally controlling the atmosphere of the whole.

> Complacencies of the peignoir, and late
> Coffee and oranges in a sunny chair,
> And the green freedom of a cockatoo
> Upon a rug mingle to dissipate
> The holy hush of ancient sacrifice.
> She dreams a little, and she feels the dark
> Encroachment of that old catastrophe,
> As a calm darkens among water-lights.
> The pungent oranges and bright, green wings
> Seem things in some procession of the dead,
> Winding across wide water, without sound.
> The day is like wide water, without sound,
> Stilled for the passing of her dreaming feet
> Over the seas, to silent Palestine,
> Dominion of the blood and sepulchre.

A great deal of ground is covered in these fifteen lines, and the more the slow ease and conversational elegance of the verse are observed, the more wonder it seems that so much could have been indicated without strain. Visually, we have a woman enjoying her Sunday morning breakfast in a sunny room with a green rug. The image is secured, however, not as in Pound's image about the gold gathering the light against it, in directly visual terms, but by the almost casual combination of visual images with such phrases as "*complacencies* of the peignoir," and "the green *freedom* of the cockatoo," where the italicized words are abstract in essence but rendered concrete in combination. More important, the purpose of the images is to show how they dissipate the "holy hush of ancient sacrifice," how the natural comfort of the body is aware but mostly unheeding that Sunday is the Lord's day and that it commemorates the crucifixion.

From her half-awareness she feels the more keenly the "old catastrophe" merging in the surroundings, subtly, but deeply, changing them as a "calm darkens among water-lights." The feeling is dark in her mind, darkens, changing the whole day. The oranges and the rug and the day all have the quality of "wide water, without sound," and all her thoughts, so loaded, turn on the crucifixion.

R. P. BLACKMUR · 67

The transit of the body's feeling from attitude to attitude is managed in the medium of three water images. These images do not replace the "complacencies of the peignoir," nor change them; they act as a kind of junction between them and the Christian feeling traditionally proper to the day. By the time the stanza is over the water images have embodied both feelings. In their own way they make a condensation by appearing in company with and showing what was already condensed.

If this stanza is compared with the tropes quoted from Pound, the principal difference will perhaps seem that while Pound's lines define their own meaning and may stand alone, Mr. Stevens' various images are separately incomplete and, on the other hand, taken together, have a kind of completeness to which Pound's lines may not pretend: everything to which they refer is present. Pound's images exist without syntax, Mr. Stevens' depend on it. Pound's images are formally simple, Mr. Stevens' complex. The one contains a mystery, and the other, comparatively, expounds a mystery.

While it would be possible to find analogues to Eliot's tropes in the stanzas of "Sunday Morning," it will be more profitable to examine something more germane in spirit. Search is difficult and choice uncertain, for Mr. Stevens is not a dramatic poet. Instead of dramatizing his feelings, he takes as fatal the drama that he sees and puts it down either in its least dramatic, most meditative form, or makes of it a simple statement. Let us then frankly take as pure a meditation as may be found, "The Snow Man," where, again, the title is integrally part of the poem:

> One must have a mind of winter
> To regard the frost and the boughs
> Of the pine-trees crusted with snow;
>
> And have been cold a long time
> To behold the junipers shagged with ice,
> The spruces rough in the distant glitter
>
> Of the January sun; and not to think
> Of any misery in the sound of the wind,
> In the sound of a few leaves,

Which is the sound of the land
Full of the same wind
That is blowing in the same bare place

For the listener, who listens in the snow,
And, nothing himself, beholds
Nothing that is not there and the nothing that is.

The last three lines are as near as Mr. Stevens comes to the peculiar dramatic emotion which characterizes the three tropes quoted from Eliot. Again, as in the passage compared to Pound's images, the effect of the last three lines depends entirely on what preceded them. The emotion is built up from chosen fragments and is then stated in its simplest form. The statement has the force of emotional language but it remains a statement—a modest declaration of circumstance. The abstract word *nothing,* three times repeated, is not in effect abstract at all; it is synonymous with the data about the winter landscape which went before. The part which is not synonymous is the emotion: the overtone of the word, and the burden of the poem. Eliot's lines,

The awful daring of a moment's surrender
Which an age of prudence can never retract,

like Pound's lines, for different reasons, stand apart and on their own feet. The two poets work in contrary modes. Eliot places a number of things side by side. The relation is seldom syntactical or logical, but is usually internal and sometimes, so far as the reader is concerned, fatal and accidental. He works in violent contrasts and produces as much by prestidigitation as possible. There was no reason in the rest of "Prufrock" why the lines about the pair of ragged claws should have appeared where they did and no reason, perhaps, why they should have appeared at all; but once they appeared they became for the reader irretrievable, complete in themselves, and completing the structure of the poem.

That is the method of a dramatic poet, who molds wholes out of parts themselves autonomous. Mr. Stevens, not a dramatic poet, seizes his wholes only in imagination; in his poems the parts are already connected. Eliot usually moves from point to point or between two termini. Mr. Stevens as a rule ends where he began; only when he is through, his beginning has become a chosen end. The differences may be exaggerated but in their essence is a true contrast.

If a digression may be permitted, I think it may be shown that the different types of obscurity found in the three poets are only different aspects of their modes of writing. In Pound's verse, aside from words in languages the reader does not know, most of the hard knots are tied round combinations of classical and historical references. A passage in one of the Cantos, for example, works up at the same time the adventures of a Provençal poet and the events in one of Ovid's *Metamorphoses*. If the reader is acquainted with the details of both stories, he can appreciate the criticism in Pound's combination. Otherwise he will remain confused: he will be impervious to the plain facts of the verse.

Eliot's poems furnish examples of a different kind of reference to and use of history and past literature. The reader must be familiar with the ideas and the beliefs and systems of feeling to which Eliot alludes or from which he borrows, rather than to the facts alone. Eliot does not restrict himself to criticism; he digests what he takes; but the reader must know what it is that has been digested before he can appreciate the result. The Holy Grail material in *The Waste Land* is an instance: like Tiresias, this material is a dramatic element in the poem.

Mr. Stevens' difficulties to the normal reader present themselves in the shape of seemingly impenetrable words or phrases which no wedge of knowledge brought from outside the body of Mr. Stevens' own poetry can help much to split. The wedge, if any, is in the words themselves, either in the instance alone or in relation to analogous instances in the same or other poems in the book. Two examples should suffice.

In "Sunday Morning," there is in the seventh stanza a reference to the sun, to which men shall chant their devotion—

> Not as a god, but as a god might be,
> Naked among them, like a savage source.
> Their chant shall be a chant of paradise,
> Out of their blood, returning to the sky; . . .

Depending upon the reader this will or will not be obscure. But in any case, the full weight of the lines is not felt until the conviction of the poet that the sun is origin and ending for all life is shared by the reader. That is why the god might be naked among them. It takes only reading of the stanza, the poem, and other poems where the fertility of the sun is celebrated, to make the notion sure. The only bit of outside information that might help is the fact that in an earlier version this stanza concluded the poem. —In short, generally, you need only the dictionary and familiarity with the poem in question to clear up a good part of Mr. Stevens' obscurities.

The second example is taken from "The Man Whose Pharynx Was Bad":

> Perhaps, if winter once could penetrate
> Through all its purples to the final slate.

Here to obtain the full meaning, we have only to consult the sixth stanza of "Le Monocle de Mon Oncle":

> If men at forty will be painting lakes
> The ephemeral blues must merge for them in one,
> The basic slate, the universal hue.
> There is a substance in us that prevails.

Mr. Stevens has a notion often intimated that the sky is the only permanent background for thought and knowledge; he would see things against the sky as a Christian would see them against the cross. The blue of the sky is the prevailing substance of the sky, and to Mr. Stevens it seems only necessary to look at the sky to share and be shared in its blueness.

If I have selected fairly types of obscurity from these poets, it should be clear that whereas the obscurities of Eliot and Pound are intrinsic difficulties of the poems, to which the reader must come well armed with specific sorts of external knowledge and belief, the obscurities of Mr. Stevens clarify themselves to the intelligence alone. Mode and value are different—not more or less valuable, but different. And all result from the concentrated language which is the medium of poetry. The three poets load their words with the maximum content; naturally, the poems remain obscure until the reader takes out what the poet puts in. What still remains will be the essential impenetrability of words, the bottomlessness of knowledge. To these the reader, like the poet, must submit.

Returning, this time without reference to Pound and Eliot, among the varieties of Mr. Stevens' tropes we find some worth notice which comparison will not help. In "Le Monocle de Mon Oncle," the ninth stanza has nothing logically to do with the poem; it neither develops the subject nor limits it, but is rather a rhetorical interlude set in the poem's midst. Yet it is necessary to the poem, because its rhetoric, boldly announced as such, expresses the feeling of the poet toward his poem, and that feeling, once expressed, becomes incorporated in the poem.

> In verses wild with motion, full of din,
> Loudened by cries, by clashes, quick and sure
> As the deadly thought of men accomplishing
> Their curious fates in war, come, celebrate
> The faith of forty, ward of Cupido.
> Most venerable heart, the lustiest conceit
> Is not too lusty for your broadening.
> I quiz all sounds, all thoughts, all everything
> For the music and manner of the paladins
> To make oblation fit. Where shall I find
> Bravura adequate to this great hymn?

It is one of the advantages of a nondramatic, meditative style, that pure rhetoric may be introduced into a poem without injuring its substance. The structure of the poem is, so to speak, a structure of loose ends, spliced only verbally, joined only by the sequence in which they appear. What might be fustian ornament in a dramatic poem, in a meditative poem casts a feeling far from fustian over the whole, and the slighter the relation of the rhetorical interlude to the substance of the whole, the more genuine is the feeling cast. The rhetoric does the same thing that the action does in a dramatic poem, or the events in a narrative poem; it produces an apparent medium in which the real substance may be borne.

Such rhetoric is not reserved to set interludes; it often occurs in lines not essentially rhetorical at all. Sometimes it gives life to a serious passage and cannot be separated without fatal injury to the poem. Then it is the trick without which the poem would fall flat

entirely. Two poems occur where the rhetoric is the vital trope—
"A High-Toned Old Christian Woman," and "Bantams in Pine-
Woods," which I quote entire:

> Chieftain Iffucan of Azcan in caftan
> Of tan with henna hackles, halt!
>
> Damned universal cock, as if the sun
> Was blackamoor to bear your blazing tail.
>
> Fat! Fat! Fat! I am the personal.
> Your world is you. I am my world.
>
> You ten-foot poet among inchlings. Fat!
> Begone! An inchling bristles in these pines,
>
> Bristles, and points their Appalachian tangs,
> And fears not portly Azcan nor his hoos.

The first and last distichs are gauds of rhetoric; nevertheless they
give not only the tone but the substance to the poem. If the reader
is deceived by the rhetoric and believes the poem is no more than
a verbal plaything, he ought not to read poetry except as a plaything.
With a different object, Mr. Stevens' rhetoric is as ferociously comic
as the rhetoric in Marlowe's *Jew of Malta,* and as serious. The ability to handle rhetoric so as to reach the same sort of intense condensation that is secured in bare, nonrhetorical language is very
rare, and since what rhetoric can condense is very valuable it ought
to receive the same degree of attention as any other use of language.
Mr. Stevens' successful attempts in this direction are what make
him technically most interesting. Simple language, dealing obviously
with surds, draws emotion out of feelings; rhetorical language, dealing rather, or apparently, with inflections, employed with the same
seriousness, creates a surface *equivalent* to an emotion by its approx-
imately complete escape from the purely communicative function
of language.[4]

[4] There is a point at which rhetorical language resumes its communicative
function. In the second of "Six Significant Landscapes," we have this
image:

> A pool shines
> Like a bracelet
> Shaken at a dance,

We have seen in a number of examples that Mr. Stevens uses language in several different ways, either separately or in combination; and I have tried to imply that his success is due largely to his double adherence to words and experience as existing apart from his private sensibility. His great labor has been to allow the reality of what he felt personally to pass into the superior impersonal reality of words. Such a transformation amounts to an access of knowledge, as it raises to a condition where it may be rehearsed and understood in permanent form that body of emotional and sensational experience which in its natural condition makes life a torment and confusion.

With the technical data partly in hand, it ought now to be possible to fill out the picture, touch upon the knowledge itself, in Mr. Stevens' longest and most important poem, "The Comedian as the Letter C." Everywhere characteristic of Mr. Stevens' style and interests, it has the merit of difficulty—difficulty which when solved rewards the reader beyond his hopes of clarity.

Generally speaking the poem deals with the sensations and images, notions and emotions, ideas and meditations, sensual adventures and introspective journeyings of a protagonist called Crispin. More precisely, the poem expounds the shifting of a man's mind between sensual experience and its imaginative interpretation, the struggle, in that mind, of the imagination for sole supremacy and the final slump or ascent where the mind contents itself with interpreting plain and common things. In short, we have a meditation, with instances, of man's struggle with nature. The first line makes the theme explicit: "Nota: man is the intelligence of his soil, the sovereign ghost." Later, the theme is continued in reverse form: "His soil is man's intelligence." Later still, the soil is qualified as suzerain, which means sovereign over a semi-independent or internally autonomous state; and finally, at the end of the poem, the sovereignty is still further reduced when it turns out that the imagination can make nothing better of the world (here called a turnip), than the same insoluble lump it was in the beginning.

---

which is a result of the startling associations induced by an ornamental, social, rhetorical style in dealing with nature. The image perhaps needs its context to assure its quality.

The poem is in six parts of about four pages each. A summary may replace pertinent discussion and at the same time preclude extraneous discussion. In Part I, called The World Without Imagination, Crispin, who previously had cultivated a small garden with his intelligence, finds himself at sea, "a skinny sailor peering in the sea-glass." At first at loss and "washed away by magnitude," Crispin, "merest minuscule in the gales," at last finds the sea a vocable thing,

> But with a speech belched out of hoary darks
> Noway resembling his, a visible thing,
> And excepting negligible Triton, free
> From the unavoidable shadow of himself
> That elsewhere lay around him.

The sea "was no help before reality," only "one vast subjugating final tone," before which Crispin was made new. Concomitantly, with and because of his vision of the sea, "The drenching of stale lives no more fell down."

Part II is called Concerning the Thunderstorms of Yucatan, and there, in Yucatan, Crispin, a man made vivid by the sea, found his apprehensions enlarged and felt the need to fill his senses. He sees and hears all there is before him, and writes fables for himself

> Of an aesthetic tough, diverse, untamed,
> Incredible to prudes, the mint of dirt,
> Green barbarism turning paradigm.

The sea had liberated his senses, and he discovers an earth like "A jostling festival of seeds grown fat, too juicily opulent," and a "new reality in parrot-squawks." His education is interrupted when a wind "more terrible than the revenge of music on bassoons," brings on a tropical thunderstorm. Crispin, "this connoisseur of elemental fate," identifies himself with the storm, finding himself free, which he was before, and "more than free, elate, intent, profound and studious" of a new self:

> the thunder, lapsing in its clap,
> Let down gigantic quavers of its voice,
> For Crispin to vociferate again.

With such freedom taken from the sea and such power found in the storm, Crispin is ready for the world of the imagination. Naturally, then, the third part of the poem, called Approaching Carolina, is a chapter in the book of moonlight, and Crispin a "fagot in the lunar fire." Moonlight is imagination, a reflection or interpretation of the sun, which is the source of life. It is also, curiously, this moonlight, North American, and specifically one of the Carolinas. And the Carolinas, to Crispin, seemed north; even the spring seemed arctic. He meditates on the poems he has denied himself because they gave less than "the relentless contact he desired." Perhaps the moon would establish the necessary liaison between himself and his environment. But perhaps not. It seemed

> Illusive, faint, more mist than moon, perverse,
> Wrong as a divagation to Peking. . . .
> Moonlight was an evasion, or, if not,
> A minor meeting, facile, delicate.

So he considers, and teeters back and forth, between the sun and moon. For the moment he decides against the moon and imagination in favor of the sun and his senses. The senses, instanced by the smell of things at the river wharf where his vessel docks, "round his rude aesthetic out" and teach him "how much of what he saw he never saw at all."

> He gripped more closely the essential prose
> As being, in a world so falsified,
> The one integrity for him, the one
> Discovery still possible to make,
> To which all poems were incident, unless
> That prose should wear a poem's guise at last.

In short, Crispin conceives that if the experience of the senses is but well enough known, the knowledge takes the form of imagination after all. So we find as the first line of the fourth part, called The Idea of a Colony, "Nota: his soil is man's intelligence," which reverses the original statement that man is the intelligence of his soil. With the new distinction illuminating his mind, Crispin plans a colony, and asks himself whether the purpose of his pilgrimage is not

> to drive away
> The shadow of his fellows from the skies,
> And, from their stale intelligence released,
> To make a new intelligence prevail?

The rest of the fourth part is a long series of synonymous tropes stating instances of the new intelligence. In a torment of fastidious thought, Crispin writes a prolegomena for his colony. Everything should be understood for what it is and should follow the urge of its given character. The spirit of things should remain spirit and play as it will.

> The man in Georgia waking among pines
> Should be pine-spokesman. The responsive man,
> Planting his pristine cores in Florida,
> Should prick thereof, not on the psaltery,
> But on the banjo's categorical gut.

And as for Crispin's attitude toward nature, "the melon should have apposite ritual" and the peach its incantation. These "commingled souvenirs and prophecies"—all images of freedom and the satisfaction of instinct—compose Crispin's idea of a colony. He banishes the masquerade of thought and expunges dreams; the ideal takes no form from these. Crispin will be content to "let the rabbit run, the cock declaim."

In Part V, which is A Nice Shady Home, Crispin dwells in the land, contented and a hermit, continuing his observations with diminished curiosity. His discovery that his colony has fallen short of his plan and that he is content to have it fall short, content to build a cabin,

> who once planned
> Loquacious columns by the ructive sea,

leads him to ask whether he should not become a philosopher instead of a colonizer.

> Should he lay by the personal and make
> Of his own fate an instance of all fate?

The question is rhetorical, but before it can answer itself, Crispin, sapped by the quotidian, sapped by the sun, has no energy for questions, and is content to realize, that for all the sun takes

it gives a humped return
Exchequering from piebald fiscs unkeyed.

Part VI, called And Daughters with Curls, explains the implications of the last quoted lines. The sun, and all the new intelligence which it enriched, mulcted the man Crispin, and in return gave him four daughters, four questioners and four sure answerers. He has been brought back to social nature, has gone to seed. The connoisseur of elemental fate has become himself an instance of all fate. He does not know whether the return was "Anabasis or slump, ascent or chute." His cabin—that is the existing symbol of his colony—seems now a phylactery, a sacred relic or amulet he might wear in memorial to his idea, in which his daughters shall grow up, bidders and biders for the ecstasies of the world, to repeat his pilgrimage, and come, no doubt, in their own cabins, to the same end.

Then Crispin invents his doctrine and clothes it in the fable about the turnip:

> The world, a turnip once so readily plucked,
> Sacked up and carried overseas, daubed out
> Of its ancient purple, pruned to the fertile main,
> And sown again by the stiffest realist,
> Came reproduced in purple, family font,
> The same insoluble lump. The fatalist
> Stepped in and dropped the chuckling down his craw,
> Without grace or grumble.

But suppose the anecdote was false, and Crispin a profitless philosopher,

> Glozing his life with after-shining flicks,
> Illuminating, from a fancy gorged
> By apparition, plain and common things,
> Sequestering the fluster from the year,
> Making gulped potions from obstreperous drops,
> And so distorting, proving what he proves
> Is nothing, what can all this matter since
> The relation comes, benignly, to its end?

> So may the relation of each man be clipped.

The legend or subject of the poem and the mythology it develops are hardly new nor are the instances, intellectually considered, very striking. But both the clear depth of conception and the extraordinary luxuriance of rhetoric and image in which it is expressed, should be at least suggested in the summary here furnished. Mr. Stevens had a poem with an abstract subject—man as an instance of fate; and a concrete experience—the sensual confusion in which the man is waylaid; and to combine them he had to devise a form suitable to his own peculiar talent. The simple statement—of which he is a master—could not be prolonged to meet the dimensions of his subject. To the dramatic style his talents were unsuitable, and if by chance he used it, it would prevent both the meditative mood and the accent of intellectual wit which he needed to make the subject his own. The form he used is as much his own and as adequate, as the form of *Paradise Lost* is Milton's or the form of *The Waste Land* is Eliot's. And as Milton's form fitted the sensibility of one aspect of his age, Mr. Stevens' form fits part of the sensibility—a part which Eliot or Pound or Yeats do little to touch—of our own age.

I do not know a name for the form. It is largely the form of rhetoric, language used for its own sake, persuasively to the extreme. But it has, for rhetoric, an extraordinary content of concrete experience. Mr. Stevens is a genuine poet in that he attempts constantly to transform what is felt with the senses and what is thought in the mind—if we can still distinguish the two—into that realm of being, which we call poetry, where what is thought is felt and what is felt has the strict point of thought. And I call his mode of achieving that transformation rhetorical because it is not lyric or dramatic or epic, because it does not transcend its substance, but is a reflection upon a hard surface, a shining mirror of rhetoric.

In its nature depending so much on tone and atmosphere, accenting precise management of ambiguities, and dealing with the subtler inflections of simple feelings, the elements of the form cannot be tracked down and put in order. Perhaps the title of the whole poem, "The Comedian as the Letter C," is as good an example as any where several of the elements can be found together. The letter C is, of course, Crispin, and he is called a letter because he is small (he is referred to as "merest minuscule," which means small letter, in the first part of the poem) and because, though small, like a letter he stands for something—his colony, cabin, and children—as a comedian. He is a comedian because he deals finally with the quotidian (the old distinction of comedy and tragedy was between everyday and heroic subject matter), gorged with apparition, illuminating plain and common things. But what he deals with is not comic; the comedy, in that sense, is restricted to his perception and does not touch the things perceived or himself. The comedy is the accent, the play of the words. He is at various times a realist, a clown, a philosopher, a colonizer, a father, fagot in the lunar fire, and so on. In sum, and any sum is hypothetical, he may be a comedian in both senses, but separately never. He is the hypothesis of comedy. He is a piece of rhetoric—a persona in words—exemplifying all these characters, and summing, or masking, in his persuasive style, the essential prose he read. He is the poem's guise that the prose wears at last.

Such is the title of the poem, and such is the poem itself. Mr. Stevens has created a surface, a texture, a rhetoric in which his feelings and thoughts are preserved in what amounts to a new sensibility. The contrast between his subjects—the apprehension of all the sensual aspects of nature as instances of fate—and the form in which the subjects are expressed is what makes his poetry valuable. Nature becomes nothing but words and to a poet words are everything.

HOWARD BAKER

WALLACE STEVENS

1935

Wallace Stevens calls his new collection of poems *Ideas of Order*, a title which, at first glance, is a rather stiff companion to that of his celebrated but too much neglected volume, *Harmonium*. And indeed the titles do suggest something of the difference between the earlier and the later work. The new poems forage the contemporary scene in their search for order; they are less blithe than the earlier ones, chiefly because they deal openly with specific problems of the last few years, going so far as to mention names like Ramon Fernandez and Karl Marx. And yet "harmonium," as a word, implies much; the earlier poems were successful quests for order, and the new work, with important differences, is a continuation of the old.

Neither the place of *Harmonium* in modern poetry nor its value has been much considered. R. P. Blackmur's excellent study on Stevens (*Hound and Horn*, Winter, 1932) is exceptional, but Mr. Blackmur was forced by the magnitude of the question of technique to let his final estimate stand in a very condensed form. Consequently the critic of Stevens is under something of an obligation to look back once again rather carefully at *Harmonium*. The follow-

. . . .

A portion of an omnibus review entitled "Wallace Stevens and Other Poets," first published in *The Southern Review*, I, Autumn, 1935, and reprinted by permission of the Louisiana State University Press, on behalf of the author.

ing pages will make a small attempt, first of all, to do this.

It is most characteristic of Wallace Stevens, as Mr. Blackmur points out, to take an incident which he has observed, to see it as an example of fate, and to set it down in a deeply meditative form. Stevens' unusual rhetoric is relevant to intense meditation; the surprising words and phrases are, as it were, squeezed out of the poet's being by the very pressure of the observation. All good poets, of course, are not forced by this pressure to use such striking diction, but they are forced to use a diction which, if inconspicuous, is nevertheless unusual. Secondly, a poem of Stevens is often ambiguous in a peculiar way—it preserves the essential ambiguity of the subject matter and of words themselves. Other good poets avoid similar ambiguity by refusing to butt up against the ultimate doubtfulness of things, or, most often, by using new or old detours, to go around it. And finally, it is peculiar to Stevens that his idiom is gay, conversational, and sometimes apparently nonsensical. This is a surface quality, but, though as a rule the poems are serious underneath, their seriousness is also suffused with the surface gaiety.

These propositions demand the careful study which Mr. Blackmur has given them; we, however, shall be able to illustrate them only briefly:

THE VIRGIN CARRYING A LANTERN

There are no bears among the roses,
Only a negress who supposes
Things false and wrong

About the lantern of the beauty
Who walks, there, as a farewell duty,
Walks long and long.

The pity that her pious egress
Should fill the vigil of a negress
With heat so strong!

The point of this poem is that a pious action is mistaken for lechery, and the feeling of the poet is directed at the fact that an incident viewed from different angles is subject to different interpretations. The clash of interpretations is gay and ironic, but it is also a serious matter; for such clashes are what make all moral decision difficult.

The juxtaposing of the virgin and the Negress insinuates the unpredictable workings of fate, and the impersonal attitude of the poet in exclaiming, "The pity that . . ." clinches the little incident as an example of fate. The rhetoric is typical of Stevens. *Bears* is an objectification of possible harms; such symbols are a part of Stevens' method, and once apprehended they give the reader satisfaction rather than trouble. The word *egress* suggests a predominant tendency in Stevens' diction—a tendency to Latin roots; most readers with some knowledge of languages will be unhampered by his vocabulary if they will look carefully at his words and postpone questions as to why he used them; other words, of course, must be tracked down.

The poem is slightly ambiguous in that we are not told specifically why the virgin walks abroad with her lantern. The question, however, borders on curiosity, and the answer lies mainly outside the margins of the poem: the poem is an incident, a bit of drama, and not a narrative. But the ambiguity is alluring; conjecture is permissible because of the hint contained in "a farewell duty," and we may guess that the virgin is concerned with her state as a virgin and intends to part from it—this, on the basis of the facts in the poem and of the similarity of the poem to the parable of the ten virgins and their lamps. The lines might have been called "two ways of looking at love," if it were not for the fact that there seem to be more than two; for there are suggestions of still other views of the material, that, for instance, ritual itself is permeated with love. Certainly the opposition of the virgin and the Negress is more complex than it may at first appear. And it is this opposition which is the heart of our specimen.

So much commentary is an unkindly burden for so short a poem. But, along with literal meaning and traits of style, the overtones— the quality and scope of Stevens' suggestiveness—must be explored as far as possible. For the aura of meaning which surrounds a poem determines very largely its worth; it is this to which all approaches are clumsy, and it is this which in Stevens' work has been misunderstood.

Clashes in points of view are the subjects of many of Stevens' poems. His ability to see things from several sides induces at once his intellectual breadth and his admirably impersonal interest in his subject matter. He also favors, as a subject of poems, the perception of order, of a superior kind of pattern, in external nature. It is significant to his mind that he can see lines "straight and swift between the stars." Similarly a wild and disorderly landscape is transformed into order by the presence of a symmetrical vase:

> I placed a jar in Tennessee,
> And round it was, upon a hill.
> It made the slovenly wilderness
> Surround that hill.
>
> The wilderness rose up to it,
> And sprawled around, no longer wild.
> The jar was round upon the ground
> And tall and of a port in air.
>
> It took dominion everywhere.
> The jar was gray and bare.
> It did not give of bird or bush,
> Like nothing else in Tennessee.

The jar acts in the imagination like one of the poles of the earth, the imaginary order of the lines of latitude and longitude projecting around the pole. The jar itself—simple and symmetrical, a product of the human consciousness and not of nature—is a very fitting symbol for man's dominion over nature. The appearance of the wilderness is deftly suggested; in contrast with it the jar is striking, but, after some familiarity with the poem, it is striking chiefly because it is so precisely an opposite to the wilderness. The spare precision of Stevens produces his initially surprising surfaces; and fortunately, since the surfaces of poems are of only momentary interest, his precision also produces that which is of lasting value in his work: the unmistakable justice of his observations and his combinations of ideas.

The range of his ideas, however, can be got at best in any of his long poems—"Sunday Morning," "Le Monocle de Mon Oncle," or "The Comedian as the Letter C." These are three examples of the finest of modern poems; but we shall be forced to confine our remarks only to the last, which is in many respects the most imposing of the three. "The Comedian as the Letter C" recounts the spiritual adventures of a poet named Crispin. Crispin is small in comparison with the regions through which he adventures, a "merest minuscule in the gales," and is therefore referred to merely by the letter which begins his name; he is a comedian in that he is concerned with "daily" things, just as comedies are, in the classical definition, concerned with daily matters. He is named after the stock valet of Italian and French comedy, he is a valet to experience, and thus he is also a varlet, a knave, etc. His adventures lead him— to resort to rough terms—through a restricted, personal Idealism into sensory realism and thence into a decline into the purely practical. The objective of his adventures is to discover means by which the human faculties can take hold of the world and reduce it to order.

Crispin, at the beginning, is a trifling person, finical and precious, a maker of poems about plums. Consequently he finds himself quite inadequate when he is confronted by the sea during an ocean voyage; his Idealistic conception of himself as the "sovereign ghost" of his experience crumbles in the face of a kind of experience which is too large for him. He is humbled by the sea, and regains his poise only after he enlarges his imagination to the point of being able to grasp the "strict austerity" of the ocean and its "one vast, subjugating, final tone." Then, landing in Yucatan, he uses his new imaginative powers to seek out the principles of order in that tropical scene. By means "of an aesthetic tough, diverse, untamed," he is able to behold "green barbarisms turning paradigm"; he is elated by a thunderstorm, for it, like the sea, strengthens his sense of elemental fate.

Crispin voyages northward. In the midst of a meditation in which he weighs the elemental force of the sun against the evasive and richly imaginative virtues of the moon, he discovers the odors that are overhanging a river bank in Carolina; he suddenly decides, in contrast with his earlier Idealistic leanings, that reality may best be grasped by tabulating sensory experience. To advance this kind of knowledge he plans to found a colony. His colony turns out to be only a cabin in which he and his wife, and then four daughters, live.

HOWARD BAKER · 85

Sapped by the daily routine, he relaxes in his search for answers to his large questions. His daughters, however, become "four questioners and four sure answerers." And Crispin concludes that life goes on, that the world, though subject to various modes of comprehension, continues to be an "insoluble lump."

The drift of this poem is unmistakable. It is not philosophical, though it does have philosophical implications. It is somewhat inconclusive, for it is content to show several attitudes toward experience rather than to choose from them: it seems to be not particularly significant that Crispin ends up a realist. But on the other hand the poem is first and last an exploration of psychological depths. The stuff out of which it is made is the stuff of basic psychological forces, ancient and powerful images, archetypes of experience. Reduced to lowest terms, it is a poem built out of the symbols in which the new psychology is interested—the sun and the moon, the sea, the voyages, the primitive, the obscure pursuit which ends in marriage.

The psychological character of this and of other poems of Stevens is obvious when we put his work beside that of other writers who are following similar bents. Here is, for instance, a passage from Thomas Mann's *Joseph and His Brothers:*

> "Much is in doubt," answered Joseph. . . . "For instance, is it the night that conceals the day, or the day the night? For it would be important to distinguish this, and often in the field and hut have I considered it, hoping, if I could decide, to draw from the decision conclusions as to the virtue of the blessing of the sun and of the moon. . . . Oil and wine are sacred to the sun, and well for him whose brow drippeth with oil and whose eyes are drunken with the shining of red wine! For his words will be a brightness and a laughing and a consolation to the peoples. . . . But the sweet fruit of the fig is sacred to the moon, and well for him whom the little mother nourisheth out of the night with its flesh. For he will grow as though beside a stream, and he should have roots whence the streams arise, and his word be made flesh and living as a body of earth, and with him shall be the spirit of prophecy. . . .

With this, compare "The Comedian as the Letter C":

> The book of moonlight is not written yet
> Nor half begun, but, when it is, leave room
> For Crispin, fagot in the lunar fire,
> Who, in the hubbub of his pilgrimage
> Through sweating changes, never could forget
> That wakefulness or meditating sleep,
> In which the sulky strophes willingly
> Bore up, in time, the somnolent, deep songs . . .
>
> Perhaps the Arctic moonlight really gave
> The liaison, the blissful liaison,
> Between himself and his environment,
> Which was, and is, chief motive, first delight,
> For him, and not for him alone . . .
>
> Thus he conceived his voyaging to be
> An up and down between two elements,
> A fluctuating between sun and moon . . .

For Stevens, as for Mann, the moon is the interpreter of things, is mental, poetic, imaginative, feminine; and the sun is the origin and destination of life, physical, masculine, "the essential prose." This information is necessary for a full understanding of many of the poems in both of Stevens' books; it is information, however, which the author gives again and again in the course of his poems. In "Sunday Morning," stanza VII, for instance, the sun appears in its usual character, and the character itself is carefully described:

> Supple and turbulent, a ring of men
> Shall chant in orgy on a summer morn
> Their boisterous devotion to the sun,
> Not as a god, but as a god might be,
> Naked among them, like a savage source.
> Their chant shall be a chant of paradise,
> Out of their blood, returning to the sky . . .

And, since night is consistently given the characteristics of the moon, many descriptive passages, like this one from "Six Significant Landscapes," have indeed more significance than mere description:

> The night is of the color
> Of a woman's arm:

> Night, the female,
> Obscure,
> Fragrant and supple,
> Conceals herself.
> A pool shines,
> Like a bracelet
> Shaken in a dance.

Just as the sun and moon are consistent symbols, so are the others. The sea, like the sun, is a source of life, but a more immediate one than the sun; and it, since it is subject to time, becomes an image of fundamental destiny—that is to say, of all things ruled by time and therefore by fate, it is the closest to being eternal and absolute and freed from fate. The various voyages and pilgrimages stand for spiritual changes. The primitive and tropical scene is explored because of its richness in broadly significant, dreamlike images. Each of these images is a problem in itself, but often an image like

> an old sailor,
> Drunk and asleep in his boots,
> Catches tigers
> In red weather.

seems to be a product of the obscurer depths of consciousness, interesting in itself but nonsignificant.

Certainly it is not a coincidence that the sun and moon have the same significance in both "The Comedian as the Letter C" and in *Joseph and His Brothers*. Nor is it a coincidence that scientists, as well as Stevens, regard the sea as a source of life; nor that many men in all ages have meditated on the patterns of the stars. Notions of this kind are as old as speculation about the world. They are at present a peculiar property of the psychologists, but they belong as well to every century—to religion and literature as well as to science.

There can well be questions as to the propriety and value of such symbolism in contemporary poetry. Our attitude to these questions depends on what we ask of poetry. If we grant that it is legitimate for poetry to explore the farthest reaches of human experience, then, I think, we have to accept precisely this symbolism. For such attempts by their very nature force the poet down into the modes of thought which men have always labored upon, and these modes of thought are lifeless without their concomitant images. At least, to support Wallace Stevens, we can insist that our best poets work very much in the fashion that he does. Yvor Winters, for instance, in "Heracles," a poem which is concerned with the modern problem of time and its attendant evils, finds his perceptions objectified in the myth which makes Hercules become a sun god, that is, timeless and absolute—properties which, as we have seen, Stevens also attaches to things of the sun. And Allen Tate, exploring the spiritual nature of an age of industry and empire, in a poem called "The Last Days of Alice," uses the fiction of Alice and the looking-glass; here, not only Tate's poem but Lewis Carroll's story draws on the ancient, mythical properties of a mirror.

To avoid ambiguity we must attempt now to state how closely we may presume the poetry of Wallace Stevens to be related to modern psychology. Certainly it is unimportant whether we think that Stevens was or was not under the direct influence of psychoanalysis. But it does seem that, as often happens, the direction of his interests has paralleled that of other important men of his time and particularly, it happens, the psychologists; just as, in a similar fashion, the interests of Proust and Einstein, for instance, seem to have paralleled each other. The times that produced psychoanalysis probably gave an emphasis to Stevens' psychical symbols, and perhaps encouraged the use to some extent of "free association" of ideas rather than strict logic in the writing of verse. But the symbols to which psychology has been attentive are the traditional materials of poetry, and no poetry is strictly logical. So we cannot hold that Stevens' poetry is "explained" by an enumeration of its psychological elements. Psychology, it must be clear, is in these pages simply one convenient instrument for criticism out of the many which would be possible. These poems could be studied and interpreted along any of the various lines that, before the day of modern psychology, the Greek myths, for instance, were studied and interpreted.

And I think that with psychology as an instrument we can go one step further toward describing the essential nature of Stevens' work.

HOWARD BAKER · 89

We observe that C. G. Jung and Wallace Stevens are contemporaries and that each is interested in his fashion in abiding images such as the sun and moon and the sea. It would be valuable to know how far the paths of their work run side by side and whether they have similar goals in view. Though it is rash even to try, without exhaustive study, to summarize achievements of this kind, still some notes may be offered tentatively.

When the human being, according to Jung, explores his consciousness in its several levels, he becomes acquainted with the sovereign images, the archetypes of racial experience, which we have been considering. These images, he begins to realize, have an influence upon his character and actions. Therefore his age is not so important as he had thought it, and the demands of his personal desires become less strong. Continuing in his explorations, he gradually comes into harmony with these psychical images. And then he perceives that he is viewing the world not from the purely egoistic point of view but from a new and more or less impersonal angle, from a spiritual platform which is built both of his personal and of racial and human values. The nonpersonal quality in this new center of consciousness is of greatest importance. For it, Jung seems to say, has the ability to mature, to empower, and to humble men as they must be empowered and humbled, and as they may be by an active social ideal or by an active religion.

The kind of poetry which we have at hand is also an exploration of consciousness. It also aims at an understanding of the archetypes of experience and doubtless does beget a harmonious relationship between the individual and such experience. Moonlight, which Stevens makes synonymous with poetry, is "the liaison, the blissful liaison" between oneself and what Stevens calls one's environment; and this is to say that poetry is a liaison between the individual and his most complex experience. This liaison, moreover, as Stevens says of Crispin,

> was, and is, chief motive, first delight,
> For him, and not for him alone . . .

The liaison effectuates a nonpersonal attitude: one sees Stevens, in the phrase "not for him alone," gliding over from the egoistic to the impersonal. We can add to our earlier remarks on the impersonal quality of Stevens' poetry that it results simply from the fact that the poet's own wishes and needs have been transformed into a sympathy with the larger figures of his poetry; it is a classical kind of detachment in which there is no lessening of human feeling, the "I" is simply enlarged.

We cannot be content merely to say that Stevens and Jung follow similar paths to similar goals. Such a statement would be both too general and too shaky in details. In Jung, for instance, we wonder how the individual can find in himself memories of racial experience, and how ideas can be inherited; we wonder at the source of the inspiration in a meditative poetry like Stevens'. On the other hand we observe that the impersonal and timeless objective is by no means confined to the poetry of Stevens or the thinking of Jung. Consequently it may be necessary to postulate, for the moment at least, an unchanging spiritual world which is independent of the time process, and with which the human being may come in touch and yet at the same time retain his individuality. Such a world might be said to draw or to pull the individual spirit toward it, and to draw thinking as a whole in the direction of absolutes. This hypothesis would account, for instance, for the fact that love appears as the motive power of the universe, not only in modern psychology, but in Hesiod and Thomas Aquinas and Dante. It would indicate the common ground between Jung's psychology and religion, and between poetry and religion. Certainly it is upon very general and difficult and important grounds that Stevens and Jung are alike.[1]

Since Stevens' poetry aims very clearly at an exploration of consciousness, one sees immediately why it has been found difficult by many readers. They have found it difficult because they expected it to do things that it had no intention of doing. But once readers are somewhat acquainted with the outlands of consciousness, the poetry will be clear. Once the modes of thought of the times which produced *Harmonium* are understood, as they will inevitably be understood, then the poetry will be understood.

[1] In this paragraph I have followed the metaphors which V. A. Demant uses in his excellent essay "Dialectics and Prophecy," in *The Criterion,* July, 1935.

We are concerned in Stevens' work with a mental poetry. It is not a poetry of "wit"—not a poetry of intellectual invention like that of the seventeenth and eighteenth centuries; it is not, that is to say, a poetry which, although it, as Dr. Johnson said, surprises and delights by producing something unexpected, aims in the large at clarity and logical progression. Stevens' poetry does not progress; instead it gradually hems in the illusive stuff of the poem. It aims not to expound familiar experience so much as to grasp fundamental experience in all its complexity. It uses a rhetoric of appositives, it encircles and closes in upon its subject matter. It seems to be more like the rhetoric of Donne's sermons than anything else:

> That God should let my soule fall out of his hand, into a bottomlesse pit, and roll an unremovable stone upon it, and leave it to that which it finds there (and it shall finde that there, which it never imagined, till it came thither), and never thinke more of that soule, never have more to doe with it; that of that providence of God, that studies the life of every weed, and worme, and ant, and spider, and toad, and viper, there should never, never any beams flow out upon me; that that God, who looked upon me when I was nothing, and called me when I was not, as though I had been, out of the womb and depth of darknesse, will not looke upon me now, when, though a miserable, and a banished, and a damned creature, yet I am his creature still, and contribute something to his glory, even in my damnation; that that God who hath often looked upon me in my foulest uncleannesse, and when I had shut out the eye of the day, the Sunne, and the eye of the night, the Taper, and the eyes of all the world, with curtaines, and windowes, and doores, did yet see me . . . that this God at last, should let this soule goe away, as a smoake, a vapour, nor a bubble, but must lie in darkness, as long as the Lord of light is light it selfe, and never sparke of that light reach my soule: What Tophet is not a Paradise, what Brimstone is not Amber, what gnashing is not a comfort, what gnawing of the worme is not a tickling, what torment is not a marriage bed to this damnation, to be secluded eternally, eternally, eternally from the sight of God?

In commenting on this passage, James M. Cline has said that "there is no advance in thought, only a refinement of it, a deepening and a gathering intensity of realization; until finally the great period crashes to a close, still reiterating, still sustaining an incremental movement of passion and of mind." [2]

And Stevens likewise. Stevens' poems are incremental movements of passionate, mental rhetoric. They are "unintelligible" in the way that the passage from Donne, if readers were unfamiliar with the notion of damnation, would be unintelligible, and for the same kind of reason. We may illustrate this incremental rhetoric, this closing in upon the stuff of the poem, and at the same time draw together our remarks on *Harmonium* by quoting one more poem, a poem about clouds:

> Gloomy grammarians in golden gowns,
> Meekly you keep the mortal rendezvous,
> Eliciting the still sustaining pomps
> Of speech which are like music so profound
> They seem an exaltation without sound.
> Funest philosophers and ponderers,
> Their evocations are the speech of clouds.
> So speech of your processionals returns
> In the casual evocations of your tread
> Across the stale, mysterious seasons. These
> Are the music of meet resignation; these
> The responsive, still sustaining pomps for you
> To magnify, if in that drifting waste
> You are to be accompanied by more
> Than mute bare splendors of the sun and moon.

Such is persistently the world as Stevens visualizes it—a small region filled with transitory but significant forms under the eternal sun. We are like clouds, we "ponderers"; we too are going to our deaths, and during our passage our best efforts are bent to brilliant words. In this poem, as very often in Stevens' work, the rhetoric itself fertilizes the thinking: the thought simply leaps from "gloomy grammarians" to "funest philosophers," from clouds to men, from the transitoriness of the speaking voice to the transitoriness of thought.

[2] "Poetry of the Mind," *Essays in Criticism* (Berkeley, Calif., 1934).

This conviction that, between the silent eternals, the transitory graces are our best possession, is the motivation of Stevens' rhetoric.

The thirty-three poems in *Ideas of Order* turn upon the same symbols that figure in *Harmonium*. The sun, for instance, appears as the eternal source of things in at least half of the new poems. And the world is still filled with "forms" that require poetic meditation. But the attitude to these symbols has changed. The sun is farther off, or is remembered from another season. The "forms" are complicated because contemporary men and their problems appear among them. The new work bespeaks a need for a practical philosophy and an active social doctrine. And since a number of these poems are expressions of a *desire* for order rather than of order, Stevens' admirable concern with contemporary problems seems unfortunately to have interfered to some extent with the writing of this collection.

In the first place there are notes of regret about the difficulties of the present:

> My old boat goes round on a crutch
> And doesn't get under way.
> It's the time of the year
> And the time of the day.
> ("Sailing After Lunch")

The tone of regret carries over into several poems on the seasons, so that Stevens could be accused of falling into one of Crispin's early faults—of writing about vanishing autumn "by way of decorous melancholy." A certain unfortunate nostalgia, in other words, has crept in to replace the fine, firm impersonality of *Harmonium*.

Despair, in some other instances, is associated with specific problems. Here the scene is the Alps:

> Panoramas are not what they used to be.
> Claude has been dead a long time
> And apostrophes are forbidden on the funicular.
> Marx has ruined Nature,
> For the moment.
> ("Botanist on Alp—No. 1")

The whole poem from which these lines are taken seems to be relaxed both in writing and in thinking. Claude does not take on the symbolic weight that such personages in Stevens' work usually have: the poem seems to slip into private references. But it does, farther along, set up momentarily a vision of lost order, of the world "resting on pillars," with which it opposes the emotion of despair. This tendency to disorganization is perhaps most painful in the long piece "Like Decorations in a Nigger Cemetery," which, doubtless because of the questionable device for holding it together, seems to be completely fragmentary.

But the greater number of the new poems are manly and stanch, and seem to overcome the new difficulties. The "Dance of the Macabre Mice" is a crisp statement of the dignity of government and its inability to change as the necessities of the people change. "Lions in Sweden" is one of the best examples of Stevens' new work. The lion is here an image or concretion of civil order; as such it has the moral qualities of faithfulness, justice, patience, and fortitude; and it has come to be a decoration for savings banks. It has also been an image for the delight of the soul. The poet, finding it now an inadequate image, discards it with the indication that better images must be hunted out. What these may be seems to remain, in this book, a little in doubt.

In general, however, the new ideas of order are not greatly different from those in *Harmonium*. One of the best poems, "Botanist on Alp—No. 2," puts into brilliant language the favorite theme of the balance between transitory graces and the tug of the eternal. The excellent sense of the power of music reappears in "The Idea of Order at Key West"; this poem ends with the following lines:

> The lights in the fishing boats at anchor there,
> As the night descended, tilting in the air,
> Mastered the night and portioned out the sea,
> Fixing emblazoned zones and fiery poles,
> Arranging, deepening, enchanting night.
>
> Oh! Blessed rage for order, pale Ramon,
> The maker's rage to order words of the sea,
> Words of the fragrant portals, dimly-starred,

HOWARD BAKER · 95

And of ourselves and of our origins,
In ghostlier demarcations, keener sounds.

This obviously is dipped from the clear spring from which *Harmonium* came.

It might well be maintained that some of the new poems have suffered not so much from a revision of ideas as from a relaxing of technique. If we put some potentially excellent lines beside those we just quoted, I think that the looseness in metrics will be noticeable first of all:

> In the far South the sun of autumn is passing
> Like Walt Whitman walking along a ruddy shore.
> He is singing and chanting the things that are part of him,
> The worlds that were and will be, death and day.
> Nothing is final, he chants. No man shall see the end.
> His beard is of fire and his staff is a leaping flame.
> ("Like Decorations in a Nigger Cemetery")

Though Whitman may not grace these lines, his name would be more welcome than his meter. And this is unfortunate, for Stevens has seized here upon that sovereign image, the sun, with a vigor that few other poets could command. But it is a fact worth insisting upon that the best work in *Harmonium* is in very strict meter and that in a different form it would be worth not at all what it is. Since, moreover, the new poems tend to be intellectual and logical, rather than passionately mental and incremental as are those in *Harmonium*, the need for rigorous form is undoubtedly just that much the greater.

One of the things that should be said about the new work is that at its best it does not deny *Harmonium*. Although it labors a little inconclusively with the social and economic problems of these disturbed years, its solutions are generally an interesting application of the earlier and larger notions to the specific difficulty. Such application is valuable and necessary. But the earlier notions—the perception of elemental structure in the universe, the balance between the individual and the impersonal—are more valuable than any applications.

HI SIMONS

"THE COMEDIAN AS THE LETTER C": ITS SENSE AND ITS SIGNIFICANCE

1940

As the culminant work of an acknowledged master's first period, "The Comedian as the Letter C" by Wallace Stevens deserves better study than it has received. Since it was brought out in *Harmonium*, in 1923, eight theories for its interpretation have been proposed. But these hypotheses are mutually contradictory, and none of them has been advanced with proof convincing enough to exclude the others. So their net effect is to cancel each other out.

In the recent issue of *The Harvard Advocate* devoted to homage to T. S. Eliot, Robert Penn Warren maintained that "the most important single contribution which Mr. Eliot has made to the cause of poetry is to define in his criticism, and to dramatize in his poetry, the terms on which we may profitably discuss the relation of poetry to the whole life of an individual and to the general society in which the individual lives." To my mind, that exactly defines the subject and the scope of "The Comedian as the Letter C," and I would suggest that if this poem had been studied as attentively as *The Waste Land*, Stevens would now be regarded as quite as significant a contemporary figure as Eliot.

·   ·   ·   ·   ·   ·   ·   ·

First published in *The Southern Review*, V, Winter, 1940, and reprinted by permission of the Louisiana State University Press, on behalf of the estate of Hi Simons.

R. P. Blackmur classified "The Comedian as the Letter C" as "a meditation"; Marianne Moore called it "an expanded metaphor." More simply and precisely, it is an allegory. It is avowedly "doctrinal." It tells both how a representative modern poet tried to change from a romanticist to a realist and how he adapted himself to his social environment. The hero's development may be summarized as a passage from (1) juvenile romantic subjectivism, through (2) a realism almost without positive content, consisting merely in recognizing the stark realities of life, (3) an exotic realism, in which he sought reality in radical sensuousness, (4) a kind of grandiose objectivism, in which he speculated upon starting a sort of local-color movement in poetry, but which he presently saw as romantic, and finally, through (5) a disciplined realism that resulted in his accepting his environment on its own terms, so to speak, and (6) marrying and begetting children, to (7) an "indulgent fatalis[m]" and skepticism. The protagonist's marriage was actual but also symbolic of complete adjustment to society. From the point of view of the poem, this homemaking was an enriching experience, for which the hero was grateful; nevertheless, he was conscious that his eventual "return to social nature" was something of a capitulation to society.

The fable is autobiographical in that it is a generalization upon the author's experience and point of view. By representing the poet in general, and himself in so far as the matter is particularized in him, as the traditional valet-comedian, Stevens characterized his work as satire and self-satire. Not only is The Poet reduced to this lowly personage, but furthermore this character is reduced to the merest designation as an initial letter. This supreme measure of ironical understatement at the outset prepares the reader for apologetics in the conclusion.

The work is divided into six parts, representing successive episodes in the comedian's career, and that is the essential design.

I: *The World Without Imagination.* Crispin's world outlook at the time the fable begins is epitomized in ten words, "man is the intelligence of his soil,/The sovereign ghost." Here *intelligence* means spirit, and *soil* is the form of synecdoche that consists in naming a part instead of the whole. Thus, man is the dominator and determiner of his milieu, the being that thinks for the rest of creation and makes it articulate.

But it is asked: is man the ruling intelligence of life at large?—does he, or fate, determine in the last resort? Crispin now was launched, to put it tritely, on the sea of life, and he found it hard sailing. Not that he missed the protective indulgence of his home environment: "What counted was mythology of self,/Blotched out beyond unblotching." That is, his imagination of himself in a multiplicity of godlike roles was threatened with extinction in the world without imagination where he was now at large. The swaggering valet who had cut such a figure among the nonentities at home began to see himself as just "A skinny sailor peering in the sea-glass." He was overwhelmed by life, "washed away by magnitude."

Another significance is added to the allegory by the personification of the sea as Triton. To the ancients Triton represented the *variability* of the ocean, and the sea is an apt scene for Crispin's adventure because it symbolizes the changefulness of life. Here, however, Triton is also represented as an old *realist*. To the question, "Could Crispin stem verboseness in the sea?" the answer implied is: no, this uncontrollable water deity, who represented real experience, kept forcing the doctrine and hard truths of realism upon him. And just as Triton was complicated to the extreme degree with that character of insistent realism that made him a sea god, just as he was so identified with the ocean that there was

> nothing left of him,
> Except in faint, memorial gesturings
> That were like arms and shoulders in the waves,
>
> .   .   .   .
>
> Just so an ancient Crispin was dissolved.
> The valet in the tempest was annulled.

The threatened catastrophe befell: the old mythology of self was "blotched out." The sea (experience, realism) drenched him through and through so that its essence saturated him—

> until nothing of himself
> Remained, except some starker, barer self
> In a starker, barer world,

and he "became an introspective voyager."

We said at the beginning that the second stage of the protagonist's development was "a realism almost without positive content, consisting merely in recognizing the stark realities of life." That is the condition Crispin has reached now. His reward for his pains was the satisfaction of knowing that he had pierced through illusion and self-delusion to the reality of the objective world and himself in relation to it. "Here was the veritable ding an sich, at last," free from any taint of the mythology of self. "Severance/Was clear." Crispin knew he was cut off from his past forever. In describing that severance by the metaphor, "The last distortion of romance/Forsook the insatiable egotist," the author equates romanticism with egotism. Crispin was undergoing a double transformation, from radical subjectivity to an objective attitude and from romanticism to philosophical and aesthetic realism. For him, both as man and as poet, to see the alternative was to make the choice: "Crispin beheld and Crispin was made new." And at the moment of complete vision the storm ceased, and the sea became a glory, a

> caparison of wind and cloud
> And something given to make whole among
> The ruses that were shattered by the large.

Nature, that heretofore had been so adverse and terrifying, now enfolded him like a beautiful and protective wrap. And he found in it, besides beauty, a balm to heal him of the loss of those ruses, those false personalities, that had been taken from him by the sea. Crispin had sacrificed all to reality; now he found that he had all of reality to recompense him.

II: *Concerning the Thunderstorms of Yucatan*. This episode describes a period in which Crispin regarded himself as an intellectual and aesthetic *avant-gardiste*, rebelling against conventions, experimenting with poetic forms, and testing, elaborating, and beginning to exploit a new conception of the relation of art to life. "The Maya sonneteers," who

> still to the night-bird made their plea,
> As if raspberry tanagers in palms,
> High up in orange air, were barbarous,

are the minor romantics who were still dealing with sentimental conventions and ignoring the crude splendors of the contemporary when Crispin entered the literary scene. Unlike them, he "was too destitute to find" the beauty in the commonplace. He had been "made vivid" and "desperately clear" by a strenuous voyage into reality. "Oracular rockings gave [him] no rest": just as "an ancient Crispin" had been "dissolved," so a new one had been presaged, in the tempest; and now he was impatient to realize that prophecy in order to clothe and feed his destitution. Therefore, "Into a savage color he went on." He saw nature as exotic and sought inspiration in the exotic aspects of the actual. His realism acquired a positive content by developing into a radical sensualism.

If this sense is pursued, the long second paragraph of this canto offers but few difficulties. The lines telling that Crispin prophetically

> sensed an elemental fate,
> And elemental potencies and pangs,
> And beautiful barenesses as yet unseen,

are important for the first occurrence of the word *fate* in this poem. It reminds us of the question raised early in Part I: does man, or fate, determine life? And *barenesses* is one of the unifying threads connecting this canto with those that precede and follow. In the thick of Crispin's first encounter with the world without imagination (I, 60–62),

> nothing of himself
> Remained, except some starker, barer self
> In a starker, barer world.

Then bareness was painful. Now he has discovered that being stripped of the husks of ruse makes things and people beautiful. In its present setting of

> savagery of palms,
> Of moonlight on the thick, cadaverous bloom
> That yuccas breed, and of the panther's tread,

the conception seems paradoxical. Crispin sought the exotic, but in nature, in reality; and he wanted to seize and hold its essence, not any simulacrum. Thus, the ascetic was joined with the exotic in his ideal. So it will be later, too, when he seeks "a sinewy nakedness"

(III, 75–76). All this is summed up, as Stevens has a talent for resuming a whole development of thought, in one metaphor, "The affectionate emigrant found/A new reality in parrot-squawks."

Despite its virtuosity and suavity of execution, the description of the thunderstorm with which the canto ends may raise the question whether a mere thunderstorm is not too ordinary an event to account for the effect this one produced in Crispin. But precisely that is the point. When he had landed in Yucatan he had been "too destitute to find/In any commonplace" what he needed. Now, this storm came to him as a revelation of "the span/Of force, the quintessential fact" of the nature which he was exploring. Like the one at sea, it was an instance of "elemental fate." Because he could now see that,

> His mind was free
> And more than free, elate, intent, profound
> And studious of a self possessing him,
> That was not in him in the crusty town
> From which he sailed. . . .

III: *Approaching Carolina.* The moonlight in that description of "the thick, cadaverous bloom/That yuccas breed" is literal moonlight. Everywhere else in this poem it stands for the "romantic" imagination, in antithesis to the sun that represents matter-of-fact realism. If "The book of moonlight" means the history, not of romanticism generally, but of Crispin's romantic phase, the opening of the canto,

> The book of moonlight is not written yet
> Nor half begun, but, when it is, leave room
> For Crispin, fagot in the lunar fire,

is, in effect, an admission that, although "The last distortion of romance" had "forsaken" Crispin during the crossing from Bordeaux, he wasn't yet an absolute realist. "Leave room, therefore," in the still unfinished record of his subjective period, for a description of his early attitude toward North America. He had known of both the grandeur and the beauty of the continent but had been a little repelled by the thought of them. This land was too "polar-purple, chilled/And lank." Crispin imagined even the Southern states as "polar":

> The green palmettoes in crepuscular ice
> Clipped frigidly blue-black meridians,
> Morose chiaroscuro, gauntly drawn.

One of the diverting ironies in the early criticism of Stevens was a controversy in *The New Republic* in 1919, in which Louis Untermeyer charged him with being precious and Conrad Aiken defended him on the grounds of—his preciosity. The present explanation of why Crispin wrote little during this period is a sufficient reply to his accuser and a disavowal of his advocate in that dispute—

> How many poems he denied himself
> In his observant progress, lesser things
> Than the relentless contact he desired . . .

This last phrase completes our justification for stressing, in regard to the "barenesses" Crispin sensed in Yucatan, the intensity of his effort "to seize and hold the essence of" reality. No superficial contact could satisfy him, nor any sham.

In a style as ornate as Stevens', occasional literal or near-literal statements or abstract or nonfigurative phrases are necessary to form a system of trusses, so to speak, that will prevent the heavy construction of imagery from sagging of its own weight. Not that the framework of sense of this poem is overweighted with decoration; but the symbolism Stevens uses as the material of his poetry makes for a massive construction requiring strong support. We now come to one of the key passages of the work. And where the weight of sense is greatest, the support is most evident.

"Perhaps," we read, "the Arctic moonlight"—Crispin's romantic notion of this "polar" America—

> Perhaps the Arctic moonlight really gave
> The liaison, the blissful liaison,
> Between himself and his environment,
> Which was, and is, chief motive, first delight,
> For him, and not for him alone.

In the interests of his psychoanalytical interpretation, Howard Baker says of these lines, "Moonlight, which Stevens makes synonymous with poetry, is 'The liaison . . .' between oneself and what Stevens calls one's environment. . . ." But no, the moonlight "seemed/Illusive, faint, more mist than moon, perverse . . ." Even more explicitly: "Moonlight was an evasion, or, if not,/A minor meeting, facile, delicate." So this paragraph does not give the solution of Crispin's problem, as Mr. Baker supposes; but it forecasts that the solution will be some theory of the milieu. The poet is trying to work out a reconciliation with his environment which so far he has felt as hostile, some adjustment that will be valid for others of his kind and time as well as himself.

Thus Crispin

> conceived his voyaging to be
> An up and down between two elements,
> A fluctuating between sun and moon,

between objectivity and subjectivity, between realism and protean romanticism that seemed to be always with him in some shape or another. Of one thing he was sure: he could not thrive in a "polar" climate. "It was a flourishing tropic he required/For his refreshment . . ." That would seem to suggest that the paradox of his ascetic exoticism was about to be resolved as he tossed between the Carolina of his juvenile imagination and the actuality that presented itself "across his vessel's prow."

It must be remembered that Crispin was still seeking "a sinewy nakedness" when he approached North America. But

> as he came he saw that it was spring,
> A time abhorrent to the nihilist
> Or searcher for the fecund minimum.

And so "The moonlight fiction"—his notion that America was essentially "polar-purple, chilled/And lank"—"disappeared." He reached the continent, not at its magnificent principal port, but through the backyard of a provincial sea town.

> A river bore
> The vessel inward. Tilting up his nose,
> He inhaled the rancid rosin, burly smells
> Of dampened lumber, emanations blown
> From warehouse doors, the gustiness of ropes,
> Decays of sacks, and all the arrant stinks
> That helped him round his rude aesthetic out.
> He savored rankness like a sensualist.

That is the point of the experience. "It made him see how much/Of what he saw he never saw at all" in the smelly everyday things about him. In Yucatan he had sought the real in the exotic; here he was persuaded to a simpler realism. The contradiction in which he had been vacillating between romanticism and realism was resolved in a new synthesis in which he discovered "the beauty in the commonplace." Therein he was to find the possibility of a realistic, an honest American poetry.

IV: *The Idea of a Colony*. The apothegm summarizing the attitude Crispin has now achieved—"his soil is man's intelligence" —means just the opposite of the egotistical maxim with which he started, "man is the intelligence of his soil." The environment determines man. In this sense it is the spirit that rules him. "That's better," said Crispin. "That's worth crossing seas to find."

And at once he strove "For application." He forswore the exotic, the effete and the insipid, and became a realist in poetry to an extent he hadn't known before.

> Here was prose
> More exquisite than any tumbling verse:
> A still new continent in which to dwell.

He purposed to give this continent a poetic expression consistent with his principle of social determinism and "To make a new intelligence prevail," that is, to substitute another dominating influence for that of the Maya sonneteers. Ever since Crispin had "Dejected his manner to the turbulence" of the sea, he had been outwardly as diffident as inwardly stoical. But now he turned more aggressive, and "planned a colony." As sketched in his "prolegomena" (III, 32–75), his conception seems to have been one of a local-color literary movement that should embrace all America. Its first principle was, "The natives of the rain are rainy men"—the inhabitants of each region have characteristics formed by the regional influences.

In retrospect, Crispin himself thought his prospectus a capricious document, "a singular collation," in which were "inscribed/Commingled souvenirs and prophecies." But the reasons why his projected regionalism came to nothing are more important than that.

HI SIMONS · 105

Crispin eventually realized that "These bland excursions into time to come" were "Related in romance to backward flights. . . ." They were fantasies of what poetry might be or ought to be. However abundant in fancy and however grandiose they may have been, their inspiration was tainted with the same fault that had repelled Crispin from his original romanticism. They were not a straightforward facing of reality.

It was because he shunned romanticism in this new guise as he had eschewed it in its earlier form that, "Preferring text to gloss, he humbly served/Grotesque apprenticeship to chance event. . . ." To one who "could not be content with counterfeit," it was better to drift than to carry on in what he knew was a false direction. And yet he felt demeaned by this passiveness; he saw himself as the lowest order of comedian, "A clown," although, still, "an aspiring clown."

This canto started in a spirit almost of triumph in the announcement of Crispin's new credo. His plan for the colony was elaborated with gusto and drollery. The tone of the verses continued vigorous through the rejection of the counterfeit "fictive flourishes." But in what we have just read it turned to a tone of apology, and in the next four lines it becomes one of frustration:

> There is a monotonous babbling in our dreams
> That makes them our dependent heirs, the heirs
> Of dreamers buried in our sleep, and not
> The oncoming fantasies of better birth.

The meaning of the images here and through the rest of the canto is this: There is an eternal recurrence of the same motifs in our dreams (our daydreams and projects, also) that makes them, not harbingers of higher attainment, but the inheritors of the weaknesses and limitations of the "stale lives" hidden within us. Crispin knew those "ruses." If he indulged in their fantasies, and still sometimes sank "down to the indulgences/That in the moonlight have their habitude," it was in spite of himself. He condemned all dreams. He was content that the common round of petty events should run its course. —Is this fable simply an amusing invention, with Crispin

in his usual role of deft entertainer? "No, no": it is, "veracious page
on page, exact," the poet's confession.

It tells us that Crispin's search for a realistic aesthetic to substitute for romanticism ended in failure. For this is the last of poetics,
in a limited sense, in "The Comedian as the Letter C." The remaining two cantos deal more particularly with that other, cognate
theme, the personal relation of the poet to society. And the tone of
frustration in the conclusion of this section is due to the poet's
failure to solve the problem he undertook to solve.

V: *A Nice Shady Home.* Harriet Monroe held that Crispin as
poet was undone by "bewildered marital allegiances" and "parental
loyalties." But Crispin's sense of frustration set in before he married. His failure to achieve as greatly as he had aspired was due not
only to his social behavior but also, and to begin with, to a defect
in his social thinking. The first two-thirds of Part V is an exposition
of a change in the character of his realism. Perhaps, we are told, if
discontent had pricked Crispin on, he might after all have carried
through his idea for a colony and so have become literary progenitor
of a school of regional bards. But his realism and his poetical Americanism failed to sustain themselves on the noble plane on which
they had been conceived. They declined to the realism of the quotidian.

> He first, as realist, admitted that
> Whoever hunts a matinal continent
> May, after all, stop short before a plum
> And be content and still be realist.

A realist, that is, may take life at its most serious and august, may
seek verity in the largest generalities, or he may recognize in the
simplest physical fact a reality as final as that of the cosmos. "So
Crispin hasped on the surviving form,/For him, of shall or ought
to be in is."

Did Wallace Stevens regard this as an advance in the development of his personage or as a compromise of his intentions? He
wrote: "Was [Crispin] to bray this in profoundest brass/Arointing
his dreams with fugal requiems"—execrating and driving off the last
vestiges of his romanticism with poems declaring its final extinction

in this new phase of realism? Why shouldn't Crispin have trumpeted out his acceptance of things as they are as proudly as he had his two earlier philosophies, "man is the intelligence of his soil" and "his soil is man's intelligence"? The answer is implied in the rhetorical questions that follow (V, 38–54). This succession of antitheses between the high things Crispin had projected and the small end to which they came expresses the poet's sense of his character's failure.

Here we are reminded that the question whether man or fate is the determiner of life was raised in the first canto (4–6), and that Crispin had prophetically "sensed an elemental fate" (II, 38) during his experience in the Yucatan jungle. When, assailed by a force he could not withstand, he had taken refuge in the church, he had been a "connoisseur of elemental fate" (II, 77). So now, confronted with a situation with which he cannot cope, he becomes a fatalist. To the self-accusation of compromise, he pleads the weakness of man in general. And that plea is continued in four lines as distinctive for their tone of melancholy as the passage on the "babbling in our dreams":

> What is one man among so many men?
> What are so many men in such a world?
> Can one man think one thing and think it long?
> Can one man be one thing and be it long?

Finally this elaborate apology leads to the catastrophe of the intellectual comedy: "For realists, what is is what should be." There is evidence, as we shall see presently, of a more than chance relationship between this aphorism and the idea that concludes the First Epistle of "An Essay on Man," by Pope:

> And spite of Pride, in erring Reason's spite,
> One truth is clear, *Whatever is, is right.*

Stevens never has been given due credit by critics of the Right for having, honestly though a trifle sheepishly, endorsed the present order of society more explicitly than any other poet of his generation.

"And so it came," the story goes on, that Crispin married: "his duenna brought/Her prismy blonde and clapped her in his hands. . . ." The duenna may be understood as Crispin's guardian angel, his fate in guise of procuress. And who, or what, allegorically, was the blonde? There is no reason for not taking this "blissful liaison" symbolically as the final reconciliation of the poet with his environment and also autobiographically as representative of the author's own marriage. In any case, it was beautifully successful. Crispin went his round

> Like Candide,
> Yeoman and grub, but with a fig in sight,
> And cream for the fig and silver for the cream,
> A blonde to tip the silver and to taste
> The rapey gouts.

There are only four literary allusions in this entire poem: the adoption of a stock character of old French comedy as hero, the two classical references, to Triton (I, 37–51) and Vulcan (II, 84), and finally this simile involving the novelette by Voltaire. Candide, too, had set out in the world with big notions of himself and life at large, had journeyed to America, undergone diverse escapades and ended "Yeoman and grub," with a fig in sight and Cunégonde— hardly a "prismy blonde," however—for bride. As Crispin abandoned his brave plans and settled down to a humdrum cottage life, so Candide finally shut off Pangloss's cheerful babble with the resolute conclusion, "*Oui, mais il nous faut cultiver nos jardins.*" Stevens could not have found in all fiction another character that would have illustrated so appositely the petit-bourgeois realism with which the intellectual development of his personage ended. This reference to *Candide* so soon after Crispin's final philosophy is epitomized in the line, "For realists, what is is what should be," helps the hypothesis that this epigram was modeled on the one in "An Essay on Man." For the optimism which Voltaire ridiculed in his romance was as much that of Pope as that of Leibnitz and Wolff. Stevens need not have had more than a college acquaintance with the eighteenth century to have known that. So his allusion to Voltaire goes far toward establishing a relationship between the English reactionary of the eighteenth century and the Stevens of the reactionary early 1920's.

HI SIMONS · 109

Well, Crispin and his girl were deeply—deliciously!—in love. Yet even in the midst of their exquisite epithalamium Stevens remembers what this adjustment to society that consisted so largely of capitulation to the dominant social values cost his hero. For he writes that "the quotidian saps philosophers/And men like Crispin. . . ." But there were compensations in such happy love; Crispin concluded:

> the quotidian
> Like this, saps like the sun, true fortuner.
> For all it takes it gives a humped return
> Exchequering from piebald fiscs unkeyed.

VI: *And Daughters with Curls.* Of course, the four girls are imaginary. They are "True daughters both of Crispin and his clay," products of the poet's union with "his soil," a general symbol of the "settling down" that follows a happy marriage. The poet summons them to forgather and chime forth Crispin's final commentary on his adventures. They come running and toddling for a jog-trot on his knee, leaving no room there for poetical offspring. Whether it be regarded as ascent or fall, Crispin's return from rebellious individualism "to social nature," once it was started, "Involved him in midwifery so dense/His cabin counted as phylactery," or, as Mr. Blackmur suggested, "His cabin— . . . the existing symbol of his colony—seems now . . . a sacred relic or amulet he might wear in memorial to his idea. . . ." Later it became a place of bothersome perambulators, then haunt of children nibbling at the sweet-coated emptiness of life, and finally "dome/And halidom for the unbraided femes," impatiently cramming themselves with the unripe fruits of the earth, yearning while waiting for life's ecstasies. *Femes* is an old Scotch legal term for women. So the "dome/And halidom" is simply the temple and sanctuary of the daughters growing toward young womanhood. On the first reading, the line, "All this with many mulctings of the man," probably will be taken to mean that Crispin's energy was sapped by the quotidian so largely composed of "midwifery." But *mulct* is, again, a legal word of which the proper definition is "to punish for any offense by imposing a fine or forfeiture." Crispin had to pay dearly for the joys of fatherhood, as he had to pay for the bliss of matrimony.

For whenever he thought he might set out again "To colonize his polar planterdom/And jig his [spiritual] chits upon his cloudy knee" (V, 8–9), he was stopped by these physical chits. And unexpectedly he found that his children helped to confirm him in the habitude of an "indulgent fatalis[m]." As Crispin aged, his attitude toward his charming girls became much like his devotion to their mother. Cost him what they might, artistically, intellectually, and otherwise, they were "Four questioners and four sure answerers"— questioners of life on their own account, answerers to his questionings that life was good.

Yet that did not obscure the fact that his life had been a compromise, when, finally, "Crispin concocted doctrine from the rout." His "grand pronunciamento"—"grand" because it prevailed over his three earlier doctrines—is this:

> The world, a turnip once so readily plucked,
> Sacked up and carried overseas, daubed out
> Of its ancient purple, pruned to the fertile main,
> And sown again by the stiffest realist,
> Came reproduced in purple, family font,
> The same insoluble lump.

After all his adventures, the condign but scarcely noble quotidian in which he ended was much like that from which he had started in Bordeaux. "A nice shady home and daughters with curls." Gelatines and jupes again. The same honest quilts. Same simple saladbeds. Well, "The fatalist/Stepped in and dropped the chuckling" —the small hard lump, the pill life had compounded for him— "down his craw,/Without grace or grumble." And that was the end of it.

Apparently this story is light comedy. But, as we noticed at the beginning, it was "Invented for its pith." Take it that way, as Crispin intended, "Autumn's compendium, strident in itself/But muted, mused, and perfectly revolved. . . ." Or if as allegory it seems false, if Crispin's example is worthless, beginning with great pretensions, "Concluding fadedly" . . . if he who, when he was still trying to solve his problems on his own terms, preferred text to gloss, now is prone to gloss over his failures with fair excuses . . . if his "anecdote," with these distortions, proves that he proves nothing— what does it matter anyway, since the story comes out well enough in the end? The fatalism and the skepticism are as abject as the "rout" was complete: "So may the relation of each man be clipped."

If this reading of it is correct, "The Comedian as the Letter C" is a greater poem than previous students have recognized. Its subject is the central artistic problem of these times, the relation of the poet to his environment and, by extension, "the relation of poetry to the whole life of an individual and to the general society in which the individual lives." Critics who have said or insinuated that Stevens' poetry is not worth reading for its contents have missed the point: anyone can dispute any of his thoughts, of course, but no one can question the seriousness of his thinking. "The Comedian as the Letter C" is Wallace Stevens' *Ulysses*. It discloses the sources of the skepticism and fatalism that run through all his later work.

Another consequence of this interpretation is to give consistency to Stevens' entire *oeuvre*. Twelve years after the appearance of "The Comedian as the Letter C" he wrote that "it is inevitable that a poet should be concerned with" "questions of political and social order," and shortly thereafter he was dealing "with the incessant conjunctions between things as they are and things imagined." But those are the subjects with which Stevens has always been concerned, and many of his seemingly precious and whimsical short poems gain in significance and power if read with this understanding.

Finally, this analysis clarifies the course Stevens has run amidst the intellectual-social currents of the past two decades. Ever since he took one, Mr. Stevens' position has been on the Right. So the major theme in the study of his work from the dialectical point of view would seem to issue from the contrast between the bland conservatism of 1923—"For realists, what is is what should be"—and the dejected realization of 1935, that "man . . ./Lives in a fluid, not on solid rock" ("Owl's Clover," V, ii, 40–43), or the still more disheartened question of 1937:

> Is this picture of Picasso's, this "hoard
> Of destructions," a picture of ourselves,
> Now, an image of our society?
> ("The Man With the Blue
> Guitar," XV, 1–3)

What happens, through fifteen years of accelerating social disintegration, to a poet who identifies himself with things as they are? The question is interesting in reference to Mr. Stevens, of course, because he is one of the best artists of our time, and because, like every first-rate poet, he is as sensitive and honest in his thought as he is expert and scrupulous in his craftsmanship.

JULIAN SYMONS

A SHORT VIEW OF
WALLACE STEVENS

1940

Wallace Stevens is the author of three books of verse, *Harmonium*, *Ideas of Order*, and *The Man With the Blue Guitar*, none of which has been published in this country. In America he is regarded as the best American-born poet writing today, next to Eliot: in England his work is even less respected than read. These notes are the basis for a more comprehensive study: their primary purpose is to introduce to English readers a poet remarkably neglected in this country.

Harmonium was first published in 1923; another edition with fourteen new poems appeared in 1931, but the book as a whole represents the first, and less valuable part of Stevens' work. A great many of the poems are written in the Imagist manner, with the sharpness and sensitiveness characteristic of the Imagist poets, but not with an Imagist seriousness; most of them contain a slightly tittery joke, or if they do not contain a joke they contain a titter, something which might have been a joke, the idea of a joke; and the joke is on Mr. Stevens as much as anyone. Here are three parts of "Thirteen Ways of Looking at a Blackbird":

·　　　·　　　·　　　·　　　·　　　·　　　·　　　·

First published in *Life and Letters Today* (London), XXVI, September, 1940, and reprinted by permission of the author.

I

Among twenty snowy mountains,
The only moving thing
Was the eye of the blackbird.

II

I was of three minds,
Like a tree
In which there are three blackbirds.

III

The blackbird whirled in the autumn winds.
It was a small part of the pantomime.

This is nearly very gentle, very observant, very charming: but it is not serious, it is in a gentlemanly way a little absurd. Mr. Stevens strolls through a world of rosy chocolate and gilt umbrellas, making little ironic notes on shapes and colors ("The houses are haunted/ By white night-gowns./None are green,/Or purple with green rings, /Or green with yellow rings,/Or yellow with blue rings"), and the delicacy of his taste and the extreme Englishness of his American accent make him look uncommonly like Philo Vance. This is "The Surprises of the Superhuman":

> The palais de justice of chambermaids
> Tops the horizon with its colonnades.

> If it were lost in Übermenschlichkeit,
> Perhaps our wretched state would soon come right.

> For somehow the brave dicta of its kings
> Make more awry our faulty human things.

Surely it is a Regie from which this cultivated American is flickin' the ash? The most successful poems in *Harmonium* are those in which the necessary irony is least obviously self-critical, "Le Monocle de Mon Oncle," "Peter Quince at the Clavier," and "The Comedian as the Letter C." This last long poem is indeed Stevens' most completely characteristic work, and conveys more nearly than any other single poem his skill and usual flippancy:

Crispin,

The lutanist of fleas, the knave, the thane,
The ribboned stick, the bellowing breeches, cloak
Of China, cap of Spain, imperative haw
Of hum, inquisitorial botanist,
And general lexicographer of mute
And maidenly greenhorns, now beheld himself,
A skinny sailor peering in the sea-glass.
What word split up in clickering syllables
And storming under multitudinous tones
Was name for this short-shanks in all that brunt?

This bears about the same relation to the best poetry of our time as the comedy of Lyly bears to the comedy of Ben Jonson. One may admire the virtuosity which is able to keep language on this level throughout a poem of more than five hundred lines: but still the whole poem remains a piece of virtuosity, a literary curio. Crispin is a comedian, he is not a serious person, and hardly a *person* even, Crispin is by his creator's account "The Comedian *as the Letter C*": Crispin is Mr. Stevens playing gracefully with the letter C and employing this imperative haw of hum to probe very gently beneath the shell of that real world which he uneasily apprehends to exist somewhere outside Crispin's range: Crispin is a figure finally unsatisfactory, even to his creator.

II

Twelve years after *Harmonium*, *Ideas of Order* was published in a limited edition. In 1936 it was brought out by Knopf, with three new poems. On the dust-wrapper of the Knopf edition Mr. Stevens says:

> We think of changes occurring today as economic changes, involving political and social changes. Such changes raise questions of political and social order.
> While it is inevitable that a poet should be concerned with such questions, this book, although it reflects them, is primarily concerned with ideas of order of a different nature, as, for example, the dependence of the individual, confronting the elimination of established ideas, on the general sense of order; the idea of order created by individ-

ual concepts, as of the poet, in "The Idea of Order at Key West"; the idea of order arising from the practice of any art, as of poetry, in "Sailing After Lunch."

This is clear, direct, and a little portentous: but the language of the poems in *Ideas of Order* is not strikingly different from that of the poems in *Harmonium*:

> Why seraphim like lutanists arranged
> Above the trees? And why the poet as
> Eternal *chef d'orchestre?*

Why indeed? Still, *Ideas of Order* represents an advance: it is less uselessly ironic, more accomplished all round. There is an increase in skill, not accompanied by any marked alteration in style.

The apparatus of Stevens' poems has changed little from 1923 to 1939; although he passed twelve years without publishing a book it is difficult to mark off his writing into periods, as the writing of Eliot and Yeats may easily (and usefully) be marked off. *Harmonium* is not noticeably less "mature" than the later books; but the title poem of *The Man With the Blue Guitar*, published in 1937, is undoubtedly Stevens' most important work. This piece contains thirty-three short poems, written in couplets, which deal with "the incessant conjunction between things as they are and things imagined." The blue guitar, which is used as "a symbol of the imagination" throughout the series of poems, is a piece of *chinoiserie*, as irritating as Yeats's occult symbols; yet Stevens' writing is so skillful, and the alternations from poem to poem are so deft, that admiration overcomes irritation, and the blue guitar is reluctantly accepted:

> I cannot bring a world quite round,
> Although I patch it as I can.
>
> I sing a hero's head, large eye
> And bearded bronze, but not a man,
>
> Although I patch him as I can
> And reach through him almost to man.
>
> If to serenade almost to man
> Is to miss, by that, things as they are,

> Say that it is the serenade
> Of a man that plays a blue guitar.

That is the second poem; the third begins: "Ah, but to play man number one," and touches the same theme a little differently; the fourth is a philosophical reflection:

> So that's life, then: things as they are?
> It picks its way on the blue guitar.
>
> A million people on one string?
> And all their manner in the thing,
>
> And all their manner, right and wrong,
> And all their manner, weak and strong?
>
> The feelings crazily, craftily call,
> Like a buzzing of flies in autumn air,
>
> And that's life, then: things as they are,
> This buzzing of the blue guitar.

The subject of the poems shifts lightly and with ease from politics to abstract morality, from abstract morality to the practical use of poetry; all the poems are written with the wit and care shown in the quotations given; and through them all the symbol of the blue guitar is maintained with wonderful ingenuity. "The Man With the Blue Guitar" is certainly one of the most notable poetic achievements of the last twenty years, an achievement that may be compared with *The Waste Land* or "Mauberley." If the language used is rarely strong, it is always delicate; if the images are not frequently powerful, they are always pleasing; if the "meaning" is sometimes flippant, it is rarely obscure: and of how many contemporary poems can one say so much?

Stevens has published several poems in the last two years, poems which seem rarely to approach "The Man With the Blue Guitar" in wit and skill: but full comment on these new poems can hardly be made with justice until they are collected into a book. Some estimate of the value of his work up to 1937 may, however, be made the more justly because his writing shows little sign of further development.

There is a point of view from which Stevens makes the painful experiments with language and subject matter through which Eliot and Pound developed in the late 'teens and the early 'twenties, seem needless and even slightly ridiculous. For Stevens' "method," though sometimes allegorical, and demanding continual attention on the reader's part, successfully avoids the "cultural-reference-rock-jumping" difficulties of *The Waste Land* and the metrical and linguistic trickery of "Mauberley" and the *Cantos*. By using an eight- or ten-syllable iambic line for all his important poems, Stevens has been able to obtain as much variation as is necessary, or even desirable, in his verse. Great interest in the *alteration* of poetic structure (distinct from interest in the use and application of technique), like that shown by Eliot and Pound in their early work, and less subtly by Cummings and William Carlos Williams, is perhaps an indication of uneasiness rather than of self-confidence. The introduction of radical novelties in poetic structure is so dangerous, it may here be pointed out, that it should be attempted only after existing structural forms have been most carefully considered and rejected. I do not suppose that anyone thinks of Eliot and Pound primarily as craftsmen; whereas it is often difficult to think of Stevens as anything else. Several of Eliot's early poems, and certainly Pound's "Mauberley," become from this point of view almost elaborate evasions of technical problems; there are no such evasions in "Le Monocle de Mon Oncle" or "Peter Quince at the Clavier." Eliot and Pound have, in fact, always had *something to say*, and they are conscientious enough artists to be troubled about a way of saying it: an unfriendly criticism of Stevens would conclude that he has not much to say, but an unusual facility in saying it.

Such a criticism would be oversimple; but still, Stevens' weakness as a poet proceeds always from a point at which an *idea* is being communicated; communicated (from lack of a creative and critical background) in unsuitably flippant language. A long and interesting article on "The Comedian as the Letter C" appeared recently in the American *Southern Review*.* The writer of the article (an enthusiastic admirer of Stevens) concludes that the poem

* The reference is to the essay by Hi Simons that is reprinted above, pp. 97-113. Eds.

tells both how a representative modern poet tried to change from a romanticist to a realist and how he adapted himself to his social environment. The hero's development may be summarized as a passage from (1) juvenile romantic subjectivism, through (2) a realism almost without positive content, consisting merely in recognizing the stark realities of life, (3) an exotic realism, in which he sought reality in radical sensuousness, (4) a kind of grandiose objectivism, in which he speculated upon starting a sort of local-color movement in poetry, but which he presently saw as romantic, and finally, through (5) a disciplined realism that resulted in his accepting his environment on its own terms, so to speak, and (6) marrying and begetting children, to (7) an "indulgent fatalis[m] and skepticism."

If one accepts this definition, which is perhaps as near an estimate of the poem's theme as can be made, it becomes necessary to point out that there is a distressing lack of relevance between the language in which the poem is written, and the meaning which is given to that language. Nor is it possible to defend the poem on the ground that it is deliberately a comic piece. Mr. Stevens' intention was no doubt to write a comic poem, but certainly not to write a flippant poem; yet the flippancy of the language (which has already been indicated) can hardly be exceeded; and it is not less true now than in the eighteenth century that flippant language used throughout a lengthy poem must debase a serious theme. An elaborate faulty good taste mars even "The Man With the Blue Guitar":

> He held the world upon his nose
> And this-a-way he gave a fling.
>
> His robes and symbols, ai-yi-yi—
> And that-a-way he twirled the thing.

It is a grave artistic error to attempt to convey the "incessant conjunction between things as they are and things imagined" in such terms.

This flippancy leads naturally to Stevens' second and most revealing fault. His work does not contain an objective view of life, nor does it express a philosophy of life; it gives instead an objective view of Mr. Stevens in various attitudes. This view may be most valuable and interesting; it may result in valuable and interesting poetry; it is still a poor substitute for a view of life. There is not one of Stevens' more important poems which does not have for its explicit or implied subject *the poet and his poetry*, rather than a consideration of a man as a social animal. The definition of "The Comedian as the Letter C" is terribly clear; poem XXII of "The Man With the Blue Guitar" begins "Poetry is the subject of the poem"; and notice also "The practice of any art, *as of poetry*" in the note on *Ideas of Order*. The reader will get a clear understanding of Stevens' approach to his material, and the nature of that material, by examining the second poem (already quoted) of "The Man With the Blue Guitar" and by asking that always reasonable question: What is said in this poem? What is it about?

The poem is a statement on the poet's part of inability to come to terms with the "real world," the world which is "quite round" (lines 1–2). He writes about man: but his writing turns man to a formal figure, a "bearded bronze" (lines 3–6). So far so bad, one could think, for the poet; but then comes the conclusion (lines 7–10) that *if* inability to come to terms with the world, to be unable to write of men as men but only as bearded bronzes, is "to miss, by that, things as they are" (there is now some doubt on that point, it seems!), then we should say that this is "the serenade/Of a man that plays a blue guitar." That is to say, since the blue guitar is "a symbol of imagination," the serenade of a man who has imagination. So that the position finally posed by Mr. Stevens here is that if you have "imagination," you will not be able to write about reality, about "things as they are." "Imagination" and "reality" are mutually contradictory; and this leads the "imaginative" man, the player of the blue guitar, into all kinds of (poetic) difficulties, for he writes about reality at one remove: and like a man who sees himself reflected endlessly between two mirrors, he writes not about life, but about the poet's reflection of life in his poetry; which becomes before long the reflection of a reflection, and at length the reflection of a reflection of a reflection.

"Poetry is the subject of the poem": if the statement were true, so much the worse for poetry; but it is not true, or it is not true of the best poetry. There is a limited sense in which poetry is the poem's subject, that sense in which reading, and not reading a book, is the object of reading, in which being a butcher, and not making a living, is the object of being a butcher; but that is not at all what Mr. Stevens means, or it is not what he means in his own poetry, where poetry is too often the subject of the poem, with results rarely sterile, but sometimes absurd.

From the failure of American literature to evolve in a hundred and fifty years a tradition useful to a poet inclined to European dandyism; from a time and a country absorbed in largely useless literary experiments; from his own natural genius and limitations; comes the work of Wallace Stevens. Eccentric and typical, irritating and urbane, his poems are not less readable than unsatisfying: and if one pays the tribute to his skill to say that they are always very well worth rereading, one must make at the same time the motion of regret that a poet with so fine a natural genius should be so frequently a fribble of taste.

J. V. CUNNINGHAM

TRADITION AND MODERNITY: WALLACE STEVENS

1949; revised 1960

I have defined tradition in such a way that every poem necessarily has a tradition, but this is not the common meaning of the term. For we distinguish between what is traditional and what is not, and in the latter case the principle is a negative one. This is a concern for tradition that is a modern concern, and provoked by something so simple as a sense of alienation from the past, a feeling for history as distinct. It is motivated by the persuasion that tradition has been lost and is only recoverable in novelty. From this arises a corollary concern with modernity in poetry, for which the poetry of Wallace Stevens will serve as an illustration. He himself writes in the poem entitled "Of Modern Poetry":

> The poem of the mind in the act of finding
> What will suffice. It has not always had
> To find: the scene was set; it repeated what
> Was in the script.
>   Then the theatre was changed
> To something else. Its past was a souvenir.

•　　　•　　　•　　　•　　　•　　　•　　　•　　　•

To be modern in this sense is not the same thing as to be contemporary, to be living and writing in our time, or to have lived and written within our normal life span. There are many contemporary poets who are not modern. The modern poet writes the new poetry, as it was called some years ago. His poetry is modern in that it is different from the old, the traditional, the expected; it is new. This is the sense in which *modern* has always been used in these contexts: the modern poets in Roman antiquity were Calvus and Catullus who wrote in new and untraditional poetic forms, in forms borrowed from another language and regarded by the traditionalists of the times as effete and decadent; whose subjects were novel and daring; and whose attitudes were in conscious distinction from those of the old morality. Again, the *moderni*, the modern thinkers in the late Middle Ages, were those who advocated and embraced the new logic of that time and whose attitudes were thought to be dangerous to the established order; it was later said that they caused the Reformation.

The modern poet, then, is modern only in the light of tradition, only as distinguished from the old. His forms, his models, his subjects, and his attitudes are different from and in opposition to the customary and expected forms, models, subjects, and attitudes of his own youth and of his readers. Consequently to be modern depends on a tradition to be different from, upon the firm existence of customary expectations to be disappointed. The new is parasitic upon the old. But when the new has itself become the old, it has lost its quality of newness and modernity and must shift for itself.

This is the situation with respect to what is still called modern poetry; it is rapidly becoming the old and the traditional. There appeared some years ago a number of articles in the leading conventional journals in this country in defense of modern poetry. Had the poetry still needed defense, the articles would never have been accepted by the editors of those journals. But modern poetry is, in fact, in secure possession of the field, and its heroes are aged men with a long public career behind them. Wallace Stevens, in fact, died recently at the age of seventy-six after a public career of forty years. Yet the attitude of modernity still persists. These poets still represent to the young writer of today the new, the adventurous, the advance-guard, the untried. Their names are still sacred to the initiate.

For it is the condition of modernity in art that it appeal to the initiate, that it provoke the opposition of the ordinary reader who has the customary and old expectations which it is the purpose of modern art to foil. Hence it lives in an attitude of defense; is close and secret, not open and hearty; has its private ritual and its air of priesthood—*odi profanum vulgus et arceo*, "I despise the uninitiated crowd, and I keep them at a distance." It is obscure, and its obscurities are largely calculated; it is intended to be impenetrable to the vulgar. More than this, it is intended to exasperate them.

There is something of this in all art that is genuine. For the genuine in art is that which attains distinction, and the distinguished is uncommon and not accessible to the many. It is different, it must be different, and as such provokes the hostility of the many, and provokes it the more in that its difference is a claim to distinction, to prestige, and to exclusion. This claim is diminished by time. Wordsworth is now regarded as quite traditional, quite stuffy and conventional. For the particular qualities of difference in an older body of poetry that has been absorbed into the tradition become part of that tradition, and so something that the reader actually need not see since he does not know it is different. He may then in his early years and through his school days develop a set of social responses to the received body of poetry; he may enjoy that poetry without effort, be pleased by his conditioned responses, and think of himself as a lover and judge of poetry. When the audience for poetry becomes satisfied with a customary response to a customary poem, when they demand of the poet that he write to their expectations, when distinction is lost in commonness, there is need for the modern in art, for a poetry that is consciously different, even if it often mistakes difference for distinction. The poet must exasperate his reader, or succumb to him.

Such was the situation out of which Stevens wrote, at least as it seemed to him and to those of his contemporaries who have become the aged fathers of modern poetry. They sought to appear different, and hence distinguished, and they succeeded perhaps too well. The first thing that strikes the reader of Wallace Stevens, and the quality for which he was for a long time best known, is the piquant, brilliant, and odd surface of his poems. They are full of nonsense cries, full of virtuoso lines, such as

> Chieftain Iffucan of Azcan in caftan
> Of tan with henna hackles, halt!

which unexpectedly make grammar and sense if you read them slowly with closed ears. They are thronged with exotic place-names, but not the customary ones of late romantic poetry; instead of "Quinquireme of Nineveh from distant Ophir" there is "a woman of Lhassa," there is Yucatan. Rare birds fly, "the green toucan," and tropical fruits abound, especially the pineapple. Odd characters appear—Crispin, Redwood Roamer, Badroulbadour, black Sly, Nanzia Nunzio—and are addressed in various languages—my semblables, Nino, ephebi, o iuventes, o filii. And they wear strange hats.

A good deal of this, of course, is simply the unexpected in place of the expected; a new and different collection of proper names, for example, instead of the old collection, but used largely for the same purpose while seeming to deny this by being designedly different.

> Canaries in the morning, orchestras
> In the afternoon, balloons at night. That is
> A difference, at least, from nightingales,
> Jehovah, and the great sea-worm.

The process is common in Stevens, and can be seen neatly in one of his most engaging stanzas. The theme of the stanza is the traditional one of Tom Nashe's

> Brightness falls from the hair,
> Queens have died young and fair.

But instead of Helen and Iseult there are references to the beauties in Utamaro's drawings and to the eighteenth-century belles of Bath:

> Is it for nothing, then, that old Chinese
> Sat tittivating by their mountain pools
> Or in the Yangtse studied out their beards?
> I shall not play the flat historic scale.
> You know how Utamaro's beauties sought
> The end of love in their all-speaking braids.
> You know the mountainous coiffures of Bath.

> Alas! Have all the barbers lived in vain
> That not one curl in nature has survived?

A woman's hair is here used as a synecdoche for her beauty. Have all those who have cared for and cherished her hair, have all the barbers, lived in vain, that though much has survived in art, none has survived in nature? The poet concludes then, expressing the sense of the couplet of a Shakespearean sonnet:

> This thought is as a death, which cannot choose
> But weep to have that which it fears to lose.

in the more specialized terms of his synecdoche, but almost as movingly:

> Why, without pity on these studious ghosts,
> Do you come dripping in your hair from sleep?

Much of this is rather amusing, and even, as we say now, intriguing. Sometimes, indeed, it is much more than that, as in the stanza just quoted, which is poetry of a rare though too precious kind. But Wallace Stevens had a public career in poetry for forty years, and forty years is a little too long for this sort of pepper to retain its sharpness and piquancy. We have to ask, then, what is the motive and purpose in this?

It is usually said that these aspects of Stevens' work derive from a study of the French poets of the latter nineteenth century, the Symbolists and Parnassians, and this explanation no doubt is true enough. But it is not a sufficient explanation. The prestige of that poetry was not so high in Stevens' youth as to serve as a motive, though it might be sufficient now. The motive is rather a more human one. It is disdain—disdain of the society and of the literary tradition in which he grew up, of himself as a part of that society, and of his readers so far as they belonged to it. He sought, he tells us:

> when all is said, to drive away
> The shadow of his fellows from the skies,
> And, from their stale intelligence released,
> To make a new intelligence prevail.

How did he go about it? He celebrated the rankest trivia in the choicest diction. He was a master of the traditional splendors of poetry and refused to exercise his mastery in the traditional way; he displayed it in the perverse, the odd:

> he humbly served
> Grotesque apprenticeship to chance event . . .

He became "a clown" though "an aspiring clown." In his own summary, in the passage that immediately follows the lines quoted above, he explains:

> Hence the reverberations in the words
> Of his first central hymns, the celebrants
> Of rankest trivia, tests of the strength
> Of his aesthetic, his philosophy,
> The more invidious, the more desired.
> The florist asking aid from cabbages,
> The rich man going bare, the paladin
> Afraid, the blind man as astronomer,
> The appointed power unwielded from disdain.

He possessed "the appointed power"—the Miltonic and Scriptural phrasing is blasphemous in this context, and deliberately so— but would not wield it from disdain. The question then is: Why should he have felt such disdain? The answer can be collected from various of his poems but is given full and detailed exposition in the one from which I have just quoted. This is "The Comedian as the Letter C," the showpiece and longest poem in his first book. The poem is sufficiently complex to have several centers of concern. I shall interpret it, however, in terms of our question, and we shall find that this will turn out to be a primary concern of the poem.

The poem consists of six sections, each of a little under a hundred lines of blank verse. It is in form and subject a poem that depicts the growth of a poet's mind, and though the main character is given the fictitious name of Crispin, he may be taken as an aspect of the author, a mask for Wallace Stevens the poet, so that the poem in effect is autobiographical. It belongs, then, to that literary form of which the model and prototype is Wordsworth's *Prelude*. It is not a wholly easy poem to read, partly because much of it is written in Stevens' fastidious and disdainful manner, partly because its structure is not adequately adjusted to its theme. The hero of the poem makes a sea voyage to a strange and exotic country, in this case Yucatan, and back to his own land. The motive for the voyage is explicitly given late in the poem in the passage already quoted:

> What was the purpose of his pilgrimage,
> Whatever shape it took in Crispin's mind,
> If not, when all is said, to drive away
> The shadow of his fellows from the skies,
> And, from their stale intelligence released,
> To make a new intelligence prevail?

His voyage is a rejection of his society as banal and trite, of its intelligence as stale, and his quest is the quest of a new intelligence. His problem was the problem that every teacher of freshman composition sets his better students, the problem of striking through routine phrasing and syntax to the genuine, the honest, the possibly distinguished.

The hero is portrayed as having been before this trip a man who was master of his environment, but he was a little man, "the Socrates of snails," "this nincompated pedagogue," and the environment itself was trivial; it was a land "of simple salad-beds,/Of honest quilts." It was, in fact, to quote Stevens' own summary of his early environment in an essay of later date, "the comfortable American state of life of the 'eighties, the 'nineties, and the first ten years of the present century." It was the time and place when the sun

> shone
> With bland complaisance on pale parasols,
> Beetled, in chapels, on the chaste bouquets.

It was that middle-class culture of business, public chastity, and official Christianity which we often call, with some historical injustice, Victorianism. In this world Crispin wrote the conventional poetry of the times. He was one

> that saw
> The stride of vanishing autumn in a park
> By way of decorous melancholy . . .
> That wrote his couplet yearly to the spring,
> As dissertation of profound delight . . .

However, he found that

J. V. CUNNINGHAM · 129

He could not be content with counterfeit . . .

It was this dissatisfaction with the conventional—in society and in poetry—"That first drove Crispin to his wandering." He alludes to it as "The drenching of stale lives," a life of "ruses" that was shattered by the experience of his voyage.

He found the sea overwhelming; he "was washed away by magnitude." "Here was no help before reality." It was not so much that he was cut off from the snug land; he was cut off from his old self:

> What counted was mythology of self,
> Blotched out beyond unblotching.

and hence from his environment. He was destitute and bare:

> The salt hung on his spirit like a frost,
> The dead brine melted in him like a dew
> Of winter, until nothing of himself
> Remained, except some starker, barer self
> In a starker, barer world . . .

From this experience he came to Yucatan. The poetasters of that land, like the poetasters at home, in spite of the vividness of experience around them,

> In spite of hawk and falcon, green toucan
> And jay . . .

still wrote conventional verses about the nightingale, as if their environment were uncivilized. But Crispin's conversion at sea—for it was obviously a conversion—had enlarged him, made him complicated

> and difficult and strange
> In all desires . . .

until he could reduce his tension only by writing an original and personal poetry, different and unconventional.

The experience at sea is now reinforced by another experience in Yucatan, of the same elemental, overwhelming sort:

> one
> Of many proclamations of the kind,
> Proclaiming something harsher than he learned

from the commonplace realism of home:

> From hearing signboards whimper in cold nights.

It was rather "the span/Of force, the quintessential fact,"

> The thing that makes him envious in phrase.

It was the experience that altered and reinvigorated his poetry, the source from which he drew that distinction of style that marks off his published work from the sentimental verses he had printed in the college magazine some twenty years before. The experience was of the type of a religious experience:

> His mind was free
> And more than free, elate, intent, profound
> And studious of a self possessing him,
> That was not in him in the crusty town
> From which he sailed.

The poetry he now wrote issued from this context. It was conditioned by the kind of dissatisfaction that drove Crispin to his wandering, by such an experience as Crispin's on the voyage and in Yucatan, and by its results. This dissatisfaction lies behind a good many of Stevens' poems, which deal, if one looks beneath the distracting surface, simply with the opposition between the aridities of middle-class convention and the vivid alertness of the unconventional, as in "Disillusionment of Ten O'clock." Some repeat in smaller compass and with other properties the subject of "The Comedian": as "The Doctor of Geneva." In others he attempts to deal directly with the experience of the sea, but this was a religious experience without the content of traditional religion. In fact, it had no content at all beyond the intuition of a bare reality behind conventional appearance, and hence was an unfertile subject for poetry since it was unproductive of detail. He treated it in one of his best short poems, "The Snow Man," but when he had stated it, there was nothing more to be done with it, except to say it over again in another place. This he has repeatedly done, though with a prodigality of invention in phrasing that is astounding.

Most of what is interesting in Stevens issues from this problem. It can be put in various terms. It is the problem of traditional religion and modern life, of imagination and reality, but it can be best put for Stevens in the terms in which it is explicitly put in "The Comedian." The problem is the relationship of a man and his environment, and the reconciliation of these two in poetry and thus in life. The two terms of this relationship are really Wordsworth's two terms: the one, what the eye and ear half create; the other, what they perceive. The reconciliation in Wordsworth is in a religious type of experience:

> With what strange utterance did the loud dry wind
> Blow through my ear! the sky seemed not a sky
> Of earth—and with what motion moved the clouds!

> Dust as we are, the immortal spirit grows
> Like harmony in music; there is a dark
> Inscrutable workmanship that reconciles

> Discordant elements, makes them cling together
> In one society.

The reconciliation in Stevens is sought in poetry, in

> those
> True reconcilings, dark, pacific words,
> And the adroiter harmonies of their fall.

For poetry is the supreme fiction of which religion is a manifestation:

> Poetry
> Exceeding music must take the place
> Of empty heaven and its hymns,

> Ourselves in poetry must take their place . . .

What Crispin is seeking is such a reconciliation, a oneness between himself and his environment. He began in the illusion that he was the intelligence of his soil, but the experience of reality overwhelmed him, and he came to believe that his soil was his intelligence. At this extreme he wrote poems in which a person is described by his surroundings. But he perceived that this too was sentimental, and so he settled for the ordinary reality of daily life, married, had four daughters, and prospered. However, he did not give up poetry entirely; he recorded his adventures in the poem, and hoped that the reader would take it as he willed: as a summary

> strident in itself
> But muted, mused, and perfectly revolved
> In those portentous accents, syllables,
> And sounds of music coming to accord
> Upon his law, like their inherent sphere,
> Seraphic proclamations of the pure
> Delivered with a deluging onwardness.

Such is Stevens' account of the source of his distinctive style and distinctive subjects. But he owed more than he acknowledged to the old and the traditional. He owed "the appointed power" which was "unwielded from disdain."

That he once had the appointed power is clear in his greatest poem, and one of his earliest, "Sunday Morning." The poem is traditional in meter—it is in eight equal stanzas of blank verse—and has as its subject a deep emotional attachment to traditional Christianity and a rejection of Christianity in favor of the clear and felt apprehension of sensory detail in this life, together with an attempt to preserve in the new setting the emotional aspects of the old values.

The poem depicts a woman having late breakfast on a Sunday morning, when of course she should have been at church. She is for the moment at one with her surroundings, which are vivid, sensory, familiar, and peaceful. All this serves to dissipate the traditional awe of Christian feeling, but the old feeling breaks through:

> She dreams a little, and she feels the dark
> Encroachment of that old catastrophe,
> As a calm darkens among water-lights.

Her mood "is like wide water, without sound," and in that mood she passes over the seas to the contemplation of the Resurrection. The remainder of the poem consists of the poet's comment and argument on her situation, on two short utterances she delivers out of her musing, and finally on the revelation that comes to her in a voice.

The poet asserts that Christianity is a religion of the dead and the unreal. In this living world of the sun, in these vivid and sensory surroundings, there is that which can assume the values of heaven:

> Divinity must live within herself:
> Passions of rain, or moods in falling snow;
> Grievings in loneliness, or unsubdued
> Elations when the forest blooms; gusty
> Emotions on wet roads on autumn nights;
> All pleasures and all pains, remembering
> The bough of summer and the winter branch,
> These are the measures destined for her soul.

The truly divine is the human and personal in this world: it consists in the association of feeling with the perception of natural landscape, in human pleasure and pain, in change, as in the change of seasons.

He then argues that the absolute God of religion was originally inhuman, but that the Incarnation by mingling our blood with His, by mingling the relative and human with the Absolute, satisfied man's innate desires for a human and unabsolute Absolute. Certainly, if "the earth" should "Seem all of paradise that we shall know," we would be much more at home in our environment:

> The sky will be much friendlier then than now . . .
> Not this dividing and indifferent blue.

At this point the woman speaks in her musing, and says that she could acquiesce in this world, that she could find an earthly paradise, a contentment, in the perception of Nature, in the feel of reality, except that the objects of her perception change and disappear. Nature is an impermanent paradise. The poet, however, answers that no myth of a religious afterworld has been or ever will be as permanent as the stable recurrences of Nature:

> There is not any haunt of prophecy,
> Nor any old chimera of the grave,
> Neither the golden underground, nor isle
> Melodious, where spirits gat them home,
> Nor visionary south, nor cloudy palm
> Remote on heaven's hill, that has endured

As April's green endures; or will endure
Like her remembrance of awakened birds,
Or her desire for June and evening, tipped
By the consummation of the swallow's wings.

The woman speaks again, and says:

"But in contentment I still feel
The need of some imperishable bliss."

There remains the desire for the eternal happiness of tradition. The lines that comment on this present some difficulties to interpretation until it is seen that the poet in his answer proceeds by developing the woman's position. Yes, he says, we feel that only in death is there fulfillment of our illusions and our desires. Even though death be in fact the obliteration of all human experience, yet it is attractive to us; it has the fatal attractiveness of the willow in old poetry for the lovelorn maiden. Though she has lovers who bring her gifts—that is, the earth and its beauty—she disregards the lovers and, tasting of the gifts, strays impassioned toward death.

Yet the paradise she would achieve in death is nothing but an eternal duplicate of this world, and lacking even the principle of change, leads only to ennui. Therefore, the poet creates a secular myth, a religion of his irreligion. The central ceremony is a chant, a poem to the sun,

Not as a god, but as a god might be . . .

It is an undivine fiction that preserves the emotions of the old religion but attaches them to a poetry in which the sensory objects of a natural landscape enter into a union in celebration of the mortality of men:

And whence they came and whither they shall go
The dew upon their feet shall manifest.

The biblical phrasing creates a blasphemous religion of mortality.

The poem now concludes with a revelation. Out of the woman's mood a voice cries to her, saying that the place of the Resurrection is merely the place where a man died and not a persisting way of entry into a spiritual world. The poet continues:

J. V. CUNNINGHAM · 135

> We live in an old chaos of the sun,
> Or old dependency of day and night,
> Or island solitude, unsponsored, free,
> Of that wide water, inescapable.
> Deer walk upon our mountains, and the quail
> Whistle about us their spontaneous cries;
> Sweet berries ripen in the wilderness;
> And, in the isolation of the sky,
> At evening, casual flocks of pigeons make
> Ambiguous undulations as they sink,
> Downward to darkness, on extended wings.

We live, in fact, in a universe suggested by natural science, whose principle is change, an island without religious sponsor, free of the specific Christian experience. It is a sensory world, it has its delights, its disorder, and it is mortal.

The poem is an argument against the traditional Christianity of Stevens' youth, and especially against the doctrine and expectation of immortality, in favor of an earthly and mortal existence that in the felt apprehension of sensory detail can attain a vivid oneness with its surroundings and a religious sense of union comparable to the traditional feeling. The former is undeniably traditional, and much of the deep feeling of the poem is derived from the exposition in sustained and traditional rhetoric of the position which is being denied. In this sense it is parasitic on what it rejects. But the positive argument is almost as traditional in the history of English poetry and in the literary situation of Stevens' youth: it is, with the important difference of a hundred years and the denial of immortality, Wordsworthian in idea, in detail, in feeling, and in rhetoric. Passages comparable to the appositive enumeration of details of natural landscape associated with human feeling, as in

> Passions of rain, and moods in falling snow;
> Grievings in loneliness, or unsubdued elations
> When the forest blooms . . .

are scattered throughout Wordsworth's poetry, especially through the blank verse. I have already quoted a short passage; let me quote another:

What want we? have we not perpetual streams,
Warm woods, and sunny hills, and fresh green fields,
And mountains not less green, and flocks and herds,
And thickets full of songsters, and the voice
Of lordly birds, an unexpected sound
Heard now and then from morn to latest eve,
Admonishing the man who walks below
Of solitude and silence in the sky?

The movement of the verse is Stevens', the syntax, and the relation of syntax to the line-ends. The kind of detail is the same. And the idea, if one reads it out of the specific context of Wordsworth's system, is Stevens' idea; for the passage in isolation says, What does man need, what need he desire, more than a live appreciation of the detail of natural landscape, for the world beyond, the birds admonish us—or, Nature tells us—is a world of solitude and silence. This is not precisely what Wordsworth would have endorsed, but certainly what a young man who was drenched in Wordsworth could make of it. And as he read on in the poem—it is "The Recluse"—he would come to the rhetoric of one of his greatest stanzas and the theme of his greatest poem: he would read in Wordsworth:

Paradise, and groves
Elysian, Fortunate fields,—like those of old
Sought on the Atlantic Main—why should they be
A history only of departed things,
Or a mere fiction of what never was?
For the discerning intellect of Man,
When wedded to this goodly universe
In love and holy passion, shall find these
The simple produce of the common day.

and he would write:

There is not any haunt of prophecy,
Nor any old chimera of the grave . . .

The central concern of Stevens' poetry, the concern that underlay Crispin's voyage and the poet's meditative argument with the woman in "Sunday Morning," as well as most of the more or less curious divergencies of his career, is a concern to be at peace with his surroundings, with this world, and with himself. He requires for this an experience of the togetherness of himself and Nature, an interpenetration of himself and his environment, along with some intuition of permanence in the experience of absoluteness, though this be illusory and transitory, something to satisfy the deeply in-grained longings of his religious feeling. Now, there is an experience depicted from time to time in the romantic tradition—it is com-mon in Wordsworth—and one that has perhaps occurred to each of us in his day, a human experience of absoluteness, when we and our surroundings are not merely related but one, when "joy is its own security." It is a fortuitous experience; it cannot be willed into be-ing, or contrived at need. It is a transitory experience; it cannot be stayed in its going or found when it is gone. Yet though fortuitous and transitory, it has in its moment of being all the persuasion of permanence; it seems—and perhaps in its way it is—a fulfillment of the Absolute:

> It is and it
> Is not and, therefore, is. In the instant of speech,
> The breadth of an accelerando moves,
> Captives the being, widens—and was there.

Stevens attempted to will it into being. He constructed a series of secular myths, like the one in "Sunday Morning," that affirm the traditional religious feeling of the nobility and unity of experience, but the myths remain unconvincing and arbitrary, and conclude in grotesqueries that betray the poet's own lack of belief in his inven-tion, as in "A Primitive Like an Orb," in which he evokes:

> A giant, on the horizon, glistening,
>
> And in bright excellence adorned, crested
> With every prodigal, familiar fire,
> And unfamiliar escapades: whirroos
> And scintillant sizzlings such as children like,
> Vested in the serious folds of majesty . . .

For, as he asks in an earlier poem:

> But if
> It is the absolute why must it be
> This immemorial grandiose, why not

138 · WALLACE STEVENS

> A cockle-shell, a trivial emblem great
> With its final force, a thing invincible
> In more than phrase?

He has attempted to contrive it by a doctrine of metaphor and resemblances, which is precisely Wordsworth's doctrine of affinities. He has sought to present in a poem any set of objects and to affirm a resemblance and togetherness between them, but all the reader can see is the objects and the affirmation, as in "Three Academic Pieces," where a pineapple on a table becomes:

> 1. The hut stands by itself beneath the palms.
> 2. Out of their bottle the green genii come.
> 3. A vine has climbed the other side of the wall . . .

> These casual exfoliations are
> Of the tropic of resemblances . . .

But there is a poem in *Transport to Summer,* one of the perfect poems, as far as my judgment goes, in his later work, that achieves and communicates this experience. It is a short poem in couplets entitled "The House Was Quiet and the World Was Calm." There is no diffle-dee-dee here. The setting is ordinary, not exotic. It is about a man reading alone, late at night. The phrasing is exact and almost unnoticeable. The style is bare, less rich than "Sunday Morning," but with this advantage over that poem, that none of its effect is drawn from forbidden sources, from what is rejected. The meter is a loosened iambic pentameter, but loosened firmly and as a matter of course, almost as if it were speech becoming meter rather than meter violated. It has in fact the stability of a new metrical form attained out of the inveterate violation of the old. It is both modern and traditional:

> The house was quiet and the world was calm.
> The reader became the book; and summer night

> Was like the conscious being of the book.
> The house was quiet and the world was calm.

> The words were spoken as if there was no book,
> Except that the reader leaned above the page,

> Wanted to lean, wanted much most to be
> The scholar to whom his book is true, to whom

The summer night is like a perfection of thought.
The house was quiet because it had to be.

The quiet was part of the meaning, part of the mind:
The access of perfection to the page.

And the world was calm. The truth in a calm world,
In which there is no other meaning, itself

Is calm, itself is summer and night, itself
Is the reader leaning late and reading there.

MARIUS BEWLEY

THE POETRY OF WALLACE STEVENS

1949

A good deal of criticism has been written by this time on the poetry of Wallace Stevens; and it is poetry that requires extensive analysis in the beginning if it is finally to be read with much intelligence. But that criticism has not been consistently accurate or helpful, and some of the best of it—an essay by the late Hi Simons in *Sewanee Review*, for example—is now forgotten in the files of literary periodicals. R. P. Blackmur's essay in *The Double Agent* is still illuminating, and, fortunately, still available; but the only other easily accessible extended essay is Yvor Winters' acrid attack, "Wallace Stevens, or the Hedonist's Progress," which is extremely misleading in its conclusions. And even these articles (Blackmur's and Winters') were written early, and deal almost exclusively with *Harmonium*. The result of this critical situation is that there has been a persistent bias in favor of Stevens' first volume, and this has led to an underestimation of the importance of meaning in his work as a whole. Yet Stevens deserves his reputation partly because his meaning is an important one, and because that meaning has been consistently developing from *Harmonium* toward the maturity of the late work. I do not wish to imply that the central meaning in

·   ·   ·   ·   ·   ·   ·   ·

First published in *Partisan Review*, XVI, September, 1949, and later collected in *The Complex Fate*, by Marius Bewley (London, Chatto & Windus, 1952); reprinted here by permission of the author and Chatto & Windus Ltd.

Stevens' poetry is not present in *Harmonium* just as much as in *Transport to Summer*, but it is present in a hidden way, and also in a less mature way, and it is sometimes extremely difficult to come by. Marianne Moore once wrote: "Wallace Stevens: the interacting veins of life between his early and late poems are an ever-continuing marvel to me." It is only by tracing out some of these veins of interaction that one can ever be *quite* sure, at least in the early poems, that one knows in fullness of detail what Stevens is talking about.

The relation, then, of Stevens' late work to his early work is not one of conflict or supersession. But neither would it be correct to say that the late work relates to the early as the sum of a problem relates to the digits it totals, for something has been added in the late work that was not present, in however piecemeal a state, before. What this addition is may be only a complex balance, an infusion of remarkable poise, but it *is* new. And despite those critics who think *Harmonium* the best of the volumes, it was needed. Its presence may have contributed to that sense of change in Stevens' work that led some critics in the late 'thirties to think he had taken up the social burden; but actually what was being taken up were the familiar meanings of the early verse, but taken up in a new way by the imagination—taken up, in fact, into what was sometimes a new dimension of poetic reality (new, at any rate, for Stevens), and occasionally one could turn aside and look downward from the new use to the old use of an identical image, and realize with a sense of delicious discovery that one now, perhaps, really read the earlier poem for the first time. Stevens' poetry shares this ability to be read profitably both forward and backward with Eliot's poetry. When the "Preludes" were first printed in *Blast* in 1915 they must have seemed little more than remarkable Imagist poems, yet Eliot had showed almost uncanny prevision in naming them, and returning now from the *Quartets* to those early opening themes, their images acquire, through the resonance of all the later work, a depth and meaning that was surely not present to their earliest readers.

In a somewhat similar manner Wallace Stevens can write in "Six Significant Landscapes" (*Harmonium*) what appears, what undoubtedly is, a charming little Imagist piece hardly beyond Amy Lowell's prowess:

Rationalists, wearing square hats,
Think, in square rooms,
Looking at the floor,
Looking at the ceiling.
They confine themselves
To right-angled triangles.
If they tried rhomboids,
Cones, waving lines, ellipses—
As, for example, the ellipse of the half-moon—
Rationalists would wear sombreros.

This contains the possibilities of a complex idea, no doubt; but in itself there is little to invite the exploration of those possibilities. Yet nearly twenty years later in another poem called "The Pastor Caballero" (*Transport to Summer*), Stevens took up the same idea, and the poem became a reflection of his deepest attitudes:

The importance of its hat to a form becomes
More definite. The sweeping brim of the hat
Makes of the form Most Merciful Capitan,

If the observer says so: grandiloquent
Locution of a hand in a rhapsody.
Its line moves quickly with the genius

Of its improvisation until, at length,
It enfolds the head in a vital ambiance,
A vital, linear ambiance. The flare

In the sweeping brim becomes the origin
Of a human evocation, so disclosed
That, nameless, it creates an affectionate name,

Derived from adjectives of deepest mine.
The actual form bears outwardly this grace,
An image of the mind, an inward mate,

Tall and unfretted, a figure meant to bear
Its poisoned laurels in this poisoned wood,
High in the height that is our total height.

The formidable helmet is nothing now.
These two go well together, the sinuous brim
And the green flauntings of the hours of peace.

The bouncy observation of the first poem has gradually moved toward this subtle statement of spiritual poise, and that Stevens is consciously aware of the transition is strongly suggested by the "becomes" of the first line. The form of a deeply complex attitude or grace is metamorphosed into the form of a particular hat, and the images that cluster around this central symbol do a good deal toward elucidating other poems in *Harmonium*. But first take the hat itself: by this time we have a somewhat elaborate idea of what it stands for, and can turn back to the last verse of "Palace of the Babies" (*Harmonium*):

> The walker in the moonlight walked alone,
> And in his heart his disbelief lay cold.
> His broad-brimmed hat came close upon his eyes.

This was certainly never one of the more difficult poems, but it had seemed a little thin. Years later Stevens enunciated a luxuriant connotation for the walker's broad-brimmed hat (a hat that obviously had no flare) and so he enabled his earlier image to explore in a more significant way the nature of the moonlight walker's disbelief. The day "The Pastor Caballero" was written the "Palace of the Babies" became a better poem than it had been the day before: one might even say that it had been revised. This is not as odd as it may sound, for if a poet creates his own language he does not cease to create it until he has ceased to be a poet—and there is a sense in which a poet rewrites his collected works every time he writes a genuinely new poem.

But "The Pastor Caballero" offers relevant insights into other early poems as well. If one reads it together with Stevens' well-known "Bantams in Pine-Woods," for example, one senses how closely united Azcan is to the more faintly evoked Most Merciful Capitan:

> Chieftain Iffucan of Azcan in caftan
> Of tan with henna hackles, halt!
>
> Damned universal cock, as if the sun
> Was blackamoor to bear your blazing tail.
>
> Fat! Fat! Fat! Fat! I am the personal.
> Your world is you. I am my world.
>
> You ten-foot poet among inchlings. Fat!
> Begone! An inchling bristles in these pines,

> Bristles, and points their Appalachian tangs,
> And fears not portly Azcan nor his hoos.

The rather brassy appeal of this poem exists at a more superficial level than its meaning, which is extremely difficult to excerpt. The poem has been relatively overpraised within the body of Stevens' work, and it would hardly be worth the trouble of interpreting, except that it provides one of the most admirable opportunities in Stevens for studying the interaction of imagery between his early and late poems. Two extreme interpretations which would contradict each other seem possible, depending on whom one chooses as the villain of the piece, Azcan or the inchling. An interpretation internally consistent, and more or less in harmony with the context provided by Stevens' poetry as a whole, can be worked out in either direction. And if Azcan seems a preferable hero to me, I am not forgetting that Mr. William Van O'Connor in a recent article on Stevens offered evidence in favor of the inchling. In actual fact, I believe that the real meaning is complex enough to release them both from the glory or responsibility of being either wholly hero or wholly villain. The poem seems to be, more than anything else, an investigation of the relationship between the imagination and reality in an anti-imaginative society. Read in this light it offers a comment on one of the more complex facets of Stevens' belief.

To begin: there is some evidence that Azcan is a symbol of the imagination. His height alone associates him with the "tall and unfretted" Capitan of the other poem, who was "high in the height that is our total height," and it associates him also with that "giant, on the horizon, glistening," who is used as the symbol for imagination in Stevens' recent poem, "A Primitive Like an Orb." But there are important differences. The Most Merciful Capitan is so successfully a state of mind that he can be visualized only as the elegant sweeping flare in the brim of a quite irresistible hat—the sort of sombrero that rationalists would wear if they studied the ellipse of the half-moon. But what is most noticeable is that the relationship of Azcan and the Capitan to their respective environment is dissimilar. Azcan is not on friendly terms with the inchling, who represents his environment, and therefore reality; but the Capitan has evidently culminated a successful resistance ("The formidable helmet is nothing now") which leaves him free to look forward to "the green flauntings of the hours of peace."

If at this point one opens Stevens' Princeton lecture, "The Noble Rider and the Sound of Words," printed in Allen Tate's *The Language of Poetry*, the following passage proves helpful in distinguishing between the plights of Azcan and the Capitan. Stevens says there that the possible poet of today

> will consider that although he has himself witnessed, during the long period of his life, a general transition to reality, his own measure as a poet, in spite of all the passions of all the lovers of the truth insist. He must be able to abstract himself, and also to abstract reality, which he does by placing it in his imagination. He knows perfectly that he cannot be too noble a rider, that he cannot rise up loftily in helmet and armor on a horse of imposing bronze.

Now the Capitan is a successful exponent of the imagination because he is able to dispense with the "formidable helmet." He knows how to deal with reality, how to subjugate it to himself by his abstracting genius. Azcan, on the other hand, is imagination mounted on too high a horse; his henna hackles are too impressive an armor, and he is out of touch with reality. "There are degrees of imagination," Stevens had said in the same lecture, "as, for example, degrees of vitality, and therefore of intensity. It is an implication that there are degrees of reality." And he further remarked that poetry represents an "interdependence of the imagination and reality as equals." But the hostile, military bearing of the inchling toward Azcan signifies that reality, in the world of this poem, is militantly out of sympathy with the imagination, and each is thereby revealed as incomplete in itself because of that hostility.

Stevens wrote in *Notes Toward a Supreme Fiction* (reprinted in *Transport to Summer*):

> How clean the sun when seen in its idea,
> Washed in the remotest cleanliness of a heaven
> That has expelled us and our images . . .

Because of the distorted dealings between them, Azcan cannot abstract from reality toward that pure idea of the sun: the sun is only a blackamoor to him, smeared over with the grimy limitations of physical fact. And yet, although prevented from functioning properly, Azcan remains a good giant at heart. When the inchling screams "Fat!" at Azcan, he applies the word in a derisive manner; but "fat" is an adjective with consistently benign connotations in Stevens' poetry. He uses it typically in *Notes Toward a Supreme Fiction* (Part III, poem 10) to describe the symbolical female embodiment of "the fiction that results from feeling," and that, as every reader of Stevens knows, is his chief reality (reality, that is, in its final, completed sense)—the synthesizing imagination itself.

It is characteristic of the elaborate conflicting connotations in this poem (representing the inchling's confusions) that the favorable word "fat" is qualified in the last line by the unfavorable adjective "portly." In *Harmonium* the page adjoining "Bantams in Pine-Woods" is occupied by "Anecdote of the Jar," in which a jar is placed on the top of a wilderness-encircled hill in Tennessee:

> The wilderness rose up to it,
> And sprawled around, no longer wild.
> The jar was round upon the ground
> And tall and of a port in air.

It has been pointed out before that the good, untrammeled wilderness is subdued by the presence of that jar to a conventional and man-made drabness ("It took dominion everywhere"), and like Azcan the jar was of a port in air. It had style (more properly, manner or affectation) rather than reality. When the inchling uses "fat" and "portly" interchangeably he serves notice that he is unable to make the necessary distinctions (connoisseur of the hard-surfaced fact that he is).

And he reveals his incapacity even more remarkably by conjoining "portly" and the Chieftain's hoos. One would hardly guess it from the poem itself, but these hoos are a symbol of Azcan's innate vitality. In *Notes Toward a Supreme Fiction* we find these verses:

> We say: At night an Arabian in my room,
> With his damned hoobla-hoobla-hoobla-how,
> Inscribes a primitive astronomy

Across the unscrawled fores the future casts
And throws his stars around the floor. By day
The wood-dove used to chant his hoobla-hoo

And still the grossest iridescence of ocean
Howls hoo and rises and howls hoo and falls.
Life's nonsense pierces us with strange relation.

Stevens always uses "primitive" to indicate the natural sources of vitality and insight which are suppressed by the academic and the insistently rational; and the stars and ocean (it is interesting to note that the ocean's "iridescence" is "gross," a synonym for "fat") are merely two items from his usual landscape that serve the same function. The Arabian, then, is seen, like Azcan and the Capitan, to be the symbol of imaginative knowledge; but it is necessary to remember that these three are not identical, for they exist under different circumstances. (Incidentally, it is rather amusing to note the diverse implications carried by Stevens' Arabian astrologist and Eliot's Madame Sosostris, whose name, oddly enough—to say nothing of dear Mrs. Equitone—might have been invented by Stevens.) It was not difficult to pass Azcan's hoos off as utter nonsense the first time one heard them, but now it is clear that Azcan and the Arabian both learned their hoos from nature itself, from the wood-dove and the ocean. And in another early poem, the frequently anthologized "Tea at the Palaz of Hoon," that exalted Personage with whom the purple-gowned and fragrant tea guest (the state of guesthood, it should be said, is not explicit in the poem, but the hospitable social implications of the title are inescapable, and are directly related to Stevens' conception of the relation between imagination and society [1]) found himself more "truly and more strange," and proceeded to create an imaginative synthesis of the world, may very well be merely the personification of Azcan's wild woodnote, which the inchling with his preference for hard facts scorns so much.

In proclaiming himself to be "the personal," the inchling has merely mistaken the part for the whole, for it is clear that a true

[1] Stevens has written: ". . . reality is life, and life is society and the imagination and reality, that is to say, the imagination and society are inseparable."

"personal" could not tolerate a dichotomy between the sensuous experience of external reality and imaginative knowledge any more than the person could be defined in terms of a single faculty. But the "scientific" bias of the inchling with his insolent cry to the imaginative life, "Begone!" reveals him content with fragmentary existence and its consequent moral isolation. When the tea guest of Hoon proclaimed:

> I was the world in which I walked, and what I saw
> Or heard or felt came not but from myself;
> And there I found myself more truly and more strange,

he meant that he had recreated the external world in his imagination, and in doing so had elevated it onto a plane in which the world of fixed objects escaped its static and excluding definition in space. And so in the world of his imagination he was at last able to emerge from his moral isolation in himself. But the inchling, being the enemy of Azcan, although he may mistake his servitude for something else, is really held incommunicado in his own identity.

Apropos of this moral isolation in the material world, it is relevant to turn back to another early poem, "Metaphors of a Magnifico" (*Harmonium*), which Mr. Winters described as "willful nonsense":

> Twenty men crossing a bridge,
> Into a village,
> Are twenty men crossing twenty bridges,
> Into twenty villages,
> Or one man
> Crossing a single bridge into a village.

So far from being "willful nonsense," this is a deeply penetrating statement about the horror of such isolation. It means much the same thing as Eliot's

> *Dayadhvam:* I have heard the key
> Turn in the door once and turn once only
> We think of the key, each in his prison
> Thinking of the key. . . .

The key for Eliot is Christianity, the key for Stevens is imagination, and in *Dayadhvam* (meaning "sympathize," as Eliot has told us) both keys fit the same lock. For sympathy is a kind of common ground between the "vivid transparence" of the imagination in which Stevens meets his friend in the poem quoted below, and the Christian charity of Eliot's later work. The poetry of both is an attempt to overcome the moral isolation imposed by the modern world: and if Stevens, Azcan, the Capitan, and the Arabian are all tea guests at the Palaz of Hoon, there is no reason to suppose that Eliot with the third walking by his side is not also on friendly calling terms with that tremendous Personage. Only the inchling must go without his tea.

So we conclude that however much Azcan seems to fail the function he ought to be performing, the blame lies with the truculent inchling, who is a most unco-operative reality. And one should note that he turns away from insulting Azcan to point the Appalachian tangs of the pines, thereby bringing the good wildness of nature under control in the same way that the gray and bare jar on the Tennessee hill domesticated the wilderness. His "Begone!" is, in a sense, self-defensive, for he instinctively knows that the kind of relationship described in one of Stevens' most beautiful poems will never bind him to Azcan. This poem (the dedication of *Notes Toward a Supreme Fiction*) describes the escape from moral isolation through the imagination:

> And for what, except for you, do I feel love?
> Do I press the extremest book of the wisest man
> Close to me, hidden in me day and night?
> In the uncertain light of single, certain truth,
> Equal in living changingness to the light
> In which I meet you, in which we sit at rest,
> For a moment in the central of our being,
> The vivid transparence that you bring is peace.

To achieve a very deep understanding of "Bantams in Pine-Woods" it must be read with some such wide range of reference to the other poems as has been indicated here. I say "some" because the references might easily have been to other poems than the ones actually selected in this paper. But this raises an extremely difficult problem of evaluation. By the time one has arrived at such a reading, it seems doubtful if one is really looking at the original poem any longer, or responding to it as it objectively exists. I said earlier that there is a sense in which a poet rewrites his collected works every time he writes a genuinely new poem, but there is also a sense in which both the poet and the interpreting critic can abuse the privileges implicit in this statement. I had chiefly in mind the increasing density of meaning in a vocabulary like Eliot's which has, as it were, passed with the inevitability of the natural world from a chilly spring to a ripening and abundant harvest. The progression in Stevens' poetry has been hardly less marked; but the vocabulary and images in his early poems are not saturated with the human experience that is the substance of Eliot's, and consequently an attempt to understand some of his poems is more like a project in archaeological reconstruction than literary analysis. Admittedly the contemplation of pure craft (whatever that is) has its delight and value, but when the complex meaning of "Bantams in Pine-Woods" is finally deciphered (if I *have* deciphered it here), its relations to its symbols and images seem largely arbitrary. On the one hand we have an arrestingly grotesque visual image, delineated with something like Swift's clean sense of deformity, and some fantastically exhilarating noises; on the other, a complex and humanly important meaning. But the hostility between Azcan and the inchling (the imagination and reality) may, I think, be taken as an adequate symbol of the ultimate failure of this poem (but I am not saying here that it does not have several remarkable *proximate successes*). If the poem means what I think it does, the meaning fails to be realized in the body of the verse. It is disowned by the very images that should proclaim it.

Before leaving, finally, this question of the interaction of images in Stevens' poetry, I should like to notice the presence of another of those "interacting veins of life" in the group of poems already quoted here. From Stevens' work as a whole we know that one of the intrinsic elements of the imagination (as of life) is motion and change. The inchling identifies himself in the second line of "Bantams in Pine-Woods" with his peremptory command to "halt!" And the principal activity manifested by the inchling is that of bristling—the characteristic behavior of animals brought to bay rather than of animals in flight. "Single, certain truth" is in constant motion, is glimpsed and realized in moments of vital, vivid apprehension, and this act of apprehension itself may constitute ontologically a part, and perhaps a large part, of the truth. Turning back, now, to "The Pastor Caballero," one discovers that the Capitan's flaring hat brim, itself the symbol of imagination and spiritual poise, is described as "grandiloquent gesture of a hand in rhapsody." We have in an astonishingly literal sense here not "language" but truth itself "as gesture." This theme of truth (or as Stevens prefers to call it, "fiction") as motion, change, gesture, recurs repeatedly throughout his poetry in varying degrees of complexity. We get it in its simplest form in a lovely early poem, "Infanta Marina" *(Harmonium)*:

> She made of the motions of her wrist
> The grandiose gestures
> Of her thought.
> .   .   .   .
> And thus she roamed
> In the roamings of her fan,
>
> Partaking of the sea,
> And of the evening,
> As they flowed around
> And uttered their subsiding sound.

The sea of which Marina partook is unmistakably the same sea that taught Azcan and the Arabian their hoos, and the evening throughout Stevens' verse has an even more suggestive connotation than the sea. One even feels a certain "prophecy" in that word "subsiding." To confine oneself to the quotations already given here, it surely carries a faint heralding of "the green flauntings of the hours of peace." But the important thing about "Infanta Marina" is that a delicate, trivial motion of the wrist is a means toward symbolizing the major end of life, and this end is conceived in terms of a motion that, from one point of view, is hardly separable from the moving wrist by which it is symbolized.

II

It was inevitable that in discussing Stevens' interaction of imagery the meaning of his poetry should have been considered; and it will be equally inevitable now that in examining primarily his meaning, a good deal will have to be said about the interaction of his images. Much has already been written on Stevens' meaning, the best article being R. P. Blackmur's; and if there has been radical disagreement among critics, there has been a consensus on certain important points, which should be enough to start the reader on his way. It is, of course, the early work that chiefly calls for elucidation. The group of poems called *Notes Toward a Supreme Fiction*, which, after Pound (and counting Eliot in the English tradition), may easily be the most distinguished work written by an American poet in this century, is not particularly difficult to understand, nor, for that matter, is his most recent poem, "A Primitive Like an Orb." If the meaning in Stevens' poetry is again submitted to some scrutiny here, it is certainly not in the belief that anything surprisingly new can be said; but the substance of Stevens' poetry can be discussed in terms that incorporate it more firmly in a traditional context, and I think that is important: for Stevens' poetry has been too much discussed in terms of relativism, misology, hedonism—even Bergsonianism. If several of these terms can be justified—and of course they can—the result is nevertheless that of dislodging Stevens' poetry from the tradition in which it seems to me most richly assimilable.

There is one difficulty to be guarded against especially in any discussion of meaning in Stevens' verse. Such a discussion is likely to get as far away from any consideration of the poetry itself as a discussion of Milton's theology can carry one away from *Paradise Lost*. The present brief examination hardly affords an opportunity for detailed discussion of the poetry, but I wish to examine two early poems with a view to seeing (at least in the second example) how much of Stevens' meaning is actually realized in terms of the verse. Beyond that concrete realization of his meaning in the body of the poetry, the further rational perspectives that may be drawn from it ought not to interest the literary critic, at least *as* critic. They are not his province. It will be seen, I think, that the part of Stevens' meaning which is poetically significant declares him to be an exponent of Coleridge's theory of the imagination; and in terms of this tradition rather than in any "modern" vocabulary one may be able to read his poetry with a new intimacy. I doubt if Stevens and

Coleridge would have been much alike in any other way, but they seem to meet perfectly in, say, the final paragraphs of the chapter "On the Imagination," in *Biographia Literaria*, or, perhaps especially, in the conclusion of the following chapter, "Philosophic Definitions." And the Coleridgean imagination has become the theme of Stevens' poetry as a whole in a way it never became the theme of Coleridge's poetry as a whole. His theme is the reconciliation of opposites by intuitive vision, the discovery of unity in diversity— and in that phrase we move back to the problem of the Many and the One, which was the great passion of the Metaphysicals: and perhaps no contemporary poet has more associations (however tenuous and qualified) with the earlier seventeenth century than Stevens. But a comparison would hardly be fair to him, for it would tend to show how much better off they were than we, both in the concrete immediacy of their language and in the controlled precision of their abstractions.

"Poetry is the supreme fiction, madame," Stevens had written in the opening line of "A High-Toned Old Christian Woman," that poem in *Harmonium* which shocked Mr. Winters so much. And with that utterance, Stevens had proceeded to attempt a reconciliation of the conventionally irreconcilable. The poem is not much more than an effective piece of rhetoric, and the fusion fails to occur imaginatively, but the intention is clear. Stevens says that the High-Toned Old Christian Woman is aiming at very much the same sort of thing—perhaps less effectually—as the low-toned artists of whom she would hardly approve. Mr. Winters says of this: "We learn that the 'moral law' is not necessary as a framework of art, but that the 'opposing law' will do just as well. . . ." Read this poem as I may, I cannot discover any more sinister meaning in it than that High-Toned (surely that adjective is suggestive of the sort of Brahminism Stevens had in mind) Old Christian Women do not hold a monopoly of spiritual experiences. Both the perspectives of the Old Christian Woman and the "disaffected flagellants" open at last into similar palm-treed vistas, for "fictive things/Wink as they will." In other words, the shaping spirit of imagination is transcendent.

To hold oneself a little longer to the progress of Mr. Winters' analysis of Stevens—the critic proceeds from a consideration of "A High-Toned Old Christian Woman" to one of the most rhythmically sensitive among Stevens' earlier poems, or for that matter, in the entire body of his work. The poem is somewhat inconsequently called, "The Man Whose Pharynx Was Bad." Mr. Winters quite rightly reprints the original version of the poem as it appeared in its periodical publication rather than the seriously mutilated version in *Harmonium*, in which its beauty is ruinously damaged. Of this poem Mr. Winters has to say:

> The poet has progressed in this poem to the point at which the intensity of emotion possible in actual human life has become insipid, and he conceives the possibility of ultimate satisfaction only in some impossible emotional finality of no matter what kind. In fact, the figurative opposites of summer and winter here offered suggest the opposites of the moral and the anti-moral which appear in "A High-Toned Old Christian Woman."

Here is the poem in its complete version as Mr. Winters reprints it:

> The time of year has grown indifferent.
> Mildew of summer and the deepening snow
> Are both alike in the routine I know;
> I am too dumbly in my being pent.
>
> The wind attendant on the solstices
> Blows on the shutters of the metropoles,
> Stirring no poet in his sleep, and tolls
> The grand ideas of the villages.
>
> The malady of the quotidian . . .
> Perhaps if summer ever came to rest
> And lengthened, deepened, comforted, caressed
> Through days like oceans in obsidian
>
> Horizons, full of night's midsummer blaze;
> Perhaps, if winter once could penetrate
> Through all its purples to the final slate,
> Persisting bleakly in an icy haze;
>
> One might in turn become less diffident,
> Out of such mildew plucking neater mould
> And spouting new orations of the cold.
> One might. One might. But time will not relent.

The ennui which is being described here is something more than the punishment meted out to hedonists. The "malady of the quotidian" which Stevens expresses with such deep poignancy is a characteristically human state that occurs at intervals in the best-regulated lives—and in spiritual writers its occurrence, or the occurrence of something very like it in a vastly aggravated form, is usually regarded as one of the more unpleasant symptoms of interior progress. But without wishing even to imply an analogy in that exalted direction, I would, at any rate, suggest that a comparison might profitably be made between this poem and Coleridge's "Dejection Ode," which it curiously, if modestly, resembles. Although the emotion of direct sensuous experience has ceased to move the poet, a new and deeper emotion arises from knowledge of his incapacity to respond in the old key. The kind of satisfaction that Stevens is looking for in the second half of the poem hardly seems as degraded as Mr. Winters thinks. The desire is to go behind the fragmentary and transitory in experience and grasp its essentiality, no longer perceived in a context in which the elements are vulgarized ("The grand ideas of the villages"), and constantly being lost again through the fitfulness of forms and faculties at the very moment of apprehension. The desire is for the "vivid transparence" of peace—and if that peace would exclude some of the things that the High-Toned Old Christian Woman stood for, I do not believe that Stevens meant her as an adequate symbol for the best that has been said and thought in the Christian world. What the ultimate nature (in rigorous philosophical language) of the reality sought in such an absolute winter and perpetual summer would be is none of the critics' business. For the purposes of the poetry it plainly involves, like the earlier poem, a reconciliation of opposites toward comprehending the largest possible degree of reality, and in so doing it would conform to Coleridge's theory of the imagination—a creative willing together into a new and unified reality of hitherto separable quantities. It is the temporary cessation of this imaginative power that Stevens is talking about in this poem, just as Coleridge was lamenting its loss in his greatest poem—"The Dejection Ode."

The imagery in this poem relates as closely to the later work as the poems previously considered here. But it is also perfectly self-contained, while its deeply personal rhythm offers a kind of satisfaction that cannot be derived from the rhetorical cadences of, say, "The Comedian as the Letter C." Mr. Blackmur at one point in his treatment of Stevens' rhetoric invoked the name of Marlowe. Taking up his suggestive remark, I should say that this poem of Stevens compares to much of the remainder of *Harmonium* (particularly "The Comedian as the Letter C") as the best passages in *Dr. Faustus* compare to *Tamburlaine*. But although "The Man Whose Pharynx Was Bad" is sufficient to itself, it is interesting to examine, in relation to it, these lines from the poem, "That Which Cannot Be Fixed" *(Transport to Summer)*:

> The human ocean beats against this rock
> Of earth, rises against it, tide by tide,
>
> Continually. And old John Zeller stands
> On his hill, watching the rising and falling, and says:
>
> Of what are these creatures, what element
> Or—yes: what elements, unreconciled
>
> Because there is no golden solvent here?

The ocean in this poem is a symbol of chaotic human experience, composed, as we learn in an unquoted part, not from one element, but from the traditional four that are unreconciled among themselves because there is no golden solvent—that is, no fire of the imagination. Now in "The Man Whose Pharynx Was Bad" the ocean that is envisaged is really a human ocean in which the discords must also be reconciled—but instead of a "golden solvent," a different image is used—"obsidian horizons." Obsidian is volcanic glass, and therefore suggests the fiery fusing power of the imagination in the Coleridgean sense, and it looks forward to that lovely recurrent image of "transparency" in the later verse. The field of the imagination is not confined within the palings of time, and therefore the reality which it creates would naturally move through timeless seasons—and we see the world and life and time itself caught and crystallized in the moment of imagination, just as the midocean is completely and eternally surrounded and defined by the encircling radiance of the sky. "The vivid transparence that you bring is peace"

—that line provides an answer to the kind of dejection and longing in this poem on whose morals Mr. Winters has been so severe.

But if Mr. Winters and others have frequently thought of Stevens as an aesthete, and even a hedonist—Stevens has not always been prudent about the poetry he has allowed to be published. Stevens used to be thought of as an unvoluminous writer, but in recent years, despite the excellence of *Transport to Summer* (undoubtedly his best volume), and what he has published since, he has allowed too many of his practice poems to appear. *Parts of a World* seems to me to number among its sixty-five titles very little of genuine distinction. For one thing, Stevens had progressed far enough in the expression of his meaning in his early volumes that a group of miscellaneous poems, all intent on saying, willy-nilly, pretty much the same thing in a wide (but related) variety of metaphors could add nothing to his achievement, and I frequently find the monotonous shadow of these poems falling over the real quality of his late work, and marring the purity of response. "A Dish of Peaches in Russia," for example, seems regrettable to me:

> The peaches are large and round,
>
> Ah! and red; and they have peach fuzz, ah!
> They are full of juice and the skin is soft.
>
> They are full of the colors of my village
> And of fair weather, summer, dew, peace.
>
> . . . .
> I did not know
>
> That such ferocities could tear
> One self from another, as these peaches do.

No doubt peaches can strike off imaginative feats in the proper observer, but that "and they have peach fuzz, ah!" leaves me uneasy. It doesn't seem to be leading up to the "ferocities" in the last verse. But Stevens' subject matter cannot be condemned because it happens, in this poem, to have failed disastrously. A good artist is entitled to his failures (if only he wouldn't publish them), and the failure here is not one of theory but one of practice. Imagination as subject matter (implicit here, of course) is bound to look a little mauve and decadent if, in a given instance, it is unable to strain beyond Fancy.

I have made a point of this poem because it seems suggestive in several ways about Stevens' development as a poet. The enameled images of *Harmonium* had carried certain limitations of expression with them, but they were sometimes of great beauty and peculiar subtlety. If in the late 'thirties Stevens did not actually, as some competent critics imagined, acquire a social consciousness, there does appear to have been a shift in his mode of experiencing—a gradual change in his verse rhythms. What was happening had nothing to do with taking up the social burden, but there was a withdrawal in Stevens' poetry from the predominance of the image, and Stevens (perhaps partly because of the shock of the war, although the change had begun earlier) began to feel increasingly in terms of an inquisitive and flexible line—a line capable of making deeper explorations and wider applications of his images to social reality than had been possible in many of his earlier saffron-starched verses. *Parts of a World* is unsuccessful (but this is said with a view only to explaining the success of his later work) because the conspicuous metaphor is still making a strong bid for controlling interest, but is steadily being supplanted by a new rhythmical interest which follows more closely the movements of the questioning and generous mind. And yet neither a balance nor an interesting tension is usually achieved in this volume between the two elements. They behave toward each other with the easy nonchalance of bar companions, and this is the more remarkable in that some of the poems treat of the nature of poetry itself with unusual insight. In *Transport to Summer* (although the dates of the composition of the poems in these two volumes must have overlapped) the balance is righted, and *Notes Toward a Supreme Fiction*, reprinted in this book, will possibly be Stevens' greatest achievement, and it should be one of the great adornments of American literature—a set of thirty meditations on the nature of the imagination.

Finally, we have another of Stevens' best poems, "A Primitive Like an Orb." In this poem the transition he has been making from an imagistically to a rhythmically controlled consciousness (this in itself implies something that might be mistaken for a social consciousness) is triumphantly completed; but not, it is interesting to note, without the assistance of Eliot's late poetry, which, without being derivative, it yet somehow resembles. It might be repetitious here to discuss this poem at any length, but I cannot drop the matter without commenting on the singular propriety of the title. We have seen how the adjective "primitive," as a term of general application, signifies the triumph of the imagination in the world of Stevens' meaning, but focused more insistently on the imagination's goal of operation. In this sense its opposition to the academic and conventional is almost rhetorical. But since the "primitive" of the title aims at achieving an imaginative unity in diversity, at seeing the wholeness behind each fragment of experience, it is a primitive shaped like an orb. And the "orb" is nothing less than the age-old circle of perfection which can be symbolized even in a little drop of dew, of which Marvell wrote:

> . . . the clear Region where 'twas born
> Round in itself encloses:
> And in its little Globes extent
> Frames as it can its native Element.

III

Harmonium, good as it is, has been praised excessively at the expense of the late work, and the late work has a habit of being confused with "transition" work; but in spite of all such confusions Stevens is almost certainly (after the two exceptions earlier noted) the most considerable figure that American poetry has produced in this century. His meaning, insofar as it is operative within the fabric of his verse, has none of the immaturity that Winters accused it of, and it is large and coherent enough to form the basis of an important body of expression. Furthermore, its meaning is traditional, and it relates, in a way unusual in American art, to a European past. I do not mean that Stevens' poetry is a sycophant of Europe, but only that the tradition in which he thinks and feels and writes is not a provincial backwater. It is part of the main current, and one does not feel strange in speaking of him in relation to the great traditional non-American poets. He is validly related.

And he has a particular significance for our time. He has been immediately and painfully aware of the cultural disintegration that has closed in with such vehemence since the end of World War I. Perhaps in as intense a way as Yeats (the subject matter of his poetry has been even more directly concerned) he has known that "the centre does not hold," and his Princeton lecture contains one or two of the most anguished passages dealing with our cultural tragedy that come to mind. It is in relation to his sense of the catastrophic fragmentariness of the contemporary world that his belief in the unifying power of the imagination has achieved such rare distinction. It cannot, in the nature of the case, offer a solution theoretically as complete as Eliot's Christianity, but it does offer a reality that sometimes seems to be almost the unbaptized blood brother of Eliot's reality—and it is a reality that finds frequent, but by no means invariable, realization in the poetry itself.

MARIANNE MOORE

"THE WORLD IMAGINED . . . SINCE WE ARE POOR"

1951

The imagination is "a roamer," Wallace Stevens says, and poetry is "a page from the tale that it tells"; this time, of "Hans by a drift-fire" near "a steamer foundered in ice," "opening the door of his mind" to the aurora borealis—to "flames." "The scholar of one candle sees an arctic effulgence flaring on the frame of everything he is, and feels afraid" but is at ease in "a shelter of the mind with supernatural preludes of his own" to enchant and hypnotize. "The stars are putting on their glittering belts. They throw around their shoulders cloaks that flash . . ." Thus happiness of the in-centric surmounts a poverty of the ex-centric. This is "the center," the satisfaction which "increases the aspects of experience" where disembodied converse is "too fragile, too immediate for any speech." The poison in the meditations of the serpent in the ferns is "that we should disbelieve" that there is a starry serpent in the heavens on which to fix the grateful mind.

Thus poetry substitutes for poverty, abundance, a spiritual happiness in which the intangible is more real than the visible and earth is innocent, "not a guilty dream" but a "holiness" in which we are

.   .   .   .

A review of *The Auroras of Autumn*, first published in *Poetry New York*, No. 4 (1951), edited by Rolf Fjelde; reprinted by permission of the author.

awake as peacefully as if we lay asleep. For the beggar "in a bad time," feeling is frozen.

> What has he that becomes his heart's strong core?
> He has his poverty and nothing more.
> His poverty becomes his heart's strong core.

Yet from illusion's paradise of unephemeral realization, the self sees "new stars . . . a foot across"; becomes someone

> On his gold horse striding like a conjured beast,
> Miraculous in its panache and swish.

Amid grandeur of this sort, surrounded by the "imagination's mercies," one knows the difference between the grand and the grandiose; is safe from "harangue," "ado," and "the ambitious page." Poetry is a "permanence of impermanence," a text concisely obscure but nutritive like the nursery rhyme: when the rain raineth and the goose winketh, little wotteth the gosling what the goose thinketh. That is to say, the child is sane however many times he asks, "What is it?" whereas the adult succumbs to an "enfantillage" of intrusiveness and asks you who you are. Safety from verbal myopia as said, is solitude in which "the bouquet is quirked and queered by lavishings of the will to see." The real is more acute by reason of an unreal; illusiveness is an intangible region in which images flit, for metaphor is a "flitter" that reflects itself in verisimilitudes of a mirror, a thing of magic surely, where "It blows a glassy brightness on the fire and makes flame flame." "The pines that were fans" and objectified fragrances emerge; we see "wheat rapturous in the wind"; the fixity in motion of the stream:

> The river kept flowing and never the same way twice,
> Through many places as if it stood still in one.

The "ultimate poem" truly is "far beyond the rhetorician's touch": is as reliably real as that river flowing, "these locusts by day, these crickets by night." It creates an illusion, peace.

> This is that figure stationed at our end,
> Always, in brilliance, fatal, final, formed
> Out of our lives to keep us in our death,
> · · · · · · · · · · · · ·

> . . . a king as candle by our beds
> In a robe that is our glory as he guards.

The Hans of these Auroras of Autumn speaks in a variety of dainty modes. Sometimes the flexible chain of sound recalls the pendulum; has ease:

> Life fixed him wondering on the stair of glass,
> With its attentive eye.

Besides rhyme and familiar statement, we have unrhyme with the effect of rhyme:

> blue as of a secret place,
> in the anonymous color of the universe;

and alliterative effects such as "a sovereign, a souvenir, a sign"; the "fidgets of a fire," "from finikins to fine finikin, edgings and inchings of final form"; the f's recalling "Bantams in Pine-Woods":

> Chieftain Iffucan of Azcan in caftan
> Of tan with henna hackles, halt!

Also: tones and pauses as carefully regulated as by La Fontaine, when Thyrsis entices the fish to forsake Naiads for Annette (Book X: Fable 10):

> *Ne craignez point, d'entrer au prison de la belle.*
> *Ce n'est qu'à nous qu'elle est cruelle*

in

> Eulalia, I lounged on the hospital porch,
> On the east, sister and nun, and opened wide
> A parasol which I had found, against
> The sun.

La Fontaine, becoming demure, says, "I leave it to the authorities"; Mr. Stevens says, "The poet mumbles," writing what for us is "the durable, the classic, the incontestable." The vulgarity of poetry is an insisting upon the subsidiary as major; sensibility imposes silence which the imagination transmutes into eloquence. Then, for the spiritual mariner, however northern, stranded, or chilled, there is society in solitude. He has it all—"the heavens, the hells, the

worlds, the longed-for lands," "the invisible tree which may hold
a serpent whose venom and whose wisdom will be one."

> That's it. The lover writes, the believer hears,
> The poet mumbles and the painter sees,
> Each one, his faded eccentricity.

It is "the spirit's speech," "a gorgeous fortitude," the "tidal inunda-
tion" in this tale of Hans, embodying the thinking of a lifetime.

DONALD DAVIE

THE AURORAS OF AUTUMN

1954

"The Auroras of Autumn" is a cycle of ten poems, each of twenty-four lines arranged in groups of three. It first appeared in book form in 1950, in a volume to which this poem gave a title. It can be taken as a typical example of the poet's recent style and of his current preoccupations.

When I first read the poem a couple of years ago it struck me as delightful and impressive, but difficult to understand. I therefore made notes on it to elucidate it for my own sake, and this is at bottom what I offer here—no more than a painstaking, deliberate, even leaden-footed elucidation of the poem from first to last. But, as often happens, the process of elucidating, of trying to understand, turned into evaluation as I proceeded with it. And I now find that the poem is not the completely assured masterpiece I thought it at first. In fact it now seems to me that the sequence breaks down just after the halfway mark. I was led to this conclusion when I found that my efforts at interpretation broke down at just this point, and suspicious readers may make of this admission what they please— may decide that the critic's inability to understand is no reflection on the poet. However I find sufficient evidence of a loss of touch in the last few poems in the sequence to make me stick to my guns.

•   •   •   •   •   •   •   •

First published in *Perspective*, VII, Autumn, 1954, and reprinted by permission of the author and Mr. Jarvis Thurston, editor of *Perspective*.

And in what remains of the poem after all my objections have been made, there is sufficient splendor to justify the close attention that I have given and that I ask for.

3) The title prepares us: Aurora = dawn = beginning; Autumn = eve = ending. "In my end is my beginning," the cyclical pattern— this is the theme of the work. The first poem exhibits this clearly. Here the autumn is said to be a snake, because the snake sloughs his skin; and is he then the beginning of a new thing or the end of an old thing? Of course he is both; and this is the paradox to be explored. But the snake is also inevitably the serpent of the Garden of Eden, who tempts to the knowledge of good and evil; and this, as we see later, looks forward to what is unique in this treatment of what is otherwise almost a poetic commonplace. The cyclical human knowledge, what it is, how it comes, how reliable it is. The verse strikes me in this first poem as not yet strung up to the pitch it is soon to reach. It is difficult in places to make expressive sense out of the rhythms, and there is also what seems to me the solecism:

> His meditations in the ferns,
> When he moved so slightly to make sure of sun,
>
> Made us *no less as sure*. . . .   [my italics]

This is important however to the meaning. Sure of what? Of some constant principle behind the elusive metamorphoses of the natural world as proffered to us by our senses? Or of there being no such underlying constancy to look for? Elsewhere in the poem we seem to learn that the changeability of that snake, the world, when it leads us to accept the second alternative, leads us astray—"This is his poison." Nevertheless, the poem ends in a cluster of images which are thoroughly and (I take it) deliberately ambiguous. We cannot tell from them whether we ought to believe that there is no principle governing the world except the principle of continual change, or that, in some way as yet unexplored, the metamorphoses of the world prove the existence of some more constant principle underlying them.

The next poem is splendid and delicate. It begins, "Farewell to an idea . . ."; but the rest of the poem is concerned with a concretely presented scene, a whitewashed cabin on a beach. The quality of its whiteness changes with changes in the light and changes in the seasons. In this context, "Farewell to an idea" can mean (1) farewell to the idea of whiteness, because "whiteness," we realize, is not the name of one idea, but a name conveniently attached to many different ideas ("idea" in this case being used, as by Berkeley, to mean "sense-impression"); or it can mean (2) farewell to the idea of summer, now that autumn has come; or it can mean (3) farewell to an idea in the more conversational sense of something that has been a governing principle in one's thought. In this last case, one may say farewell to the idea, not when it is proved unsound, but as soon as it comes to seem less important, to move out of the center of one's mind; and if so, then the changes in the landscape drawn in the poem are metaphors for a mental process:

> The wind is blowing the sand across the floor.

> Here, being visible is being white,
> Is being of the solid of white, the accomplishment
> Of an extremist in an exercise . . .

> The season changes. A cold wind chills the beach.
> The long lines of it grow longer, emptier,
> A darkness gathers though it does not fall

> And the whiteness grows less vivid on the wall.
> The man who is walking turns blankly on the sand.
> He observes how the north is always enlarging the change,

> With its frigid brilliances, its blue-red sweeps
> And gusts of great enkindlings, its polar green,
> The color of ice and fire and solitude.

I sympathize with any reader who insists on taking this for what it so beautifully is on the surface, an astonishingly felicitous description, offered for its own sake. But the more one looks at the poem, the more one is forced to see that every item so lovingly and precisely offered has a function beyond the merely descriptive. Thus, "The wind is blowing the sand across the floor" is a piece of information interrupting the detailed charting of the changing play of color in the scene, and it says in effect that the change of color seems just as aimless as the blowing of the sand, or the movements of the walker who turns "blankly" (how else, in this context?) on the beach. And the question whether these changes are in fact as aimless as they seem is, as we have seen, precisely the question that is being discussed throughout.

The last stanza, that seems at first merely decorative, though beautiful, in fact links up with the images of the next poem in the sequence, and not just with its images but with its themes (*e.g.*, solitude). This third poem is again very beautiful indeed. This too begins, "Farewell to an idea." It paints the picture of a family gathering at home in a tranquillity and security that centers on the mother and is in contrast to the bitter weather outside, which seems to invade the members of the family as they say "Goodnight" to the mother and separate to their beds. The simplest reading of this is: summer gives way to autumn as a mother leaves her family when they all retire to rest. It is a beautiful simile, but it is not the whole of the poem. For as we are concerned not with summer but with the idea of summer, so we are concerned not with the mother but with the idea of the mother. This epistemological element is much more prominent here, so much so that one may read the poem as an account, not of an actual domestic occasion, but of how the poet writes a poem about such an occasion, present only in his imagination. The point is indeed that the actual occasion is no more "real" than the imagined occasion. In either case:

> The necklace is a carving not a kiss.

> The soft hands are a motion not a touch.
> The house will crumble and the books will burn.
> They are at ease in a shelter of the mind

> And the house is of the mind and they and time,
> Together, all together.

So, throughout, "their present peace" is presented as precarious and partial. The theme once again is the hackneyed but permanent one of transience, seen alike in the autumn poised on the change to winter, in the poem that slides out of the mind once it is written, in the mother who grows older and more remote as her family grows up. In this last connection, a possible reading would be: Children accept the mother as a presence; adults necessarily see in the presence *the idea* of a mother and so they possess her less completely. The meaning is clinched in the consummate wit and beauty of:

> Upstairs
> The windows will be lighted, not the rooms.
>
> A wind will spread its windy grandeurs round
> And knock like a rifle-butt against the door.
> The wind will command them with invincible sound.

That is, the watchers are inevitably *outside* the thing they watch, watching not a home but the idea of a home. How scrupulous this poet is through all his brilliance may be seen from the audacious and difficult image, "The necklace is a carving not a kiss." The necklace, one of the mother's charms, being a carving, is cold. Our idea of a mother's charm, just because it *is* an idea, is an artifact, something we have constructed for ourselves; and to that extent it is inevitably cold, colder than the warm presence itself as the child understands it. Moreover, this strikes off against the images that follow—being a congealing where these others express dissolution. The change, that is, may be from fluid to rigid as well as the other way round.

The fourth poem is difficult. As the third poem was concerned with the mother, this concerns the father; as that was elegiac, this is affirmative; as that dealt with the world of feeling, this deals with the world of intellect. The father, of course, is the idea of the father or, if you like, Father-principle, among other things God the Father. The poem affirms His constancy beneath and despite the cycles of change; hence it affirms in particular the existence of a body of reality set over against us, not the projection of our own feelings. Here is a new note, which can best be defined by using an unfashionable word and calling it the sublime. I quote the poem in full:

> Farewell to an idea . . . The cancellings,
> The negations are never final. The father sits
> In space, wherever he sits, of bleak regard,
>
> As one that is strong in the bushes of his eyes.
> He says no to no and yes to yes. He says yes
> To no; and in saying yes he says farewell.

He measures the velocities of change.
He leaps from heaven to heaven more rapidly
Than bad angels leap from heaven to hell in flames.

But now he sits in quiet and green-a-day.
He assumes the great speeds of space and flutters them
From cloud to cloudless, cloudless to keen clear

In flights of eye and ear, the highest eye
And the lowest ear, the deep ear that discerns,
At evening, things that attend it until it hears

The supernatural preludes of its own,
At the moment when the angelic eye defines
Its actors approaching, in company, in their masks.

Master o master seated by the fire
And yet in space and motionless and yet
Of motion the ever-brightening origin,

Profound, and yet the king and yet the crown,
Look at this present throne. What company,
In masks, can choir it with the naked wind?

Seeing it laid before us like that, we are naturally tempted to try
the fatal and impossible task of appreciating it in full, word by word
and line by line. Instead, one can only comment on one or two
points, taken almost at random. First, "As one that is strong in the
bushes of his eyes." This gives a flavor at once exotic and primitive,
almost as of the Old Testament. The primitive idea that eyes exert
power ("he has the evil eye") is being vindicated after a fashion
in this poem, as in many others by this poet. If, as Berkeley believed, nothing exists except as it is perceived, or if, as Berkeley did
not believe, the eye created the things it sees, then the eye obviously has all the power in the world. "Bush" suggests, given the
biblical flavor, the burning bush—so that the eyes are fiery. But
there may be a hint of that other kind of bush that is a piece of
machinery. "Masks," in line 18 and also in line 24, looks forward to
the theatrical metaphors of the next poem. But again, to know
Wallace Stevens' work as a whole is to know that he bears very
heavily on the old idea of life as a stage whereon we play our parts;
and that he means by it something very precise which rejuvenates
the old commonplace. All men have parts to play; the eminent per-

son is he who elects to play his part with a vengeance, with panache —but this is to digress. "The fire," of course, in line 19, reminds us of the domestic scene drawn in the previous poem. In the last stanza, "this throne," together with "wind," seems to refer back to the terms in which the question was first posed, of autumn poised on the brink of winter. Finally, a carping comment, on the lines,

> From cloud to cloudless, cloudless to keen clear
>
> In flights of eye and ear, the highest eye . . .

The alliteration in the first of these lines, and the play on the "i" sound in the other, are obvious, rather vulgar effects. It is worth making this point here because, if I am right, when the poet's touch fails him, this is one of the ways in which it shows itself and this sort of thing is found, later in the sequence, in places where it does more damage.

It occurs, for that matter, in the very next poem. But here it is fully under control, and, judiciously exaggerated, is used very successfully for a specific purpose. For, following up the hint at the end of the preceding poem, the poet now introduces the human being called to play his part in the universe thus constituted of female and male principles, which have been defined in poems III and IV respectively. Much is made of the abundant provision made for him by the father. But what *is* his part? What is the play? What is the plot?

> What festival? This loud, disordered mooch?
> These hospitaliers? These brute-like guests?
> These musicians dubbing at a tragedy,
>
> A-dub, a-dub, which is made up of this:
> That there are no lines to speak? There is no play.
> Or, the persons act one merely by being here.

To convey this idea of the human actor as bewildered, out of his element, unbriefed, the effect of a lumpish vulgarity in the diction is of course splendidly appropriate.

Instead of answering these questions just posed, the next poem (VI) tells us of the theater in which the play, whatever it is, takes place. It is Shakespeare's "insubstantial pageant," massive and evanescent at once, impermanent because continually changing, out of nothing else it seems but a splendid abundance for ever expressing itself. This is still a hymn to the glory of God the Father, but in the last two stanzas there is a sudden return on man, and therefore (by implication) on the mother. All this sublimity is as nothing until it is perceived, and the perceiving of it is man's role, or part of it. Very aptly, the images of III (the home, the winter night) make a memorable reappearance in these last lines:

> This is nothing until in a single man contained,
> Nothing until this named thing nameless is
> And is destroyed. He opens the door of his house
>
> On flames. The scholar of one candle sees
> An arctic effulgence flaring on the frame
> Of everything he is. And he feels afraid.

"This is nothing until in a single man contained." In Berkeleyan terms, there is no *esse* where there is no *percipi*. Nothing *is* until it enters some consciousness. But now comes the twist, for having perceived a thing one gives it a name. Yet to name is, as W. R. Rodgers says, in some way to numb. The thing once labeled can be put away or at a distance, shelved. It is then no longer "in a single man contained." It must be "felt upon the pulses," and cannot be so felt until it is nameless, all the accredited names discarded as inadequate. In the last splendid stanza, the "one candle" seems to stand for the individual consciousness, which has to acknowledge that every star is an intelligence, that everywhere there are modes of consciousness —by no means only human ones—foreign to its own.

We now approach the crux, for the next poem (VII) seems to me the turning point in the sequence—at least in the sense that the three poems which follow fall far short of the brilliant assurance of what has gone before. On this showing, it is significant that the poem should be, as it appears to me, the most obscure of the whole group. The piece pursues in more splendid and metaphysical terms the same arc of thought as the preceding poem—ultimate reality may be a Divine Imagination which barely needs, and yet does just need, the collaboration of a human mind to perceive its workings. But there is rather suddenly a much narrower range of feeling ex-

DONALD DAVIE · 173

pressed and appealed to. The fear invoked in the last line of the previous poem ("And he feels afraid") seemed, in the context of that piece, equivalent to awe, a sort of *frisson* in the face of abundant glory, including fear certainly, but also worship, even a kind of rapture. But in this, the next poem, the mood darkens to a sort of resentful terror at a universe ruled by a transience considered as predetermined law. And this is not only a darkening but also a narrowing of mood. The Father here becomes almost exclusively the "bad angel" which in IV was seen as only one of his aspects or his roles. The last two stanzas move up and out of this trough of dejection (this pattern, incidentally, is to be found in other poems of the sequence, with a change of direction before the last six lines, rather as before the sextet of a sonnet):

> But it dare not leap by chance in its own dark.
> It must change from destiny to slight caprice.
> And thus its jetted tragedy, its stele
>
> And shape and mournful making move to find
> What must unmake it and, at last, what can,
> Say, a flippant communication under the moon.

The argument here is difficult but seems to be something like this: an iron law of continual change *does* govern nature, but the presiding genius, the Father, has to make exceptions to this—"must change from destiny to slight caprice"—just so as not to be ruled by his own law. The obvious fallacy in this argument (for if the Father *has* to introduce caprice, he is thereby constrained just as much as if he never acted capriciously) would not matter if the poetry were powerful enough to carry us over it and make us content with paradox. But I doubt if it is so. Such a locution as "jetted tragedy" surely gives it away. To call "tragedy" dark or black would be lame enough, but "jetted" is worse since it adds nothing to the idea of "black" except the taint of the precious and the poetical; and on top of that seems dishonestly to be trying to cover up the poverty of an idea that "black" would reveal altogether too nakedly.

The eighth poem appears, again, to go off at a tangent, in a discussion of "innocence," which (the poet affirms excitedly) *exists*; whether in actual time and space or only as idea, makes no difference. The link with what has gone before appears if we remember the title of a book by Sir Herbert Read, *The Innocent Eye*. One mode of innocence is the child's capacity for seeing immediately— seeing a white thing without needing an idea of whiteness. To say that innocence *exists* means, in this connection and among other things, that adults can achieve the ability to see with this childlike eye. And at the end of the poem this is asserted all but explicitly. Randall Jarrell has objected to the "philosophizing" in some of the recent poetry of Wallace Stevens, and this poem is open to attack on those grounds. But we need to be clear what we are objecting to, and why. I think we should not object to a certain amount of quite unashamedly lean and dry "philosophizing" in verse, so long as it makes no pretense to be anything else. (If the New Critics are forced to object to it even then, so much the worse, I would say, for their doctrine.) One objects to it, surely, when it is ashamed of itself and pretends to be the poetic concrete thinking which it is not. This sort of thing has impaired for me some of Mr. Stevens' earlier work, notably the frequently magnificent early poem, "Le Monocle de Mon Oncle." It occurs in this poem in conjunction with the too-obvious play on sounds, which I have already objected to as "vulgarity." The specious concreteness is to be seen here, along with the facile alliteration, in "pinches the pity of the pitiful man," where I suspect we have "pinches" rather than "touches," partly because it contributed to a jingle of sound too obvious to be interesting, but partly because it gives the illusion of a greater "concreteness." In fact, to consider this phrase in its context is to see that some part of the meaning of "pinch"—as when we say, "pinched with the cold"—works against the meaning apparently aimed for, by introducing a pointless ambiguity.

Next comes a difficult rather wayward piece. The imagery already established, of warm home (the mother) and the winter night (the father), is crossed with another image, of two brothers. The reason for the entry of brothers is not far to seek—the examination of man's role toward God the Father is to be supplemented now with an account of his role toward his neighbor; and, as in the Gospels, the one is a corollary of the other. The first four stanzas create the impression of "taking other people for granted"; the remainder as-

DONALD DAVIE · 175

sert the far from novel truth that we cease to do so under the stress of a common calamity. On the level of epistemology, calamity is change—and (this is the point) the pain of change, e.g., from summer to autumn, bringing the message of our own frailty, sharpens our innocence and makes us draw closer to our neighbor. It is when the beauty is about to depart that we see it more expansively and poignantly, as a child sees it.

But I must here admit that I have no such confidence in my own readings of these later poems as in those at the beginning of the sequence. It goes without saying that in offering my own summary notions of the import of every one of these pieces I am disregarding a wealth of implication which is precisely what gives the work at its best an easy richness that can be savored only in properly sympathetic reading. But if in this way I am throughout doing less than justice to the poetry, it seems to me that in another way I am doing more than justice to these last poems, putting the best face on the matter for the poet's sake, in a way that he doesn't altogether deserve. For here I am no longer so sure that the poet is in complete control of his material; the implications that I have to ignore strike me hereabouts as a fuzz of vagueness rather than meaningful ambiguities. My discomfort is justified by such a passage as this:

> We were as Danes in Denmark all day long
> And knew each other well, hale-hearted landsmen,
> For whom the outlandish was another day
>
> Of the week, queerer than Sunday. We thought alike
> And that made brothers of us in a home
> In which we fed on being brothers, fed
>
> And fattened as on a decorous honeycomb.
> The drama that we live—We lay sticky with sleep.
> The sense of the activity of fate—
>
> The rendezvous when she came alone,
> By her coming became a freedom of the two,
> An isolation which only the two could share.

I have fought shy throughout of describing these three-line groups as "stanzas." And yet in the first half of the sequence they are genuine stanzas, no less truly so for not being self-contained. The sense is

176 · WALLACE STEVENS

cunningly made to run over from one stanza to another (note how often I have had to start a quotation with the last line of a stanza rather than the first), and this weaving through and over the divisions between stanzas enacts very often just the theme that is being presented, of flux, continual transition, and change. In the passage just quoted, however, the sense is no longer run over but wrenched across the gap between stanzas; and because I can find no significance in the violent effect thus attained, I cannot help thinking that the apparent stanza-form here is no more than a typographical convenience. There is, in the penultimate stanza quoted, what seems like an analogous breakdown in syntax.

The last poem in the sequence stands back and tries to see for what it is, this whole picture of the nature of the world and man's destiny in it. What phrase will cover it? "An unhappy people in an unhappy world"—no, the case is not so bad as that. "A happy people in an unhappy world"—no, that means nothing. "A happy people in a happy world"—that's mere comic opera. Nothing will do to define it but, "An unhappy people in a happy world." And the reason for this? The poet decided that man's destiny is as it is because God requires in His Creation, before it can satisfy Him, an element of conflict to be reconciled, and hence a margin of freedom for man that leaves him capable of heroism:

Like a blaze of summer straw, in winter's nick.

This is the last line of the whole poem, a fine full close in which the heroic affirmative tone is mixed with an acknowledgment of man's smallness, and so is shot through with pathos. This recovery at the end is effected in nearly every one of these poems, but some of them, as we have seen, start very lamely indeed, and this last poem is no exception:

An unhappy people in a happy world—
Read, rabbi, the phases of this difference.
An unhappy people in an unhappy world—

Here are too many mirrors for misery.
A happy people in an unhappy world—
It cannot be. There's nothing there to roll

On the expressive tongue, the finding fang.
A happy people in a happy world—
Buffo! A ball, an opera, a bar.

Turn back to where we were when we began:
An unhappy people in a happy world.
Now, solemnize the secretive syllables.

Is it really presumptuous to think that, in this consideration of possible formulae, the judgments that we made on each in the course of paraphrase are clearer, more succinct than those the poet passes in his verse? "No, that means nothing," or "No, this formula is meaningless"—isn't that natural phrasing better, even as poetry, than lame poeticisms such as "finding fang"? And in the last stanza quoted, with the pointless vulgarity of the alliterative sibilants in the last line, is the poet not telling himself what he ought to do, rather than doing it?

At this point my admittedly summary analysis is complete. I have no wish, nor do I see the need, to draw a moral. That can be safely left to persons more interested in the arguments of poems, or in the personalities of their authors, than in the poems themselves. One point only may not be clear. I treat this poem in its two aspects, as communication and as artifact, because it seems to me to deserve such treatment. Most poems, especially poems so ambitious in intention as "The Auroras of Autumn," deserve nothing better than to be brought in as evidence of a common or characteristic tendency or pattern or dilemma. All the poems of Wallace Stevens deserve the more rigorous scrutiny that we give to poems in and for themselves, not as material for making a case or advancing an argument. They demand this sort of attention by virtue of a power in them which makes itself felt immediately, when we have hardly begun to understand them. If I had to define this power in a word, I should fall back upon one that I have already used more than once, though loosely. It is *splendor*. There is splendor in "The Auroras of Autumn," and it is that which forces us to get quite clear in our own minds what we understand by these poems, and (quite precisely) what we think of them.

RANDALL JARRELL

THE COLLECTED POEMS OF
WALLACE STEVENS

1955

Back in the stacks, in libraries; in bookcases in people's living rooms; on brick-and-plank bookshelves beside studio couches, one sees big books in dark bindings, the *Collected Poems* of the great poets. Once, long ago, the poems were new: the book went by post—so many horses and a coach—to a man in a country house, and the letter along with it asked him to describe, evaluate, and fix the place in English literature, in 12,000 words, by January 25, of the poems of William Wordsworth. And the man did.

It is hard to remember that this is the way it was; harder to remember that this is the way it is. The *Collected Poems* still go out —in this century there have been Hardy's and Yeats's and Frost's and Eliot's and Moore's, and now Stevens'—and the man who is sent them still treats them with rough, or rude, or wild justice; still puts them in their place, appreciates their virtues, says *Just here thou ail'st*, says *Nothing I can say will possibly* . . . and mails the essay off.

It all seems terribly queer, terribly risky; surely, by now, people could have thought of some better way? Yet is it as different as we

.   .   .   .

First published in *The Yale Review*, XLIV, Spring, 1955, copyright 1955 by Yale University Press; reprinted by permission of the author and *The Yale Review*.

think from what we do to the old *Poems* in the dark bindings, the poems with the dust on them? Those ruins we star, confident that we are young and they, they are old—they too are animals no one has succeeded in naming, young things nothing has succeeded in aging; beings to which we can say, as the man in Kafka's story says to the corpse: "What's the good of the dumb question you are asking?" They keep on asking it; and it is only our confidence and our innocence that let us believe that describing and evaluating them, fixing their places—in however many words, by whatever date—is any less queer, any less risky.

The *Collected Poems* of such a poet as Stevens—hundreds and thousands of things truly observed or rightly imagined, profoundly meditated upon—is not anything one can easily become familiar with. Setting out on Stevens for the first time would be like setting out to be an explorer of Earth. Fortunately, I knew some of the poems well, and the poems I didn't know at all—the new ones in *The Rock*—I fell in love with. I have spent a long time on the book, and have made lists (of what seemed to me the best poems, and the poems almost as good) that I hope will be of help to those who want to get to know Stevens' poetry, and of interest to those who already know it. But I too want to say *Nothing I can say will possibly* . . . before I mail my essay off.

This *Collected Poems* is full of extraordinary things, and the most extraordinary of all is the section of twenty-eight new—truly new—poems called *The Rock*. One begins

> It makes so little difference, at so much more
> Than seventy, where one looks, one has been there before.
>
> Wood-smoke rises through trees, is caught in an upper flow
> Of air and whirled away. But it has been often so.

In "Seventy Years Later," Stevens can feel that "It is an illusion that we were ever alive"; can feel that the old, free air "is no longer air"—that we, the houses, our shadows, their shadows, "The lives these lived in the mind are at an end./They never were." To him, now, "The meeting at noon at the edge of the field seems like/An invention, an embrace between one desperate clod/And another in a fantastic consciousness,/In a queer assertion of humanity . . ." Custom, the years, lie upon the far-off figures, and the man remembering them, "with a weight/Heavy as frost, and deep almost as life"; and this weight and depth are in the poems, but transfigured, transcendent—are themselves a part of the poems' life. When Stevens says, as he looks at an old man sleeping, that "The two worlds are asleep, are sleeping now./A dumb sense possesses them in a kind of solemnity," the motion of his words is as slow and quiet as the sleep of the worlds. These are poems from the other side of existence, the poems of someone who sees things in steady accustomedness, as we do not, and who sees their accustomedness, and them, as about to perish. In some of the poems the reader feels over everything the sobering and quieting, the largening presence of death. The poems are the poems of a very old man, "a citizen of heaven though still of Rome"; many of their qualities come naturally from age, so that the poems are appropriately and legitimately different from other people's poems, from Stevens' own younger poems. These poems are magnanimous, compassionate, but calmly exact, grandly plain, as though they themselves had suggested to Stevens his "Be orator but with an accurate tongue/ And without eloquence"; and they seem strangely general and representative, so that we could say of them, of Stevens, what Stevens himself says "To an Old Philosopher in Rome":

> each of us
> Beholds himself in you, and hears his voice
> In yours, master and commiserable man.

How much of our existence is in that "master and commiserable man"! When we read even the first stanzas of this long poem,

> On the threshold of heaven, the figures in the street
> Become the figures of heaven, the majestic movement
> Of men growing small in the distances of space,
> Singing, with smaller and still smaller sound,
> Unintelligible absolution and an end—
>
> The threshold, Rome, and that more merciful Rome
> Beyond, the two alike in the make of the mind.
> It is as if in a human dignity
> Two parallels become one, a perspective, of which
> Men are part both in the inch and in the mile.

RANDALL JARRELL · 181

> How easily the blown banners change to wings . . .
> Things dark on the horizons of perception,
> Become accompaniments of fortune, but
> Of the fortune of the spirit, beyond the eye,
> Not of its sphere, and yet not far beyond,
>
> The human end in the spirit's greatest reach,
> The extreme of the known in the presence of the extreme
> Of the unknown. . . .

it seems to us that we are feeling, as it is not often possible for us to feel, what it is to be human; the poem's composed, equable sorrow is a kind of celebration of our being, and is deeper sounding, satisfies more in us, than joy; we feel our own natures realized, so that when we read, near the end of the poem,

> It is a kind of total grandeur at the end
> With every visible thing enlarged, and yet
> No more than a bed, a chair and moving nuns . . .
>
> Total grandeur of a total edifice
> Chosen by an inquisitor of structures
> For himself. He stops upon this threshold . . .

we feel that Santayana is Stevens, and Stevens ourselves—and that, stopping upon this threshold, we are participating in the grandeur possible to man.

This is a great poem of a new kind. The completeness and requiredness of the poem's working-out; the held-back yet magically sure, fully extended slowness with which these parallel worlds near each other and meet, remind one of the slow movements of some of Beethoven's later quartets and sonatas. But poems like these, in their plainness and human rightness, remind me most of a work of art superficially very different, Verdi's *Falstaff*. Both are the products of men at once very old and beyond the dominion of age; such men seem to have entered into (or are able to create for us) a new existence, a world in which everything is enlarged and yet no more than itself, transfigured and yet beyond the need of transfiguration.

When Stevens writes, in "The World as Meditation," of Penelope waiting for Ulysses, it is not Penelope and Ulysses but Stevens and the sun, the reader and the world—"two in a deep-founded sheltering, friend and dear friend." At dawn "a form of fire approaches the cretonnes of Penelope," a "savage presence" awakes within her her own "barbarous strength." Has Ulysses come? "It was only day./It was Ulysses and it was not. Yet they had met,/ Friend and dear friend and a planet's encouragement"; and she combs her hair, "repeating his name with its patient syllables."

Some of the phrases of the poems describe the poems better than any I can invent for them. "St. Armorer's Church from the Outside" shows us the stony majesty of the past, man's settled triumphs:

> St. Armorer's was once an immense success.
> It rose loftily and stood massively; and to lie
> In its church-yard, in the province of St. Armorer's,
> Fixed one for good in geranium-colored day . . .

but it leaves them for "the chapel of breath," for "that which is always beginning because it is part/Of that which is always beginning, over and over," for the new creation that seems to us "no sign of life but life,/Itself, the presence of the intelligible/In that which is created as its symbol." And the poems' wish for themselves, at the end—"It was not important that they should survive./ What mattered was that they should bear/Some lineament or character,/Some affluence, if only half-perceived,/In the poverty of their words,/Of the planet of which they were part"—is touching as Keats's "writ in water" is touching, and endears them to us more than our own praise.

Stevens has always looked steadily at the object, but has looked, often, shortly and with a certain indifference, the indifference of the artist who—as Goethe says—"stands above art and the object; he stands above art because he utilizes it for his purpose; he stands above the object because he deals with it in his own manner." But now that the unwanted, inescapable indifference of age has taken the place of this conscious indifference, Stevens is willing to be possessed by "the plain sense of things," and his serious undeviating meditation about them seems as much in their manner as in his. His poetry has had "the power to transform itself, or else/And what meant more, to be transformed." The movement of his poetry has changed; the reader feels in it a different presence, and is touched by all that is no longer there. Stevens' late-nineteenth-century orchestration has been replaced, most of the time, by plain chords from a few instruments—the stir and dazzle of the parts is lost in the sense of the whole. The best of these late poems have a calm, serious certainty, an easiness of rightness, like well-being. The barest and most pitiable of the world's objects—"the great pond,/ The plain sense of it, without reflections, leaves,/Mud water like dirty glass, expressing silence/Of a sort, silence of a rat come out to see"—have in the poems "the naked majesty . . . of bird-nest arches and of rain-stained vaults," a dignity and largeness and unchange-ableness; on the winter day "the wind moves like a great thing tottering."

I had meant to finish this section on *The Rock* by quoting the marvelously original "Prologues to What Is Possible," but it is too long; I had better quote "Madame La Fleurie," a particularly touching treatment of a subject that is particularly Stevens':

> Weight him down, O side-stars, with the great weightings of the end.
> Seal him there. He looked in a glass of the earth and thought he lived in it.
> Now, he brings all that he saw into the earth, to the waiting parent.
> His crisp knowledge is devoured by her, beneath a dew.
>
> Weight him, weight, weight him with the sleepiness of the moon.
> It was only a glass because he looked in it. It was nothing he could be told.
> It was a language he spoke, because he must, yet did not know.
> It was a page he had found in the handbook of heartbreak.
>
> The black fugatos are strumming the blacknesses of black . . .
> The thick strings stutter the finial gutturals.
> He does not lie there remembering the blue-jay, say the jay.
> His grief is that his mother should feed on him, himself and what he saw,
> In that distant chamber, a bearded queen, wicked in her dead light.

When the reader comes to aberrant poems like "Page of a Tale" and "A Rabbit as King of the Ghosts," he realizes how little there is in Stevens, ordinarily, of the narrative, dramatic, immediately active side of life, of harried actors compelled, impelled, in ignorant hope. But how much there is of the man who looks, feels, meditates, in the freedom of removedness, of disinterested imagining, of thoughtful love! As we read the poems we are so continually aware of Stevens observing, meditating, creating, that we feel like saying that the process of creating the poem is the poem. Surprisingly often the motion of qualification, of concession, of logical conclusion—a dialectical motion in the older sense of *dialectical*—is the movement that organizes the poem; and in Stevens the unlikely tenderness of this movement—the one, the not-quite-that, the other, the not-exactly-the-other, the real one, the real other—is like the tenderness of the sculptor or draftsman, whose hand makes but looks as if it caressed.

Few poets have made a more interesting rhetoric out of just fooling around: turning things upside-down, looking at them from under the sofa, considering them (and their observer) curiously enough to make the reader protest, "That were to consider it too curiously." This rhetoric is the rhetoric of a kaleidoscope, a kaleidoscope of parts; and when it is accompanied, as it sometimes is, by little content and less emotion, it seems clear, bright, complicated, and inhuman. When the philosopher is king, his subjects move like propositions. Yet one is uneasy at objecting to the play—to the professional playfulness, even—of a large mind and a free spirit.

I have written, in another essay, about the disadvantages of philosophizing (in verse) as inveterately and interminably as Stevens has philosophized. But his marvelous successes with his method, in its last bare anomalous stages in *The Rock*, make me feel that the hand of the maker knows better than the eye of the observer, at least if it's my eye. Without his excesses, his endless adaptations and exaggerations of old procedures, how could he ever have learned these unimaginable new ways of his? A tree is justified in its fruits: I began to distrust my own ways, and went back to the poems (in *The Auroras of Autumn*) that had seemed to me monumental wastes; transcendental, all too transcendental études; improvisations preserved for us neither by good nor by bad, but by middle fortune. I read them over and over, relishing in anticipation the pleasures of an honest reformation. I could see how much familiarity this elaborate, almost monotonously meditative style requires of the reader; I managed, after a while, to feel that I had not been as familiar with the poems, or as sympathetic to the poems, as I ought to have been. And there I stuck. Whatever is wrong with the poems or with me is as wrong as ever; what they seemed to me once, they seem to me still.

Stevens' poetry makes one understand how valuable it can be for a poet to write a great deal. Not too much of that great deal, ever, is good poetry; but out of quantity can come practice, naturalness, accustomed mastery, adaptations and elaborations and reversals of old ways, new ways, even—so that the poet can put into the poems, at the end of a lifetime, what the end of a lifetime brings him. Stevens has learned to write at will, for pleasure; his methods of writing, his ways of imagining, have made this possible for him as it is impossible for many living poets—Eliot, for instance. Anything can be looked at, felt about, meditated upon, so Stevens *can* write about anything; he does not demand of his poems the greatest concentration, intensity, dramatic immediacy, the shattering and inexplicable rightness the poet calls inspiration. (Often it is as if Stevens didn't want the poetic equivalent of sonata form, and had gone back to earlier polyphonic ways, days when the crescendo was still uninvented.) His good poems are as inspired as anybody else's— if you compare *The Auroras of Autumn* with *The Rock*, you will decide that the last poems come from a whole period of the most marvelous inspiration; but Stevens does not think of inspiration (or whatever you want to call it) as a condition of composition. He too is waiting for the spark from heaven to fall—poets have no choice about this—but he waits writing; and this—other things being equal, when it's possible, if it's possible—is the best way for the poet to wait.

Stevens' rhetoric is at its worst, always, in the poems of other poets; just as great men are great disasters, overwhelmingly good poets are overwhelmingly bad influences. In Stevens the reign of the dramatic monologue—the necessity to present, present! in con-

186 · WALLACE STEVENS

centrated dramatic form—is over, and the motion of someone else's speech has been replaced by "the motion of thought" of the poet himself. Ordinarily this poet's thought moves (until *The Rock*) in unrhymed iambic pentameter, in a marvelously accomplished Wordsworthian blank verse—or, sometimes, in something akin to Tennyson's bland lissome adaptation of it. If someone had predicted to Pound, when he was beginning his war on the iambic foot; to Eliot, when he was first casting a cold eye on post-Jacobean blank verse; to both, when they were first condemning generalization in poetry, that in forty or fifty years the chief—sometimes, I think in despair, the only—influence on younger American poets would be this generalizing, masterful, scannable verse of Stevens', wouldn't both have laughed in confident disbelief? And how many of the youngest English poets seem to want to write like Cowper! A great revolution is hardest of all on the great revolutionists.

At the bottom of Stevens' poetry there is wonder and delight, the child's or animal's or savage's—man's—joy in his own existence, and thankfulness for it. He is the poet of well-being: "One might have thought of sight, but who could think/Of what it sees, for all the ill it sees?" This sigh of awe, of wondering pleasure, is underneath all the poems that show us the "celestial possible," everything that has not yet been transformed into the infernal impossibilities of our everyday earth. Stevens is full of the natural or Aristotelian virtues; he is, in the terms of Hopkins' poem, all windhover and no Jesuit. There is about him, under the translucent glazes, a Dutch solidity and weight, he sits surrounded by all the good things of this earth, with rosy cheeks and fresh clear blue eyes, eyes not going out to you but shining in their place, like fixed stars—or else he moves off, like the bishop in his poem, "globed in today and tomorrow." If he were an animal he would be, without a doubt, that rational, magnanimous, voluminous animal, the elephant.

As John Stuart Mill read Wordsworth, to learn to feel, so any of a thousand logical positivists might read Stevens, to learn to imagine: "That strange flower, the sun,/Is just what you say./Have it your way./The world is ugly,/And the people are sad./That tuft of jungle feathers,/That animal eye,/Is just what you say./That savage of fire,/That seed,/Have it your way./The world is ugly,/And the people are sad." But such a poem does more than imagine—it sees, it knows; so perhaps imagining is a part of seeing and knowing. Stevens finishes "Tea at the Palaz of Hoon" by admitting that it has all been imaginary, that his ears have made the hymns they heard, that "I was the world in which I walked, and what I saw/Or heard or felt came not but from myself;/And there I found myself more truly and more strange"—he has seen his own being, in truth and in strangeness, as he could never have seen it if he had looked at it directly.

When I read the first two lines of a poem, "Place-bound and time-bound in evening rain/And bound by a sound which does not change"; or of something "in which/We believe without belief, beyond belief"; or of the people of the future beginning to "avoid our stale perfections, seeking out/Their own, waiting until we go/To picnic in the ruins that we leave"; or that "Time is a horse that runs in the heart, a horse/Without a rider on a road at night"; or of "armies without/Either drums or trumpets, the commanders mute, the arms/On the ground, fixed fast in a profound defeat," these low grave notes are more to me, almost, than any of the old bright ones. But then I remember that some of the old ones were as grave: "The Snow Man" or "The Death of a Soldier" or that haunting poem no one seems haunted by, "Autumn Refrain":

> The skreak and skritter of evening gone
> And grackles gone and sorrows of the sun,
> The sorrows of sun, too, gone . . . the moon and moon,
> The yellow moon of words about the nightingale
> In measureless measures, not a bird for me
> But the name of a bird and the name of a nameless air
> I have never—shall never hear. And yet beneath
> The stillness of everything gone, and being still,
> Being and sitting still, something resides,
> Some skreaking and skrittering residuum,
> And grates these evasions of the nightingale
> Though I have never—shall never hear that bird.
> And the stillness is in the key, all of it is,
> The stillness is all in the key of that desolate sound.

But how charming Stevens' jokes are, too! When he uses little cultural properties unexpectedly, with mocking elegiac humor; when we—so to speak—discover that the part of the collage we thought a washrag is really a reproduction of the Laocoön, we are pleased just as we are in Klee. This Dawn *is* one of Klee's little watercolor-operas, isn't it?

> An opening of portals when night ends,
> A running forward, arms stretched out as drilled.
> Act I, Scene I, in a German Staats-Oper.

And when Stevens begins, "O that this lashing wind was something more/Than the spirit of Ludwig Richter!"; when he thinks, looking out upon a prospect of the Alps, "Claude has been dead a long time/And apostrophes are forbidden on the funicular"; when he says of "Lions in Sweden" that he too was once

> A hunter of those sovereigns of the soul
> And savings banks, Fides, the sculptor's prize,
> All eyes and size, and galled Justitia,
> Trained to poise the tales of the law,
> Patientia, forever soothing wounds,
> And mighty Fortitudo, frantic bass . . .

—when Stevens does all this, I am delighted; and I am more delighted with these souvenirs, these ambiguous survivals, because in other poems the other times and the other peoples, the old masters and the old masterpieces, exist in fresh and unambiguous magnificence.

Stevens does seem a citizen of the world. The other arts, the other continents, the other centuries are essential not merely to his well-being but to his own idea of himself, his elementary identity. Yeats called Keats a schoolboy with his nose pressed against the window of a sweetshop; we Americans stand with our noses pressed against the window of the world. How directly, in *The Cantos* and *The Waste Land,* Pound and Eliot appropriate that world! stones from the Coliseum, drops of water from the Jordan, glitter from the pages like a built mirage. (The only directer procedure would have been to go to Europe and stay there.) If Stevens could stay home, except for trips, it was because he had made for himself a Europe of his own, a past of his own, a whole sunlit, and, in the end, twilight—world of his own. It is an extremely large world, the world that an acute mind, varied interests and sympathies, and an enormous vocabulary can produce. (I know what an abject, basely material anticlimax that *enormous vocabulary* is; but the bigger a poet's effective natural vocabulary is, the larger his world will seem.) And Stevens has an extraordinarily original imagination, one that has created for us—so to speak—many new tastes and colors and sounds, many real, half-real, and nonexistent beings.

He has spoken, always, with the authority of someone who thinks of himself as a source of interest, of many interests. He has never felt it necessary to appeal to us, make a hit with us, nor does he try to sweep us away, to overawe us; he has written as if poems were certain to find, or make, their true readers. Throughout half this century of the common man, this age in which each is like his sibling, Stevens has celebrated the hero, the capacious, magnanimous, excelling man; has believed, with obstinancy and good humor, in all the heights which draw us toward them, make us like them, simply by existing. A few weeks ago I read, in Sacheverell Sitwell, two impressive sentences: "It is my belief that I have informed myself of nearly all works of art in the known world. . . . I have heard most of the music of the world, and seen nearly all the paintings." It was hard for me to believe these sentences, but I wanted Sitwell to be able to say them, liked him for having said them—I believed. While I was writing this essay the sentences kept coming back to me, since they seemed to me sentences Stevens would say if he could. In an age when almost everybody sold man and the world short, he never did, but acted as if joy *were* "a word of our own," as if nothing excellent were alien to us.

I should like, now, to give a list of eighteen or twenty of Stevens' best poems, and a list of twenty or thirty of his better. Reading the poems in these lists will give anyone a definite—dazzlingly definite —idea of the things I think exceptional about Stevens' poetry, and the lists can be of help to people just beginning to make, from this big *Collected Poems,* a "Selected Poems" of their own. Some of his best poems are, I think: "The Snow Man," "To an Old Philosopher in Rome," "Esthétique du Mal," "The World as Meditation," "Peter Quince at the Clavier," "Autumn Refrain," "Angel Surrounded by Paysans," "Sunday Morning," "The Death of a Soldier," "Prologues to What Is Possible," "Madame La Fleurie," "Sea Surface Full of Clouds," "The Man on the Dump," "Some Friends From Pascagoula," "The Brave Man"—but now I begin to be very confused about where the best ends and the better begins —"Dutch Graves in Bucks County," "Seventy Years Later," "The Comedian as the Letter C," "The Emperor of Ice-Cream," "Mrs. Alfred Uruguay," "Page from a Tale," "The Common Life," "Sailing After Lunch," "Le Monocle de Mon Oncle." And now I begin, however uneasily, on my second list: "To the One of Fictive Music," "St. Armorer's Church from the Outside," "Disillusionment of Ten O'Clock," "The Plain Sense of Things," "The Good Man Has No Shape," "Lions in Sweden," "Gubbinal," "Sonatina to Hans Christian," "The American Sublime," "A Quiet Normal Life," "Tea at the Palaz of Hoon," "Bantams in Pine-Woods," the first of "Six Significant Landscapes," Part IX of "Credences of Summer," "A Lot of People Bathing in a Stream," "Metaphors of a Magnifico," "Cy Est Pourtraicte, Madame Ste Ursule, et Les Unze Mille Vierges," "The Idea of Order at Key West," "Anecdote of the Prince of Peacocks," "No Possum, No Sop, No Taters," "Martial Cadenza," "Anglais Mort à Florence," "Mozart, 1935," "A Rabbit as King of the Ghosts," "Poetry Is a Destructive Force," "A Woman Sings a Song for a Soldier Come Home," "Less and Less Human, O Savage Spirit."

Stevens has spoken with dignity and elegance and intelligence—with eloquence—of everything from pure sensation to pure reflection to pure imagination, from the "elephant-colorings" of tires to the angel of reality, the "necessary angel" in whose sight we "see the earth again /Cleared of its stiff and stubborn, man-locked set"—the angel who asks as he departs:

> Am I not
> Myself, only half of a figure of a sort,
>
> A figure half seen, or seen for a moment, a man
> Of the mind, an apparition apparelled in
>
> Apparels of such lightest look that a turn
> Of my shoulder and quickly, too quickly, I am gone?

RANDALL JARRELL · 191

These lines, so pure and light and longing, remind me of the other figures which, in the second of the *Duino Elegies*, touch us lightly on the shoulder before they turn and go. "A man/Of the mind": in this end of one line and beginning of another, and in the suspension between them, the angel has spoken an epitaph for Stevens.

SAMUEL FRENCH MORSE

THE NATIVE ELEMENT

1958

Poetry, for Wallace Stevens, was the essence of "a quiet normal life," "the one reality in this imagined world." He flirted for years with these paradoxes and quasi-paradoxes: they fill the poems, the essays, the notebooks. If they do not define his poetry, they at least characterize a great deal that he wrote, and they frame his attitude toward poetry. The notebooks in which he recorded the "Adagia" give us the paradoxes stripped of context—one cannot say the naked paradox, because in Stevens nothing is naked and everything bears the mark of metaphor. But the "Adagia" furnish some significant clues to the definition in which he was interested. He writes, for example: "I have no life except in poetry. No doubt that would be true if my whole life was free for poetry." Or again: "An evening's thought is like a day of clear weather." Or, finally: "The collecting of poetry from one's experience as one goes along is not the same thing as merely writing poetry."

Such statements point to an obvious fact and what, for Stevens, was the primary fact: that a man writes because he needs to; and the

.   .   .   .

A paper delivered at The English Institute in September, 1957, Mr. Morse's essay was first published in *The Kenyon Review*, XX, Summer, 1958, copyright 1958 by *The Kenyon Review*; it is reprinted by permission of the author and Mr. Robie Macauley, editor of *The Kenyon Review*.

need is the basic premise upon which everything else depends and from which every other fact follows in all of his writing about poetry. As the great categorical imperative of his life, it accounts for the peculiar character not only of the poems but also of the essays; and nothing could be more typical of him than the comment on a note on "Cézanne at the Lefèvre," by Graham Bell: "I note [this] both for itself and because it adds to subject and manner the thing that is incessantly overlooked: the artist, the presence of the determining personality. Without that reality no amount of other things matters much."

The essays belong neither to the theory of literature nor to criticism in the ordinary sense in which we use those words. Stevens states his judgments in terms of the satisfactions of poetry or a given poem, and almost always under the self-protective guise of metaphor, which is a poet's inevitable and preternatural way of expressing himself. It is familiar testimony in any case, nor does it differ greatly from the testimony of many other poets. The *Ars Poetica* and the *Essay on Criticism*, after all, are poems. A *Vision* is an extended metaphor. The essays of Robert Frost speak directly in parables of "the constant symbol," "the figure a poem makes." But although the uses to which a poet puts metaphor in what he writes about poetry do not vary much from the uses to which he puts metaphor in his poems, they suggest different conclusions. A *Vision*, for example, gives us insights into the needs which Yeats wrote his poems to satisfy; the poems themselves reveal the satisfactions of those needs.

With Stevens these differences tend constantly to disappear. Even his most discursive essays, such as "Imagination as Value" and "A Collect of Philosophy" or "The Irrational Element in Poetry," strain toward the condition of poetry; and in one instance—"Three Academic Pieces"—the discursive element disappears altogether: what begins as an essay ends literally as poetry. His introductions to books and his tributes to fellow artists, painters as well as poets, and friends such as Henry Church and Paul Rosenfeld, show the same impulse at work. A review of the *Selected Poems* of Marianne Moore concentrates on those aspects of her work which, for him, demonstrate its character and remain untranslatable; he calls atten-

194 · WALLACE STEVENS

tion to them as evidence, a proof that "poetry and materia poetica are interchangeable terms," a test of the proposition he noted down more than once: "Literature is the better part of life," with the humorously rueful qualification: "To this it seems inevitably necessary to add, provided life is the better part of literature." It is not that Miss Moore's poems leave Stevens tongue-tied, as they do many of her critics, for his review illuminates her work with great perspicacity; rather he is interested in pointing out those qualities which make her poetry for him "the veritable thing." The text of his broadcast for the Voice of America is a prose-poem; and so are his responses to the National Book Award, the Poetry Society of America, and Bard at the time the college gave him an honorary degree. The notebooks comprise a collection of proverbs and about three hundred and fifty titles and metaphors for poems.

"The presence of the determining personality" is thus apparent everywhere. Typically, a note on Marcel Gromaire begins with the observation that "Catalogues for exhibitions of paintings are the natural habitat of the prose-poem." After stating that "in the case of Marcel Gromaire one feels that the need for definition comes first," Stevens goes on to define the artist in a prose-poem similar to Léon-Paul Fargue's *"portrait de famille"* of Segonzac, of which Stevens made a paraphrase not long after he had completed his text on Gromaire. To symbolize the painter's principles and convictions, he selects from Gromaire's own words half a dozen key phrases which he combines with salient facts about Gromaire's background and life, in order to characterize as well as define the man and his work. Gromaire's words, Stevens says, "help us to look at his pictures as they are." So it is with the biographical details. More than this, the note as a whole conveys the impression that it is intended to be a true image in words of Gromaire's painting. A true "seeing" of Gromaire—that is, of his painting, is a true evaluation or criticism, and therefore a true appreciation, of Gromaire. It is as close as one can come, in words, to the thing itself. It is the thing seen that becomes what we later think about it. Although the image is no more than a metaphor, it is its own justification because "what we see," for Stevens, "is what we think," and "what we think is never what we see." As a metaphor meant to demonstrate that the man is in all important respects indistinguishable from his work, the note on Gromaire is grounded in the conviction that "The poet seems to confer his identity on the reader"; to which he adds by way of explanation: "It is easiest to recognize this when listening to music—I mean this sort of thing: the transference." The doctrine implicit in this attitude is even more transcendentalist than it is Mallarméan. "Whenever a true theory appears," says Emerson at the beginning of *Nature*, "it will be its own evidence."

The note on Gromaire, however, chiefly typifies the way in which Stevens blurs the distinctions between poetry and criticism. Nevertheless, the discursive element does not disappear; the transformation is not complete nor is it intended to be. The occasion, and possibly the painting itself, at least for Stevens, did not warrant anything more specific than the kind of prose-poem he refers to at the beginning of his essay. It did not provide, it may be, the satisfactions that produced the actual poems which form the great body of his work. Gromaire was not, for him, a painter whose pictures made life complete in itself. But there were other occasions and other paintings; music, landscapes, "things chalked/On the sidewalk" for the "pensive man" who is the "connoisseur of chaos" to see; "the dreadful sundry of this world" catalogued in "O Florida, Venereal Soil":

> Convolvulus and coral,
> Buzzards and live-moss,
> Tiestas from the keys. . . .

> The Cuban, Polodowsky,
> The Mexican women,
> The negro undertaker
> Killing the time between corpses
> Fishing for crayfish.

The satisfactions these experiences produced in themselves gave rise to the satisfactions expressed in the poems. Frequently the correspondences between the original experience and the experience given its being in the poem are vivid, direct, and easy to account for, as in the poems that concentrate on landscape and atmospheres in celebration of "the great interests of man: air and light, the joy of having a body, the voluptuousness of looking." "Evening Without Angels," the poem for which these words from Mario Rossi form an epigraph, is a superb example of the way in which a phrase casually come upon in his reading could "confer its identity" upon Stevens, arranging the world for him in a poem, and achieving the "transference" which gave life its point, not in terms of what life lacks but by making life "complete in itself."

> Why seraphim like lutanists arranged
> Above the trees? And why the poet as
> Eternal *chef d'orchestre?*
>
>   Air is air,
> Its vacancy glitters round us everywhere.
> Its sounds are not angelic syllables
> But our unfashioned spirits realized
> More sharply in more furious selves.
>
>   And light
> That fosters seraphim and is to them
> Coiffeur of haloes, fecund jeweller—
> Was the sun concoct for angels or for men?
> Sad men made angels of the sun, and of
> The moon they made their own attendant ghosts,
> Which led them back to angels, after death.
>
> Let this be clear that we are men of sun
> And men of day and never of pointed night,
> Men that repeat antiquest sounds of air
> In an accord of repetitions. Yet,
> If we repeat, it is because the wind
> Encircling us, speaks always with our speech.
>
> Light, too, encrusts us making visible
> The motions of the mind and giving form
> To moodiest nothings, as, desire for day
> Accomplished in the immensely flashing East,
> Desire for rest, in that descending sea
> Of dark, which in its very darkening
> Is rest and silence spreading into sleep.
>
> . . . Evening, when the measure skips a beat
> And then another, one by one, and all
> To a seething minor swiftly modulate.
> Bare night is best. Bare earth is best. Bare, bare,

Except for our own houses, huddled low
Beneath the arches and their spangled air,
Beneath the rhapsodies of fire and fire,
Where the voice that is in us makes a true response,
Where the voice that is great within us rises up,
As we stand gazing at the rounded moon.

Such is the satisfaction that Stevens felt most deeply the need to express. As the world is round, so the poems compose and re-compose by what he called repetition, not by a deliberate and self-conscious search for new subjects. Furthermore, it was a principle with Stevens that "A man cannot search life for unprecedented experiences." He often wrote a new poem because one poem suggested another: the "Two Letters" published in *Vogue* in celebration of his seventy-fifth birthday he did not consider inseparable parts of a whole; and although *Notes Toward a Supreme Fiction* and "An Ordinary Evening in New Haven" are more impressive as wholes than in their parts, they seem to have been composed in much the same way. They are illustrations of "the pleasures of circulating," although not of "merely circulation," unless one catches here Stevens' implicit agreement with Marianne Moore that "one's sense of humor is the clue to the most serious part of one's nature." Unlike a great many of his contemporaries, he was never afraid of repeating himself. As early as 1917 or 1918 he wrote to William Carlos Williams:

> My idea is that in order to carry a thing to the extreme [necessary] to convey it one has to stick to it. . . . Given a fixed point of view, realistic, imagistic, or what you will, everything adjusts to that point of view; and the process of adjustment is a world in flux, as it should be for a poet. But to fidget with points of view leads always to new beginnings and incessant new beginnings lead to sterility. A single manner or mood thoroughly matured and exploited is that fresh thing.

In the light of such a statement, some of the "Adagia" acquire special significance, particularly those that deal with the poet's world and the perspective from which he views it. Almost without exception Stevens makes of the inevitable limitation of the individual a crowning virtue. It is in the poems, however, that his mastery of repetition achieves its fullest effect. Among the early poems, there is no better example than "Ploughing on Sunday," with its extraordinary evocation of wind and light and that excitement in such experiences which is so intense as to suggest that it is almost a secret and forbidden pleasure. "Some Friends From Pascagoula," written more than ten years later, repeats the pattern of "Ploughing on Sunday" so closely that one is at first simply bewildered to know by what means Stevens managed to perform the feat. The repetitions are, of course, variations, like the three versions of a line from Baudelaire, which appear in the essay "Two or Three Ideas." Each is final for the moment, but each differs from the other, so that one is almost tempted to say that it is when things are most nearly the same that they change most often in Stevens. Obviously the "presence of the determining personality" is one essential element here; "the world in flux" is another. It is the rapport between them that produces a poetry whose "words are of things that do not exist without the words." That relationship between the poet and his world is most vividly set forth in "The Comedian as the Letter C," but it finds its most perfect form near the end of the *Notes Toward a Supreme Fiction*:

> Whistle aloud, too weedy wren. I can
> Do all that angels can. I enjoy like them,
> Like men besides, like men in light secluded,
>
> Enjoying angels. Whistle, forced bugler,
> That bugles for the mate, nearby the nest,
> Cock bugler, whistle and bugle and stop just short,
>
> Red robin, stop in your preludes, practicing
> Mere repetitions. These things at least comprise
> An occupation, an exercise, a work,
>
> A thing final in itself and, therefore, good:
> One of the vast repetitions final in
> Themselves and, therefore, good, the going round
>
> And round and round, the merely going round,
> Until merely going round is a final good,
> The way wine comes at a table in a wood.

And we enjoy like men, the way a leaf
Above the table spins its constant spin,
So that we look at it with pleasure, look

At it spinning its eccentric measure. Perhaps,
The man-hero is not the exceptional monster,
But he that of repetition is most master.

There are times in the later poems especially when the correspondences between the original satisfaction and the satisfaction given
substance in words are apparent only as a faint shadow. One example
will suffice. Characteristically, the original satisfaction came from
"the voluptuousness of looking" at one of the paintings in his
own collection: a still-life by Tal Coat, which he acquired in 1949.
Stevens' letters to his Paris bookseller, who was also his buyer of
pictures, reveal his original satisfactions in the painting when he
first received it:

> The picture came this morning in perfect condition. I
> had feared that it was going to be low in tone, having in
> mind your drawing and color indications, and I was happy,
> therefore, to find that it is so much cooler and richer and
> fresher than I had expected. It is young and new and full
> of vitality. The forms and the arrangement of the objects
> are, both, full of contrariness and sophistication. It is a
> fascinating picture. For all its in-door light on in-door
> objects, the picture refreshes one with an out-door sense of
> things. The strong blue lines and the high point of the
> black line in the central foreground collect the group. The
> wine in the glass at the right-hand edge warms, without
> complicating, the many cool blues and greens. This is
> going to give me a great deal of pleasure, and I am most
> grateful to you. Since you will want to know about the
> frame, let me say that it is completely successful, and no
> doubt Tal Coat himself would agree that it is a very happy
> complement—a part of the good fortune of the picture.

A few days later he wrote again:

> Now that I have had the new picture at home for a few
> days, it seems almost domesticated. Tal Coat is supposed
> to be a man of violence but one soon becomes accustomed

to the present picture. I have even given it a title of my own: *Angel Surrounded by Peasants*. The angel is the Venetian glass bowl on the left with the little spray of leaves in it. The peasants are the terrines, bottles, and the glasses that surround it. This title alone tames it as a lump of sugar might tame a lion. I shall study everything that I see concerning Tal Coat. If you see anything, I shall be grateful to you if you will send it to me.

In a final comment, about a month later, the particulars have broadened into generalizations:

Since my last letter to you about the Tal Coat I have reached what I think is my final feeling about it, although one never knows what prompts an artist to do what he does. It is obvious that this picture is the contrary of everything that one would expect in a still-life. Thus it is commonly said that a still-life is a problem in the painting of solids. Tal Coat has not interested himself in that problem. Here all the objects are painted with a slap-dash intensity, the purpose of which is to convey the vigor of the artist. Here nothing is mediocre or merely correct. Tal Coat scorns the fastidious. Moreover, this is not a manifestation of the crude strength of a peasant, to use that word merely to convey a meaning. It is a display of imaginative force: an effort to attain a certain reality purely by way of the artist's own vitality. I don't know that all these words will mean much, but I think they disclose the reason why Tal Coat is well thought of. He is virile and he has the naturalness of a man who means to be something more than a follower.

The delight in "contrariness and sophistication," "slap-dash intensity" and "imaginative force," are commonplace in the poetry. The precision with which these characteristics are expressed, even in his letters, is a commonplace of the man himself. But the only clearly visible links between Stevens' satisfactions in the painting and the poem that can be identified with it are the title they share: "Angel Surrounded by Paysans," and the "contrariness and sophistication" of everything about the poem itself.

SAMUEL FRENCH MORSE · 201

One of the countrymen:
                                          There is
    A welcome at the door to which no one comes?

The angel:
    I am the angel of reality
    Seen for a moment standing in the door.

    I have neither ashen wing nor wear of ore
    And live without a tepid aureole,

    Or stars that follow me, not to attend,
    But of my being and its knowing, part.

    I am one of you and being one of you
    Is being and knowing what I am and know.

    Yet I am the necessary angel of earth,
    Since, in my sight, you see the earth again,

    Cleared of its stiff and stubborn, man-locked set,
    And, in my hearing, you hear its tragic drone

    Rise liquidly in liquid lingerings,
    Like watery words awash; like meanings said

    By repetitions of half-meanings. Am I not,
    Myself, only half of a figure of a sort,

    A figure half seen, or seen for a moment, a man
    Of the mind, an apparition apparelled in

    Apparels of such lightest look that a turn
    Of my shoulder and quickly, too quickly, I am gone?

The poem undoubtedly expressed Stevens's "final feeling" about
the picture; and it seems likely that the statement that "one never
knows what prompts an artist to do what he does" applies to the
poem as well as to the picture. This is not to say that Stevens did
not know what he was doing when he wrote the poem, but it does
imply a respect for the fortuitousness of the poetic impulse, which,
for him, finds its best source in "the aspects of earth" that he
describes as "the casual ones, as light or color, images." In other
words, as "a display of imaginative force: an effort to attain a
certain reality purely by way of the artist's own vitality," the poem
is much more than a page of illustrations. Nor is it in any sense an

imitation. Even as an analogue of the painting, it has its own character, despite the fact that everything Stevens says in his letter to Mlle. Vidal of the intentions and qualities of Tal Coat applies to Stevens himself.

It is important to keep these distinctions in the realm of resemblance clear; otherwise, the poem becomes a series of symbols dependent for their meaning on a purely private frame of reference. The necessary angel of reality in the poem can be considered the equivalent of "the Venetian glass bowl . . . with the little spray of leaves in it," but it is no more than an equivalent. The poem creates a "new reality," although not necessarily a reality "from which the original appears to be unreal." Nor should the poem be considered a metaphor of the painting which, in its own right as a work of art, is an imaginative transcript of reality. "There is no such thing," Stevens says, "as a metaphor of a metaphor. One does not progress through metaphors. Thus reality is the indispensable element of each metaphor. When I say that man is a god it is very easy to see that if I also say that a god is something else, god has become a reality." Elsewhere he says that "the word must be the thing it represents, otherwise it is a symbol." In any comparison of the poem and the painting, then, the question is one of identity rather than correspondence or symbolic representation. Each has its own identity in its own terms and its own medium. Each has its own reality. The whole drift of such ideas is away from systematic patterns of thought and even, in some respects, as much away from an acceptance of a clearly ordered symbolism as from allegory; and it is toward perception and insight as the measure of the poetic mind. In both theory and practice, for Stevens, "Thought tends to collect in pools." This was one reason, perhaps, for the interruptions in his career as a poet, the partial explanations, at least, of the fact that he wrote almost nothing between 1924 and 1929, although it is also true that these were the years in which he was consolidating his position in the business world. Later on he came to feel that too much had been made of his having pursued two careers successfully; and it is no exaggeration to say that his material success made it possible for him to sit still in order to discover the world, to indulge his imagination, and spend more and more time in "looking." Although he had "no life except in poetry," he could also write: "Money is a kind of poetry." His characterization of "the whole man" includes the observation that: "More often than the satirists admit, the man who can afford to buy pictures is entirely competent to take their measure and at the same time to take the measure both of the artist and of the dealer." And "The Noble Rider and the Sound of Words" includes, almost incidentally, a wonderfully accurate description of "the normal aspect" of the everyday life most of us live, which defeats all but the best of us; and among other observations, the following: "Democritus plucked out his eye because he could not look at a woman without thinking of her as a woman. If he had read some of our novels, he would have torn himself to pieces." Whatever his personal fortunes, Stevens knew, as a poet, that "Materialism is an old story and an indifferent one."

This knowledge vivifies not only the best of his last poems—the poems that in time will come to be regarded as his greatest—but also the casual improvisations and exercises of "an extremist in an exercise," such as the "Five Grotesque Pieces," which he never included in any of his books, or the "Things of August," which stands near the end of *The Auroras of Autumn*.

> We'll give the week-end to wisdom, to Weisheit, the rabbi,
> Lucidity of his city, joy of his nation,
> The state of circumstance.
>
> The thinker as reader reads what has been written.
> He wears the words he reads to look upon
> Within his being,
>
> A crown within him of crispest diamonds,
> A reddened garment falling to his feet,
> A hand of light to turn the page,
>
> A finger with a ring to guide his eye
> From line to line, as we lie on the grass and listen
> To that which has no speech,
>
> The voluble intentions of the symbols,
> The ghostly celebrations of the picnic,
> The secretions of insight.

A phrase like "The secretions of insight" momentarily binds together all the loose strands of the poetry; it is both "the thing it represents" and "the sum of its attributes."

Herein lies the great ambiguity of Stevens. He is both a symbolist and not a symbolist, logician and anti-logician, a player of things as they are and as they are imagined. The "Adagia" furnish the simplest and most powerful evidence in support of this hypothesis. The inconsistencies they reveal can, of course, be broadly resolved under the loose designation of the romantic. Romantic Stevens certainly is; and in many respects his romanticism resembles that of his great predecessors and contemporaries who have shaped and given the doctrine its continuing vitality. He is eclectic, idiosyncratic, self-centered, and, as many self-styled classicists say, a little contemptuously, an amateur. Yet his interest in and quarrel with philosophy did not prevent him from enthusiastically supporting a plan for a Chair of Poetry at Princeton, when Henry Church suggested the idea. He wrote for Church a "Memorandum" in which he set forth a "theory of poetry" in the most far-ranging of terms, although they were terms he could make intelligible only by way of illustration. "The subject-matter of poetry," he wrote, "is the thing to be ascertained. Offhand, the subject-matter is what comes to mind when one says of the month of August . . . 'Thou art not August, unless I make thee so.' "

As examples of this conflict between the general and the particular, the abstract and the concrete, proliferate, it becomes clear that his inconsistencies and contradictions matter less than the tone in which they are uttered. It is a tone that reveals the presence of the poet's determining personality and at the same time safeguards its detachment. If tone holds things together, it amounts almost to style in its penetration of poems, essays, plays, and even letters. If the poetry lacks drama, nevertheless it is rich with the inflections of a mind speaking aloud, for which "Words are the only melodeon."

The pithiness and raciness of his words deepens in the later poems, only to reassert itself in *The Rock* and the final works written in 1954 and 1955, not quite so intensely as in the great show-pieces of *Harmonium*, but with a certitude the more compelling because of its serenity. The ambiguity, the irony, the detachment are ultimately resolved in a handful of poems which speak with an unexpected directness. One of these, "As You Leave the Room," was nearly ten years in the making:

> *You speak. You say:* Today's character is not
> A skeleton out of its cabinet. Nor am I.
>
> That poem about the pineapple, the one
> About the mind as never satisfied,
>
> The one about the credible hero, the one
> About summer, are not what skeletons think about.
>
> I wonder, have I lived a skeleton's life,
> As a disbeliever in reality,
>
> A countryman of all the bones in the world?
> Now, here, the snow I had forgotten becomes
>
> Part of a major reality, part of
> An appreciation of a reality
>
> And thus an elevation, as if I left
> With something I could touch, touch every way.
>
> And yet nothing has been changed except what is
> Unreal, as if nothing had been changed at all.

And yet, too, for all this, no poet is ever satisfactorily defined in his own words. It is also true that "What criticism wants poetry to be, and what poetry as a result wants consciously to be, it cannot be," as Mark Van Doren has said. Furthermore, everything Stevens wrote he wrote from the inside. "Life cannot be based on a thesis," he asserted, "since by nature, it is based on instinct," to which he added the qualification: "A thesis, however, is usually present and living in the struggle between thesis and instinct." Thus his comments on his own work are inevitably evasive. When asked about the meaning of a particular poem, he generally set down the first thing that came into his head. He was once asked by the National Association of Ice-Cream Manufacturers whether he was for or against ice-cream, and his answer was nearly as much to the point as his replies to some of his more solemnly academic questioners who were equally troubled by "The Emperor of Ice-Cream." A comment on the poem—one of a half a dozen Stevens wrote at various times—published in *The Explicator* is altogether pertinent here:

> Things that have their origin in the imagination or in the emotions (poems) very often have meanings that differ in nature from the meanings of things that have their origin in reason. They have imaginative or emotional meanings, not rational meanings, and they communicate these meanings to people who are susceptible to imaginative or emotional meanings. They may communicate nothing at all to people who are open only to rational meanings. In short, things that have their origin in the imagination or in the emotions very often take on a form that is ambiguous or uncertain. It is not possible to attach a single, rational meaning to such things without destroying the imaginative or emotional ambiguity or uncertainty that is inherent in them and that is why poets do not like to explain. That the meanings given by others are sometimes meanings not intended by the poet or that were never present in his mind does not impair them as meanings. On the inside cover of the album of Mahler's Fifth Symphony recently issued by Columbia there is a note on the meanings of that work. Bruno Walter, however, says that he never heard Mahler intimate that the symphony had any meanings except the meanings of the music. Does this impair the meanings of the commentators as meanings? Certainly this music had no single meaning which was the meaning intended and to which one is bound to penetrate. If it had, what justification could the composer have had for concealing it? The score with its markings contains any meaning that imaginative and sensitive listeners find in it. It takes very little to experience the variety in everything. The poet, the musician, both have explicit meanings but they express them in the forms these take and not in explanation.

The astuteness of the comment is equaled only by its evasions—even, one can say, its own poetry. Incidentally it documents the "fixed point of view" and the "world in flux" of his early letter to William Carlos Williams as the late poems document the early ones. If such documentation is little more than the kind of criticism which makes poetry "what criticism wants poetry to be," it can serve the richer purpose of "helping us to see the poetry as it is." It is the poet, after all, rather than the critic, who finds it easy to say: "It takes very little to experience the variety in everything," unless the critic happens to be something of a poet too. It is the poet who says: "It is not that I am a native, but that I feel like one"; who says:

> If we were all alike; if we were millions of people saying do, re, mi in unison, one poet would be enough and Hesiod himself would do very well. Everything he said would be in no need of expounding or would have been expounded long ago. But we are not all alike and everything needs expounding all the time because, as people live and die, each one perceiving life and death for himself, and mostly by and in himself, there develops a curiosity about the perceptions of others. This is what makes it possible to go on saying new things about old things. The fact is that the saying of new things in new ways is grateful to us. If a bootblack says that he was so tired that he lay down like a dog under a tree, he is saying a new thing about an old thing in a new way. His new way is not a literary novelty; it is an unaffected statement of his perceptions of the thing.

It is the man for whom poetry is the essence of life, who says:

> One turns with something like ferocity toward a land that one loves, to which one is really and essentially native, to demand that it surrender, reveal, that in itself which one loves. This is a vital affair, not an affair of the heart (as it may be in one's first poems), but an affair of the whole being (as in one's last poems), a fundamental affair of life, or, rather, an affair of fundamental life; so that one's cry of O Jerusalem becomes little by little a cry to something a little nearer and nearer until at last one cries out to a living name, a living place, a living thing, and in crying out confesses openly all the bitter secretions of experience. This is why trivial things often touch us intensely. It is why the sight of an old berry patch, a new growth in the woods in spring, the particular things on display at a farmers' market, as, for example, the trays of poor apples, the few boxes of black-eyed peas, the bags of dried corn, have an emotional

power over us that for a moment is more than we can control.

It is in passages such as these, and again and again in the poems—and in the last poems especially, when the merely superficial eccentricities of manner and form drop away—that we begin to see the poetry for what it is. The repetitions, the gaiety of language, the integrity of emotion, the power to improvise: these are triumphant qualities that set Stevens apart from all but a handful of modern poets. In an age in which, as life has become more terrible, its literature has grown increasingly bleak, his comic vision, touched with melancholy but seldom warped out of shape by contemporary configurations of violence, is almost unique. Only one other American poet so impresses us by his conviction that life itself is poetry. Like Stevens, he seems to have had no life except in poetry. Like Stevens, too, he provides an example of the poet whose singular vision—whose romanticism, if you like—sets him apart from the ordinary strategies of contemporary criticism, and whose defenders have sometimes been his worst enemies.

Even to mention his name here is to leave these remarks ragged at the edge. But to mention him provides at least one way in which to characterize Stevens in terms other than his own. Surely his name must have occurred to some of you in the course of this paper, although on the surface no poets seem to have less in common, and even if, as was undoubtedly true, he was never an "influence" on Stevens. He appears once as a figure in Stevens' poetry, at the beginning of "Like Decorations in a Nigger Cemetery":

> In the far South the sun of autumn is passing
> Like Walt Whitman walking along a ruddy shore.
> He is singing and chanting the things that are part of him,
> The worlds that were and will be, death and day.
> Nothing is final, he chants. No man shall see the end.
> His beard is of fire and his staff is a leaping flame.

Howard Baker, whose comment is the only one I know on the poem, has said that the figure of Whitman is more appropriate to Stevens than Whitman's manner. Perhaps so; but the implication that Whitman is nothing more than an isolated phenomenon, a poet whose successes are unique and largely accidental, beyond the pale of serious literary criticism, may prove, in the long run, as inadequate to an understanding of Stevens as they have proved to any real understanding of Whitman himself. Like Whitman, Stevens lends himself to any number of excesses and difficulties; but in spite of their obvious differences, Stevens and Whitman share a great deal both in theory and practice. They have in common that sense of place and that loneliness which is so often its complement, in their lives as much as in their poems. And the closer one looks, the closer the resemblances between them become. The "slap-dash intensity," the "contrariness," and even the "sophistication" run like streams through their work. We have made too much of certain aspects of Stevens—his debt to Mallarmé and the Symbolist tradition; his debt to Wordsworth—and too little of the native element. I do not mean any sort of factitious Americanism; but I do mean a quality of mind, a sense of the world and of the character of the poet. Who else except Whitman, Randall Jarrell asks, would have thought of using language (and here he has in mind Whitman's use of French and his characteristic catalogues) in the way Whitman does? And I should answer, Wallace Stevens. The evocation of Whitman in a single instance is too slender a thread to support any conclusions here, though the Old Testament figure is as apt to Stevens as it is to Whitman; and the words Stevens puts into Whitman's mouth, like the beard and the staff, are wonderfully appropriate to them both.

> He is singing and chanting the things that are part of him,
> The worlds that were and will be, death and day.
> Nothing is final, he chants. No man shall see the end.
> His beard is of fire and his staff is a leaping flame.

Though no more than a thread, it may be a golden one.

LOUIS L. MARTZ

WALLACE STEVENS: THE WORLD
AS MEDITATION

1958

"In an age of disbelief," says Wallace Stevens in a late essay, "it is for the poet to supply the satisfactions of belief, in his measure and in his style." It is my purpose here to explore the nature of those satisfactions, to examine the measure and the style that Stevens achieved in his later poetry, and in this way to suggest the answer that Stevens found to his own blunt question: "What, then, is the nature of poetry in a time of disbelief?" [1]

The answer is implicit in the late poem that provides my theme and title here: "The World as Meditation" (1952) seems to sum up the poetical discoveries of Stevens since that time, some thirty years earlier, when his Paltry Nude started on her Spring Voyage through the world of *Harmonium,* to become at the close of that volume a complete Nomad Exquisite, fully attuned to the harmonies of nature, creating as nature herself creates:

[1] "Two or Three Ideas" (1951), in *Opus Posthumous,* ed. by Samuel French Morse (New York, 1957), pp. 206, 211. (Cited hereafter as OP.)

· · · · · · · ·

As the immense dew of Florida
Brings forth
The big-finned palm
And green vine angering for life,
. . . .
So, in me, come flinging
Forms, flames, and the flakes of flames.

"The World as Meditation," on the other hand, finds its central proposition, not in any text from the surface of things, but in certain words of a human composer, Georges Enesco: *"J'ai passé trop de temps à travailler mon violon, à voyager. Mais l'exercice essentiel du compositeur—la méditation—rien ne l'a jamais suspendu en moi. . . . Je vis un rêve permanent, qui ne s'arrête ni nuit ni jour."* With those words as epigraph, the poem presents as its symbol of human achievement the figure of Penelope, awaiting the return of Ulysses. As the sun rises she awakens to the meditation that has composed her life:

A form of fire approaches the cretonnes of Penelope,
Whose mere savage presence awakens the world in which
she dwells.

She has composed, so long, a self with which to welcome
him,
Companion to his self for her, which she imagined,
Two in a deep-founded sheltering, friend and dear friend.
. . . .

But was it Ulysses? Or was it only the warmth of the sun
On her pillow? The thought kept beating in her like her
heart.
The two kept beating together. It was only day.

It was Ulysses and it was not. Yet they had met,
Friend and dear friend and a planet's encouragement.
The barbarous strength within her would never fail.

There is, we see, a "savage presence" outside her, the primitive force of the sun, which arouses within her a "barbarous strength," some primitive human power that makes it possible for her to compose a self, with the sun's encouragement; and so she dwells in a world of belief created by her will. This sounds like the conception found at the close of Stevens' essay "The Noble Rider" (1942), where he mentions a certain nobility of mind that constitutes "a violence from within that protects us from a violence without. It is the imagination pressing back against the pressure of reality." Thus the violence of the sun might have aroused Penelope to the violent, ugly pressure of those outward suitors; but her imagination of Ulysses, her constant meditation of reunion with the man she constantly creates in her mind, this power presses back, composes within herself a world of value and order. Thus, as Stevens concludes in that essay, imagination "seems, in the last analysis, to have something to do with our self-preservation." [2]

I have used two terms, both prominent in Stevens' writings: *imagination, meditation*; they are not synonymous. Meditation is the essential exercise which, constantly practiced, brings the imagination into play, releases creative power, enables the human being to compose a sensitive, intelligent, and generous self. It is the sort of self that Stevens has found fully represented in the person of George Santayana, as he points out in an essay of 1948. "Most men's lives," he regretfully concedes, "are thrust upon them" by the outward violence; but, he insists:

> There can be lives, nevertheless, which exist by the deliberate choice of those that live them. To use a single illustration: it may be assumed that the life of Professor Santayana is a life in which the function of the imagination has had a function similar to its function in any deliberate work of art or letters. We have only to think of this present phase of it, in which, in his old age, he dwells in the head of the world, in the company of devoted women, in their convent, and in the company of familiar saints, whose presence does so much to make any convent an appropriate refuge for a generous and human philosopher. (NA, 147-48.)

And so in his late poem "To an Old Philosopher in Rome" (1952) he finds the fulfillment of human existence in Santayana's reconciliation of flesh and spirit on the threshold of death:

[2] *The Necessary Angel* (New York, 1951), p. 36. (Cited hereafter as NA.)

The sounds drift in. The buildings are remembered.
The life of the city never lets go, nor do you
Ever want it to. It is part of the life in your room.
Its domes are the architecture of your bed.

. . . .

It is a kind of total grandeur at the end,
With every visible thing enlarged and yet
No more than a bed, a chair and moving nuns,
The immensest theatre, the pillared porch,
The book and candle in your ambered room,

Total grandeur of a total edifice,
Chosen by an inquisitor of structures
For himself. He stops upon this threshold,
As if the design of all his words takes form
And frame from thinking and is realized.

Such admiration for the power of *thinking*, for the constructive power of deliberate choice—this is not the sort of values that were being attributed to Stevens fifteen or twenty years ago. The central impact of Stevens' poetry up to about 1940 has been, I think, admirably summed up by Yvor Winters in his famous essay "Wallace Stevens or The Hedonist's Progress." There Winters, basing his thesis primarily on *Harmonium*, saw in Stevens the cultivation of "the realm of emotion divorced from understanding," the commendation of "the emotions as a good in themselves." It was, he felt, a point of view that had led Stevens from the great poetry of *Harmonium* into a "rapid and tragic decay" of style, the sad, inevitable progress of the hedonist, "unable to think himself out of the situation into which he has wandered." [3]

Winters has made a brilliant diagnosis of the malady; but he underestimated the patient's will to live. Looking back now, with the immense advantage of all that Stevens has published since Winters wrote, and with the equally great advantage of the recent *Opus Posthumous*—looking back now, we can see that something quite different happened. We can see something analogous to the course of Yeats's poetry. We can see a poet, by a deliberate process of self-knowledge, rebuilding himself and his poetry, rebuilding him-

[3] *The Anatomy of Nonsense* (Norfolk, Conn., 1943), pp. 89, 91, 97.

self through his poetry, and achieving, in *Transport to Summer* (1947), a volume of meditative poetry that is in every way the equal of his great, first volume of hedonist poetry. It is not a question of setting up divisions, but of watching recessive elements in the early poetry develop into dominance.

Let us try to sketch, now, this different progress. Stevens' second volume, *Ideas of Order*, appeared in 1935; its slimness, its dominant tone, and its title are all significant of a change in the poet's outlook. The buoyancy that gave forth the bounty of *Harmonium* is gone; that force within, like "the immense dew of Florida," that had brought forth "Forms, flames, and the flakes of flames" is subsiding, although here and there it reappears, the old gay defiance of Winters:

> But what are radiant reason and radiant will
> To warblings early in the hilarious trees
> Of summer, the drunken mother?

Or:

> What is there here but weather, what spirit
> Have I except it comes from the sun?

The trouble is that the younger Nomad Exquisite had lived by a view that the poet of the 1930s could no longer accept, for reasons he suggests in the late essay cited at the outset of this discussion: "If in the minds of men creativeness was the same thing as creation in the natural world, if a spiritual planet matched the sun, or if without any question of a spiritual planet, the light and warmth of spring revitalized all our faculties, as in a measure they do, all the bearings one takes, all the propositions one formulates would be within the scope of that particular domination"—as they were, for the most part, in *Harmonium*. "The trouble is, however, that men in general do not create in light and warmth alone," he continues. "They create in darkness and coldness. They create when they are hopeless, in the midst of antagonisms, when they are wrong, when their powers are no longer subject to their control. They create as the ministers of evil" (OP, 210). *Ideas of Order* moves in this different world; it is filled with the tones of evening:

LOUIS L. MARTZ · 215

"A Fading of the Sun," "Gray Stones and Gray Pigeons," "Autumn Refrain," "Winter Bells," "Sad Strains of a Gay Waltz."

> There is order in neither sea nor sun.
> The shapes have lost their glistening.
> There are these sudden mobs of men.

In this new atmosphere one poem stands out to control the chaos: the famous "Idea of Order at Key West." Here the speaker, significantly, stands at the far edge of Florida, his back upon that world of flame and green. The physical world now offers none of its old "comforts of the sun," but exists here as

> The meaningless plungings of water and the wind,
> Theatrical distances, bronze shadows heaped
> On high horizons, mountainous atmospheres
> Of sky and sea.

The object of wonder and admiration is now a human figure, that singer by the shore whose voice made

> The sky acutest at its vanishing.
> She measured to the hour its solitude.
> She was the single artificer of the world
> In which she sang.

This is more than the Palace of Hoon, the solipsist of *Harmonium;* for the idea of order here resides in more than mental landscapes, in "More even than her voice, and ours": the idea of order is found in a unique conjunction of landscape, singer, and listener, a situation in which the listener's mind, exulting in the full strength of its powers, is able to assert the controlling force of consciousness, "Fixing emblazoned zones and fiery poles" upon the outer atmosphere, "Arranging, deepening, enchanting night"—while realizing fully that the outer universe goes its inhuman way.

The fierce strength of mind in that poem, its clipped and muted language before the final exultation, prepares the way for a striking addition to the volume *Ideas of Order,* when it appeared in a trade edition in the next year, 1936. The volume no longer opens with the curiously fatigued poem, "Sailing After Lunch," where Stevens truly says, "My old boat goes round on a crutch/And doesn't get under way," and where he ends with the sentimental desire:

To expunge all people and be a pupil
Of the gorgeous wheel and so to give
That slight transcendence to the dirty sail.

No, the volume now opens with the stirring "Farewell to Florida," in which Stevens renounces all that "Florida" has symbolized in his earlier poetry: that world of vivid physical apprehension, where man created within the bounds of the natural order. "Her mind had bound me round," he says, but now he cries:

Go on, high ship, since now, upon the shore,
The snake has left its skin upon the floor.
Key West sank downward under massive clouds
And silvers and greens spread over the sea. The moon
Is at the mast-head and the past is dead.
Her mind will never speak to me again.

And he looks forward to his engagement with a new, a tough, bitter, and turbulent subject:

My North is leafless and lies in a wintry slime
Both of men and clouds, a slime of men in crowds.
The men are moving as the water moves,
This darkened water cloven by sullen swells
Against your sides, then shoving and slithering,
The darkness shattered, turbulent with foam.
To be free again, to return to the violent mind
That is their mind, these men, and that will bind
Me round, carry me, misty deck, carry me
To the cold, go on, high ship, go on, plunge on.

Stevens, it is clear, has determined to take his old boat out of The Pleasures of Merely Circulating, to plunge into the turmoil of the mid-'thirties, to engage it somehow in his poetry. In fact, he had already begun the effort. The year before "Farewell to Florida" appeared he had already published the first part of what was to become his longest poetical effort, Owl's Clover, which appeared in 1936 in its original version of 861 lines. It is a poem that caused Stevens immense labor and, finally, intense dissatisfaction. In 1937 it reappeared with nearly 200 lines cut out; and in 1954 Stevens omitted it entirely from his Collected Poems, on the grounds that it was "rhetorical," Mr. Morse tells us (OP, xxiii). As a result of this drastic omission, the reader of the Collected Poems may emerge with a sense of the poet's steady self-possession, an ideal progress from the old gaudy style toward a sober, muted, thoughtful, pruned, and thoroughly re-made poetry: for we move from *Ideas of Order* directly into *The Man With the Blue Guitar*, where

> The man bent over his guitar,
> A shearsman of sorts.

A shearsman indeed, a sort of tailor, cutting his cloth anew and shearing away the excess.[4] But the effect is too neat. We need *Owl's Clover*, preferably in its first version, to tell us all the trouble of the change; and fortunately we have it all now before us once again, in the new posthumous volume. It is not a successful poem, though it contains great passages and opens remarkably well, with the firmly controlled symbols of "The Old Woman and the Statue." There the magnificent statue in the park represents the soaring, noble imagination of the past, "leaping in the storms of light": the statue is a work of art subtly and powerfully arranged for the human mind to grasp and be exalted. One thing, one thing only, the sculptor "had not foreseen": the old woman, "the bitter mind/In a flapping cloak," a woman so depressed that she cannot apprehend the statue's action:

> A woman walking in the autumn leaves,
> Thinking of heaven and earth and of herself
> And looking at the place in which she walked,
> As a place in which each thing was motionless
> Except the thing she felt but did not know.

That thing is the "harridan self," "Crying against a need that pressed like cold,/Deadly and deep." It is not simply physical poverty that tortures this suffering self: it is that she lives, as the second part tells us, amid "the immense detritus of a world"

> That is completely waste, that moves from waste
> To waste, out of the hopeless waste of the past
> Into a hopeful waste to come.

[4] See Stevens' explanation of this figure in a letter to his Italian translator, Renato Poggioli: "This refers to the posture of the speaker, squatting like a tailor (a shearsman) as he works on his cloth." *Mattino Domenicale ed Altre Poesie* (Turin, 1954), p. 174.

The hopeful waste of the future, I think, alludes to the sort of world proffered by Mr. Burnshaw, whose name adorns the original title of the second part: "Mr. Burnshaw and the Statue" (later altered to "The Statue at the World's End"). Stanley Burnshaw was the Marxist critic who in 1935 had reviewed *Ideas of Order* with considerable acuteness, though with a condescending tone: he had seen it as a book of "speculations, questionings, contradictions"— "the record of a man who, having lost his footing, now scrambles to stand up and keep his balance." [5] The critique, being so largely true, left the mark, as *Owl's Clover* shows in its derisive rejection of all mass solutions that offer only "an age of concentric mobs." But what can be offered instead to the suffering self? The offering in this long second section turns out, in spite of its high rhetoric, to be surprisingly meager: it is simply the old pleasures of Florida, chanted in a weak imitation of the old hieratic style of "Sunday Morning," as this passage (later removed) indicates:

> Dance, now, and with sharp voices cry, but cry
> Like damsels daubed and let your feet be bare
> To touch the grass and, as you circle, turn
> Your backs upon the vivid statue. Then,
> Weaving ring in radiant ring and quickly, fling
> Yourselves away and at a distance join
> Your hands held high and cry again, but cry,
> This time, like damsels captured by the sky,
> Seized by that possible blue.

But those waltzes had ended, long since. Clearly, the poet must try another way, and so, in his third section, Stevens turns to develop a contrast between two ways of life. One is the old way of religious meditation, where "each man,"

> Through long cloud-cloister-porches, walked alone,
> Noble within perfecting solitude,
> Like a solitude of the sun, in which the mind
> Acquired transparence and beheld itself
> And beheld the source from which transparence came.

And the other is something that seems to have arisen or to be aris-

[5] *New Masses*, October 1, 1935, p. 42.

LOUIS L. MARTZ · 219

ing in place of the old religious way, something he calls Africa, a world of dense, savage, mindless animality, where

> Death, only, sits upon the serpent throne:
> Death, the herdsman of elephants,
> To whom the jaguars cry and lions roar
> Their petty dirges of fallen forest-men,
> Forever hunting or hunted, rushing through
> Endless pursuit or endlessly pursued,
> Until each tree, each evil-blossomed vine,
> Each fretful fern drops down a fear like dew.

From here on, in the middle of the poem, *Owl's Clover* provides less and less sustenance for the troubled mind trying to feed in the dark. It becomes increasingly turgid and incoherent. The old religion cannot cope with "Africa," nor can the old art of the statue; nor can the problems be met by the believers in necessity, the nostalgic admirers of the old pioneer spirit, or the worshipers of the "newest Soviet réclame." "How shall we face the edge of time?"

> Where shall we find more than derisive words?
> When shall lush chorals spiral through our fire
> And daunt that old assassin, heart's desire?

"Lush chorals"—the backward glance toward the days of *Harmonium*—is ominous, and we are not surprised to find the poem ending with a Sombre Figuration in which the poet attempts to find refuge in a vague, semi-Jungian concept of the "subman." This subman is some inner man of imagination, who lies below the torments of thought: "The man below the man below the man,/ Steeped in night's opium, evading day." But the subman has a precarious tenure, for he seems to reside only in a rhetoric of empty assertion:

> And memory's lord is the lord of prophecy
> And steps forth, priestly in severity,
> Yet lord, a mask of flame, the sprawling form
> A wandering orb upon a path grown clear.

It is a relief to turn from this evasive subman to the daylight figure who shears away this outworn pomp. The sounds made by *The Man With the Blue Guitar* (1937) show that Stevens, within a year's hard thought, has taken quick, firm strides toward the position thoroughly established in his prose essays and his later poetry: that "the poet must get rid of the hieratic in everything that concerns him," that he must abolish "the false conception of the imagination as some incalculable *vates* within us, unhappy Rodomontade" (NA, 58, 61)—i.e., the opium-drugged subman must be erased, along with the style in which he had been expressed. In his place we will have something like Picasso's clear, clean image of the old Guitar Player, a product of his "blue period" (though the guitar itself happens to be tan), which was, incidentally, exhibited in Hartford in 1934. We will have an image of life explored, discovered and developed through a language made out of "things exactly as they are," a language moving now with a tough intent toward the discovery of a self:

> Ah, but to play man number one,
> To drive the dagger in his heart,
>
> To lay his brain upon the board
> And pick the acrid colors out,
>
> To nail his thought across the door,
> Its wings spread wide to rain and snow,
>
> To strike his living hi and ho,
> To tick it, tock it, turn it true,
>
> To bang it from a savage blue,
> Jangling the metal of the strings . . .

This is as far as we can get from the puzzled, ruminative ebb and flow of *Owl's Clover*, with its dissolving, eddying, and often turbid blank verse: note here the crisp common diction, the strict, driving rhythm of the short couplets, subtly bound together by irregular rhymes and half-rhymes, all focused on one aim: a definition of the *self* as the only province of poetry:

> Ourselves in the tune as if in space,
> Yet nothing changed, except the place
>
> Of things as they are and only the place
> As you play them, on the blue guitar,

LOUIS L. MARTZ · 221

Placed, so, beyond the compass of change,
Perceived in a final atmosphere;

For a moment final.

We have returned to the central position of the "Idea of Order at
Key West": man's inner rage for order as the ultimate constructive
force in man's universe, and hence the never-ending effort of the
mind to control, within the mind, that outer monster, the inhuman
universe:

That I may reduce the monster to
Myself, and then may be myself

In face of the monster, be more than part
Of it, more than the monstrous player of

One of its monstrous lutes, not be
Alone, but reduce the monster and be,

Two things, the two together as one.

From this effort, he says, "I shall evolve a man."

This sequence of thirty-three tightly argued, tightly ordered
meditations on a theme establishes the altered style of the later
Stevens. He has here, in a deliberate act of choice, sheared away
the kind of writing that he later calls "The romantic intoning, the
declaimed clairvoyance," since this, he says, is the "appropriate
idiom" of apotheosis; and this is not at all his subject now. Apotheosis elevates the mortal to the stature of divinity; it glorifies; and
the appropriate poetry of apotheosis is therefore the hymn, the ode,
the celebration, the chant. In a peculiar sense, this had been the
appropriate idiom of his earlier poetry, since he was there attempting to show, as he tells the lady in "Sunday Morning," that "Divinity must live within" the human realm: "Passions of rain, or moods
in falling snow." Hence he uses the idiom of romantic intoning to
glorify the satisfactions of this earth, often with deliberate irony:
the Comedian speaks of his "first central hymns, the celebrants/Of
rankest trivia"; and indeed the whole mock-heroic effect of the
Comedian arises from the application of such grand intoning to the
achievements of this "merest minuscule."

But in his new effort to evolve a man, a new idiom must be invented, since "apotheosis is not/The origin of the major man" for whom the poet is now searching. "He comes," says Stevens, "from reason,/Lighted at midnight by the studious eye,/Swaddled in revery." He is the meditative man, master of the essential exercise, student, scholar, rabbi of a new idiom, which Stevens in "Of Modern Poetry" (1940) calls "The poem of the mind in the act of finding/What will suffice." There has never been a better definition of what might be called the genre of meditative poetry. It is not, we note, a poem celebrating what suffices; nor is it any lamentation for the lack of what suffices. The difference between the true meditative poem and other poetic genres seems to be exactly this: that it alone represents "The poem of the act of the mind," the poem of the mind, in the very act of finding. One thinks of Emily Dickinson, of Hopkins, of George Herbert, and especially of Donne, in his *Divine Meditations* (Holy Sonnets).

But further definition of the genre, if there is really such a genre, is necessary, and Stevens suggests it all in "Of Modern Poetry":

> It has to be living, to learn the speech of the place.
> It has to face the men of the time and to meet
> The women of the time. It has to think about war
> And it has to find what will suffice. It has
> To construct a new stage. It has to be on that stage
> And, like an insatiable actor, slowly and
> With meditation, speak words that in the ear,
> In the delicatest ear of the mind, repeat,
> Exactly, that which it wants to hear, at the sound
> Of which, an invisible audience listens,
> Not to the play, but to itself, expressed
> In an emotion as of two people, as of two
> Emotions becoming one.

Let me expand, with only a little liberty, the possible implications of that text. This kind of poetry must know the common speech; it must make contact with men in their normal existence, through its language, its images, and its consideration of urgent problems, such as war, of whatever kind, whether between man and man, or between body and soul, good and evil, man and his environment—the "war between the mind and sky" that Stevens describes at the end of his *Notes Toward a Supreme Fiction*. It has to find what

LOUIS L. MARTZ · 223

will suffice, but in order to do this, it must construct a stage on which an actor may enact the process of this finding. And as this actor speaks his meditated words, they find a growing response in a certain invisible audience, which is not simply us, the readers or listeners, but is first of all the larger, total mind of the poet himself, controlling the actor, who is some projected aspect of himself. Then, in the close, that actor and that audience, projected self and larger self, come together in a moment of emotional resolution— for a moment final. It is a process that Stevens describes thus in his *Adagia*: "When the mind is like a hall in which thought is like a voice speaking, the voice is always that of someone else." The voice is that of some projected self: the audience is the whole self. "It is necessary to propose an enigma to the mind," he says in another adage. "The mind always proposes a solution" (OP, 168). All this seems to describe something very like the action in "The Idea of Order at Key West": the landscape is the stage, the singer by the shore is the actor, and the poet's larger mind is the audience. It is also very like the action that one finds in Donne's *Holy Sonnets*, which we may take as a prime example of pure meditative poetry, since they seem to arise directly from the rigorous meditative exercises commonly practiced by religious men of the seventeenth century. Recall how Donne projects some aspect of himself upon a stage: the deathbed, the round earth's imagined corners, the Cross; how he then allows that self to ponder the given situation; and how, at the close, the projected self makes a subtle union with the whole mind of the poet, concluding all in the finding of what will suffice.

One can only ponder the possibilities here, and pause to stress one point. In formal religious meditation, as developed during Donne's time and later practiced (certainly) by Hopkins and (presumably) by Eliot, the process of meditation consists of something akin to that just described by Stevens. It begins with the deliberate creation of a setting and the placing of an actor there: some aspect of the self; this is the famous composition of place recommended by the Jesuit exercises. This is followed by predominantly intellectual analysis of some crucial problem pertaining to that self; and it all ends in a highly emotional resolution where the projected self and the whole mind of the meditator come together in a spirit of devotion. This threefold process is related to the old division of the soul into memory, understanding, and will; the exercise of meditation integrates these faculties.

How is it that a modern poet such as Wallace Stevens, so vastly different from the seventeenth century in the objects of his belief, should come to describe the need for a kind of poetry to which Donne's *Holy Sonnets* seem to belong: a kind that we might call the genre of meditative poetry? Donne's strenuous cultivation of this kind of poetry seems to be part of his lifelong effort to transcend and resolve his grievous sense of the fickleness, the dissolution, the transiency and fragility of all physical things. In Stevens, I think, an analogous situation called forth the analogous discipline. Stevens, in midcareer, recognized the dissolution, or the inadequacy, of his old poetic self—a recognition recorded with a wry gaiety in "The Comedian as the Letter C." His later poems represent a rigorous search for ways and means of evolving another kind of poetic self, in accord with the outlook expressed in the late essay dealing with the "time of disbelief": "There was always in every man the increasingly human self, which instead of remaining the observer, the nonparticipant, the delinquent, became constantly more and more all there was or so it seemed; and whether it was so or merely seemed so still left it for him to resolve life and the world in his own terms" (OP, 207).

Allusions in his prose essays indicate that in this effort Stevens engaged in broad reading among tough thinkers, while all his later poetry displays a new respect for the "radiant idea" and the "radiant will." This is clear in the first part of *Notes Toward a Supreme Fiction* (1942), which insists that the fiction must be, in some sense, "abstract." Not, I think, abstract in the usual sense of a philosophical abstraction; Stevens has told us plainly what he thinks of this in his "Landscape with Boat," where he decries the man who "wanted imperceptible air," who "wanted the eye to see"

> And not be touched by blue. He wanted to know,
> A naked man who regarded himself in the glass
> Of air, who looked for the world beneath the blue,
> Without blue, without any turquoise tint or phase,
> Any azure under-side or after-color.

LOUIS L. MARTZ · 225

By "abstract" Stevens seems rather to imply a quality of being taken out, abstracted in the root sense, from that world we call the outer universe: something concrete taken out of this and taken into the mind through a process of full, exact realization. From that "local abstraction" the turquoise tints and azure undersides can then radiate in all directions. This is the process that Stevens vividly describes in section VII of "Credences of Summer," where he begins by scorning those who have found it too hard "to sing in face/Of the object," and have therefore fled to the woods, where they could sing "their unreal songs,/Secure." In a violent reversal of mood, he advocates a fiercely opposite process:

> Three times the concentred self takes hold, three times
> The thrice concentred self, having possessed
>
> The object, grips it in savage scrutiny,
> Once to make captive, once to subjugate
> Or yield to subjugation, once to proclaim
> The meaning of the capture, this hard prize,
> Fully made, fully apparent, fully found.

If this bears some resemblance to the old threefold process of formal meditation, it is only because Stevens has discovered for himself the same faculties, and has taught himself a way of using them for his own meditative ends. He has, in an essay of 1943, come to define the imagination as "the sum of our faculties," and has gone on to speak of "The acute intelligence of the imagination, the illimitable resources of its memory, its power to possess the moment it perceives" (NA, 61).

Indeed, it appears that Stevens has been thoroughly aware of the analogy I am suggesting, for in a newly published essay, written about 1937, we find him declaring: "The poet who wishes to contemplate the good in the midst of confusion is like the mystic who wishes to contemplate God in the midst of evil. . . . Resistance to the pressure of ominous and destructive circumstance consists of its conversion, so far as possible, into a different, an explicable, an amenable circumstance." And in this search, he adds, the poets "purge themselves before reality . . . in what they intend to be saintly exercises" (OP, 225, 227).

But if we accept Stevens' use of the term *meditation* as a proper description of his own secular exercises, we may appear to be stretching the word beyond any useful signification. Cannot any poem that contains any degree of hard thinking be thus called meditative? I do not think so, if we keep in mind the careful distinctions made by the old spiritual writer, François de Sales. "Every meditation is a thought," he says, "but every thought is not a meditation; for we have thoughts, to which our mind is carried without aim or design at all, by way of a simple musing. . . . And be this kind of thought as attentive as it may be, it can never bear the name of meditation." On the other hand, he says, "Sometimes we consider a thing attentively to learn its causes, effects, qualities; and this thought is named study." But "when we think of heavenly things, not to learn, but to delight in them, that is called to meditate; and the exercise thereof meditation." "So that meditation," he concludes, "is an attentive thought repeated or voluntarily maintained in the mind, to arouse the will to holy and wholesome affections and resolutions." [6]

It seems valid to adapt this definition to the meditations of earthly things, since meditation is a process, not a subject. If we do this, then Stevensian meditation becomes: attentive thinking about concrete things with the aim of developing an affectionate understanding of how good it is to be alive. We can see the process working everywhere in his later poetry, but nowhere better than in "The World as Meditation," which now needs to be read entire as an example of the full development of Stevens' meditative style. Note first how far the poem's range extends beyond the "comforts of the sun": the verbal beauty of Enesco's French draws in the cosmopolitan world of the musician, as the figure of Penelope draws in the ancient world of legend. Yet the sun exists as first cause; without it there would be nothing. Thus the poem is phrased to allow a double reference: the sun is Penelope's companion, along with Ulysses. Note too how the poem fulfills all of Stevens' requirements for this modern poetry: common speech, common images, common problems; the establishment of a stage, the placing of Penelope as actor on that stage, the imputed working of her meditative thoughts,

[6] François de Sales, A *Treatise on the Love of God* (1616), Book VI, chap. ii; adapted from the translation of 1630.

along with the constant presence of the poet's larger mind, controlling all, and concluding all with an affectionate understanding of what will suffice.

> Is it Ulysses that approaches from the east,
> The interminable adventurer? The trees are mended.
> That winter is washed away. Someone is moving
>
> On the horizon and lifting himself up above it.
> A form of fire approaches the cretonnes of Penelope,
> Whose mere savage presence awakens the world in which
>   she dwells.
>
> She has composed, so long, a self with which to welcome
>   him,
> Companion to his self for her, which she imagined,
> Two in a deep-founded sheltering, friend and dear friend.
>
> The trees had been mended, as an essential exercise
> In an inhuman meditation, larger than her own.
> No winds like dogs watched over her at night.
>
> She wanted nothing he could not bring her by coming
>   alone.
> She wanted no fetchings. His arms would be her necklace
> And her belt, the final fortune of their desire.
>
> But was it Ulysses? Or was it only the warmth of the sun
> On her pillow? The thought kept beating in her like her
>   heart.
> The two kept beating together. It was only day.
>
> It was Ulysses and it was not. Yet they had met,
> Friend and dear friend and a planet's encouragement.
> The barbarous strength within her would never fail.
>
> She would talk a little to herself as she combed her hair.
> Repeating his name with its patient syllables,
> Never forgetting him that kept coming constantly so near.

The world of *Harmonium* has not been discarded here, but its reliance on the natural force of "sensibility" has been modified, and the pleasures of that world have been included within a larger structure of existence. By 1951 Stevens could strongly question "the dogma that the origins of poetry are to be found in the sensibility," and could suggest: "if one says that a fortunate poem or a fortunate painting is a synthesis of exceptional concentration . . . we find that the operative force within us does not, in fact, seem to be the sensibility, that is to say, the feelings. It seems to be a constructive faculty, that derives its energy more from the imagination than from the sensibility"—imagination being, as we have seen, the "sum of our faculties." But he adds, in his cautious way, "I have spoken of questioning, not of denying" (NA, 164). That is because the old dews of Florida have never ceased to affect him. One of his very last poems, "Prologues to What Is Possible," suggests that the value of existence may have resided in

> A flick which added to what was real and its vocabulary,
> The way some first thing coming into Northern trees
> Adds to them the whole vocabulary of the South,
> The way the earliest single light in the evening sky, in
> spring,
> Creates a fresh universe out of nothingness by adding itself,
> The way a look or a touch reveals its unexpected magnitudes.

There is no inconsistency here. The look, the touch, the flick of feeling, the "times of inherent excellence," "incalculable balances," "not balances/That we achieve but balances that happen"—these are things worth recognizing, and Stevens never ceases to celebrate them as part of the wonder of human consciousness. But he is quick to recognize that "the casual is not/Enough": it does not attain the full "freshness of ourselves"; it does not satisfy the "will to make iris frettings on the blank." Beyond the casual apprehensions there lie the willed and reasoned structures of the mind, which Stevens presents in two forms. One structure occurs when the mind thoroughly and fully concentrates upon the realization of some composition that appears to be inherent in the external scene, as in "Credences of Summer."

> Let's see the very thing and nothing else.
> Let's see it with the hottest fire of sight.
> Burn everything not part of it to ash.
>
> Trace the gold sun about the whitened sky
> Without evasion by a single metaphor.

LOUIS L. MARTZ · 229

Thus:

> One of the limits of reality
> Presents itself in Oley when the hay,
> Baked through long days, is piled in mows. It is
> A land too ripe for enigmas, too serene.

This seems to be what Stevens means by seeing things in their "first idea," their "ever-early candor"; this is the adequacy of landscape— for a moment final. It exists beyond us, it is no metaphor, and yet, Stevens insists, "the first idea is an imagined thing," since it is achieved by a calculated effort of the mind. It is part, then, "of the never-ending meditation," a poem of the mind in the act of finding what will suffice. It may be, he says, "of a man skating, a woman dancing, a woman/Combing," a Woman Looking at a Vase of Flowers, a Dish of Peaches in Russia, or a Large Red Man Reading: it may be found "in the crackling summer night,"

> In the *Duft* of towns, beside a window, beside
> A lamp, in a day of the week, the time before spring,
> A manner of walking, yellow fruit, a house,
> A street.

They are acts available to any man, a sort of poetry, "an imaginative activity that diffuses itself throughout our lives" (NA, 149). You return, say, from a long vacation with your family in the mountains, dog-tired, addle-brained, and feeling the whole expedition was a huge mistake. Two weeks later snapshots return, developed in full color: you are amazed at the beauty, the order, the focus; the trip is a success, after all. Such a realization would be, in Stevens' terms, a poetic action.

And finally, beyond such compositions, there lies the inexhaustible "realm of resemblance," in which the faculties of the imagination, using all their powers, "extend the object" by analogy, by metaphor. It is a realm in which the whole mind, like Stevens' Penelope, uses the world of sensory experience as a base upon which to construct a total edifice involving and demanding the whole stretch of human experience. By the use of such analogies man connects the external and the internal; the action of analogy is the mind's ultimate way of establishing its dominant, controlling position amid the "moving chaos that never ends." And this, too, is an activity that Stevens sees as available to everyone.

You sit in a chair, say, admiring the beauty of your four-year-old daughter: you call to mind certain resemblances between her and her absent mother, between her and your imagined image of yourself, between her and your memories and pictures of grandparents. You think, too, of certain painted images of children by Renoir or Romney; you think of Andrew Marvell's "Picture of Little T. C. in a Prospect of Flowers"; you think of the dogwood that bloomed last spring and of the zinnias now blooming outside. And for a moment the object toward which all these resemblances converge, or from which they infinitely extend—for a moment the object becomes a vital center through which the sense of life is composed, final: "completed in a completed scene," as Stevens says. Such is Wallace Stevens' "World as Meditation," a world where the poet may adopt the words of Valéry's Architect and say, "By dint of constructing, . . . I truly believe that I have constructed myself."

MICHEL BENAMOU

WALLACE STEVENS: SOME RELATIONS BETWEEN POETRY AND PAINTING

1959

Whether the influence of painting on poetry is desirable might seem an old question and possibly an otiose one. With the advent of Impressionism and succeeding schools, the poetic principles underlying art have become more visible; less "word painting" (in the awkward sense of much eighteenth-century description and Parnassian verse for art's sake) has been taking place, and more sharing in the imaginative metamorphosis wrought upon nature by the painter's brush. Many modern poets, in whose rank I muster at random Baudelaire, Mallarmé, Rilke, Apollinaire, John Peale Bishop, and Wallace Stevens, have acknowledged their debt to painters or sculptors and their poetry has grown the richer by that debt. The point no longer is whether the critics should compare poetry and painting, but how they can do so without being "laocoönized."

This risk may be taken the more cheerfully since Stevens himself showed the way in his critical writing. He was—like Valéry, another poet with a painter's eye and a refined mental museum—extremely

.   .   .   .

A paper delivered at the English Institute in September, 1957, Mr. Benamou's essay was first published in *Comparative Literature*, XI, Winter, 1959; it is reprinted by permission of the author and Mr. Chandler B. Beall, editor of *Comparative Literature*.

conscious of the processes of creation. We can avail ourselves of a paper entitled "The Relations Between Poetry and Painting," which Stevens read at the Museum of Modern Art in 1951, and in which he defined four main areas of influence: sensibility, subject matter, technique, and aesthetics. He did not cite his own work as illustration, but he was so careful to keep to the craftsman's viewpoint, discarding any mysterious *Zeitgeist*, that his words bear the sigil of self-analysis. He said, in effect, that a poet can learn his trade by reading what painters reveal about theirs, and by looking at their pictures. It is not irrelevant that Stevens was a great reader of exhibition catalogues. He called them "the natural habitat for prose poems" [1] and wrote notes for catalogues in praise of Dufy, Gromaire, and the obscure Jean Labasque. He took equal heed of studio oracles and the doctrines of Croce, Berenson, and Focillon. Not only his lectures but his poems abound in references to Cézanne, Picasso, and many others. He was probably among the first in America to see Cubist paintings, thanks to his Harvard acquaintance Walter C. Arensberg, who knew Duchamp and Gleizes, and whose studio on West Seventh Street was a favorite haunt of the Kreymborg sodality.[2] Stevens' own eclectic collection of French paintings ("I have a taste for Braque and a purse for Bombois," he once complained in a letter to his Paris art dealer) displayed his attraction to Impressionism and Cubism. But his poems tell even more about his dependence on art than his lectures and pictures do.

I

One feels in the poetic universe of Wallace Stevens a sort of pulse that alternately dilates and narrows the field of vision. At its widest it resembles the world of an open-air landscapist; at the other extreme, it has the limits of a painter's studio. One pole corresponds to the broad landscapes of the Impressionists, its opposite to the still-lifes and the compositions of decorative Cubism.

[1] *Opus Posthumous,* edited by Samuel French Morse (New York, 1957), p. 290. (Cited hereafter as OP.)
[2] See Alfred Kreymborg, *Troubadour* (New York, 1957), p. 220.

MICHEL BENAMOU · 233

The more lasting influence on Stevens' vision was perhaps that of Impressionism, which he called "the only great thing in modern art." He regarded it as "poetic," ("Notes on Jean Labasque," OP, 293). By this, it seems to me that he meant an element of sensibility, a sensitiveness to the flux and change of nature. Both Monet and Stevens express the poetry of a fluent universe, a vast stage for the wind, rain, sun, and moonlight, a poem of skies and waters in which the key word is weather. Their insistence on weather, season of year, and time of day stems from an acute sense of visible changes caused by the condition of lighting. The great Impressionists, Monet, Sisley, and Pissarro, carried this concern to the extreme that they no longer painted objects so much as the light on them and the air round them. Stevens, who dubbed himself "pundit of the weather," wrote "Evening Without Angels" as a hymn to "the great interests of man: air and light." Blue shadows, "Blue Building in the Summer Air," a gold tree which is blue—air is everywhere. And a chameleon light plays in dozens of poems with suggestive titles: "Variations on a Summer Day," "Of Hartford in a Purple Light," and, most magnificent of all, "Sea Surface Full of Clouds." Presumably, the poet never saw the whole series of the "Water Lilies" in the Orangerie Museum, for he never went to Paris. Yet all the feeling of the old painter of Giverny for the fleeting reflections of light in iridescent water inspires this picture of the ocean:

> The sea-clouds whitened far below the calm
> And moved, as blooms move, in the swimming green
> And in its watery radiance, while the hue
>
> Of heaven in an antique reflection rolled
> Round those flotillas. And sometimes the sea
> Poured brilliant iris on the glistening blue.

The fascination of this spectacle results in a fusion of the consciousness with the external world. It is hard to say whether the five different aspects of the sea bring about the succeeding moods of the poem, or the reverse. Visual appearance and mental reality are one.

Stevens' saying in "Men by the Thousand" that "the soul is composed of the external world" gives a clue to what happens in

"Sea Surface Full of Clouds," "The Snow Man," and countless other poems in which the mind of the beholder mirrors his surroundings and fluctuates with the slightest change of light. This impressionistic theory of environment culminates in the fourth section of "The Comedian as the Letter C," with its anti-intellectual statement that "his soil is man's intelligence," an extreme, although not unnatural, consequence of Stevens' delight in the sheen and bloom "of the surface of things."

A constant preoccupation of the impressionist, whether painter or poet, is to restore the innocence of the eye. Monet wished he were temporarily blind, to experience sight again and see the world anew. Similarly, Wallace Stevens yearned to be the giant on Mount Chocorua, whose sensibility strikes us as thoroughly impressionistic:

> The feeling of him was the feel of day,
> And of a day as yet unseen, in which
> To see was to be.
> ("Chocorua to Its Neighbor")

His impulse toward transparence, his desire to be "at the center of a diamond," his obsession with the freshness, or, in his own refreshing phrase, the *fraicheur* of sight, bespeak the impressionist's dream of a translucent vision, free from memory and artifice. He wrote, in an unpublished letter to a Paris art dealer: "I share your pleasure in the Impressionistic school. In the pictures of this school: so light in tone, so bright in color, one is not conscious of the medium. The pictures are like nature. . . ." [3]

But very often what he saw was "Nature as pinakothek" and what he felt was "weather by Franz Hals." The freshness of Stevens' poetry is largely due to what Delmore Schwartz called "a vision instructed in the museums," rather than to the glass-pane purity of naked sight. Was not the very transparence which he praised in impressionistic landscapes a product of artifice? The recently published "Anecdote of the Abnormal" (OP, 23-24) gives a revealing documentation of Stevens' attitude:

[3] Letter to Mlle. Paule Vidal, January 30, 1948 (by courtesy of Samuel F. Morse).

The common grass is green.
But there are regions where the grass
Assumes a pale Italianate sheen—
Is almost Byzantine.
. . . new colors make new things
And new things make old things again.

This voluptuary of the eye needed an ever-renewed flow of novel sensations. Art was his remedy against "the malady" of the quotidian; its colors dispelled the slate color of habit, were a vital part of his poetic diet. He may very well go on record as a naturalist who thrived on artificiality.

Harmonium and later collections, too, seem cluttered with the paraphernalia of Cubism, the guitars and mandolins, the still-lifes arranged on tables, the plaster heads, the bits and odds that painters hoard for their collages, parts of a world rescued from the dump. To the reader looking for Stevens' subject, it may appear that the use of art as a source of inspiration entails a narrowing of the poetic range, limited as it is to studio objects. There is some truth in this opinion, and much superficiality. Certainly, the absence of man as a pictorial theme seems to me as conspicuous in Stevens' poems as in modern painting since Monet, excepting Picasso's Ingrist period. No nudes in the traditional sense, only grotesque caricatures. The human shape has lost its supremacy and its dignity. For an analysis of this fact, we have only to look at Projection A of "So-and-So Reclining on a Couch," a mere mechanism of curves and color, "completely anonymous." In like fashion, the figure in the first stanza of "Sunday Morning" has not the slightest, even suggested, feature; as in a picture by Matisse, it is sacrificed to a decorative pattern.

But the real subject of Stevens' poetry and the real subject of Cubist painting is not immediately perceptible: it is poetic imagination. The merit of the poem or picture arises from the degree of concentration with which the imagination refracts the object. The meanest and most derelict thing can thus be made significant, beautiful. "A Postcard from the Volcano" typifies this procedure; it shows

A dirty house in a gutted world,
A tatter of shadows peaked to white,
Smeared with the gold of the opulent sun

—a gold that performs the same imaginative function as the chrome yellow enhancing the dried-up fishes painted by Georges Braque. Stevens teaches us that the center of modern art is metamorphosis.

"To increase the aspects of experience" sometimes demands an artifice of perception. The multiple perspective of the Cubist, the dance round the object which causes Picasso to add an eye to his profiles, or the shifting optics of Cézanne, by virtue of which a saucer seems to bulge on either side of a bottle placed in front of it—these new modes of vision stress the role of an imaginative eye exploring the hidden facets of an object. This method can also serve in poetry, as evidenced by "Thirteen Ways of Looking at a Blackbird" or, in a more pictorial vein, the twelve views of a pineapple encompassed in "Someone Puts a Pineapple Together." The latter poem documents Picasso's saying, twice cited by Stevens, that a picture is a hoard of destructions.[4] Originally this phrase described the procedure of analytical Cubism, exploding the object into prismatic fragments. The effect was one of complexity; the picture became a simultaneous enumeration of related aspects. Stevens' pineapple is treated in much the same way. It is the "sum of its complications." By this, the poet means that the total reality of the fruit will be recomposed from the twelve pieces which make up its epistemological profile: a hut and palms, an owl covered with eyes, nailed-up lattices, etc. Nine of the twelve resemblances are visual. The complete poem adds up to a performance as witty as any Picasso *circa* 1910.

Why write a poem about a pineapple, this "incredible subject for poetry"? Stevens chose it for the same reason as the Cubist chooses his studio arrangement, because it was

[4] In "The Man With the Blue Guitar," sec. xv, it reads "hoard of destructions"; in "The Relations Between Poetry and Painting," it is "horde." The first spelling appears again in Renato Poggioli's translation, with Stevens' comment that he found the saying in Christian Zervos' book on Picasso.

A wholly artificial nature in which
The profusion of metaphor has been increased.

. . . .

. . . fertile with more than changes of the light

On the table or in the colors of the room.

This comes in defense of artificiality. Some privileged objects, however meaningless to the unpoetic, have such a shape as lends itself to metamorphosis: palms, fans, the open hand, certain fruit and flowers, a blackbird, and the sinuous guitar, friendly to the Cubist's dreams. But some other things resist imagination, defeat the poet's will. Among them certain roses in sunlight, "too much as they are to be changed by metaphor" ("Bouquet of Roses in Sunlight"), and two obdurate pears that will "resemble nothing else" ("Study of Two Pears"). Sister M. Bernetta Quinn rightly called our attention to this "victory of the real over the fictive." [5] Only when nature imitates art is it favorable to pictorial transmutation.

Thus the poetry of Wallace Stevens incorporates conflicting elements from Impressionism and Cubism: naturalness and artificiality, delight in appearances and metamorphosis of appearances. A baffling sum of relations—for where in these extreme ranges is the identity of a poet's sensibility?

The identity is in Stevens' concern with change. Impressionism shows the *passive* principle of change. The eye must be as candid as possible and merely relay the variations of light and colors. But in Cubism, "more than changes of light" are involved. Imagination is the *active* principle which transforms and extends the object by multiplying resemblances. The metaphors of poetry and the metamorphoses of painting tap the same reservoir of analogies.

II

At first glance any attempt to compare the form of a poem and that of a picture seems either futile or faulty. The ghosts of Lessing and Irving Babbitt loom before us voicing fearful interdictions. Yet, if we are to heed Stevens' hint about relating his poetic tech-

[5] Sister M. Bernetta Quinn, "Metamorphosis in Wallace Stevens," *Sewanee Review*, Spring, 1952.

nique to painting, we must cross the old barrier between arts of space and arts of time, and the new one between discursive and presentational forms.[6]

What is meant by form? A poem with its sequence of vowels and consonants offers a temporal medium entirely alien to the spatial medium of a picture: lines, tone value, and colors. The otherness, the radical heterogeneity of these pure, basic, *primary* forms cannot be overemphasized. At their level, beauty seems divorced from what is generally understood by meaning—it has only formal significance. But a poem and a picture have a *secondary* form which is intimately fused with their meaning. It is in this sense of the word form that the composition of an ode by Keats may strike Allen Tate as pictorial, that Marcel Proust wrote about the metaphors in Elstir's seascapes, that Wallace Stevens may speak of the diction of a portrait by Giorgione. So long as they do not involve primary forms, such comparisons are enlightening and legitimately drawn. The structure, imagery, and diction of Stevens' poems afford many relations of this kind with the devices and effects of painting.

The best example of Stevens' pictorial method of composition is to be found in the structure of "Sunday Morning," his most celebrated long poem. Its form is a meditative monologue, now in the first, now in the third person. Superficially the poem is tied together by references to the central character: she dreams, she says, etc. But is it really a discursive presentation of arguments with dialectic progression? It must have seemed so in the form of its first appearance in the November, 1915, issue of *Poetry*. There, the poem had five stanzas, and this five-stanza version has had fairly wide currency ever since. But the truth is that Stevens originally wrote "Sunday Morning" in the eight-stanza version which was to appear in the first edition of *Harmonium* in 1923. It was Miss Harriet Monroe who persuaded Stevens to publish the five-stanza version.[7] In assenting to this disfigurement of his work, the poet tried to make the best

[6] Cf. in John Peale Bishop's *Collected Essays* (New York, 1948), "Poetry and Painting," an essay showing the time element in pictures and the spatial element in poems. This essay was pointed out to me by Allen Tate.
[7] I owe many thanks to Samuel F. Morse for this important bit of information.

of an editorial botch by putting immediately after stanza I the final stanza of his original version. But this alteration made the poem look like a discursive argument, with the first four stanzas referring to the central character and the fifth as a possible answer to her questions.

The form of the poem as we have it in *Harmonium* erases the discursive quality and restores the original design. The central character loses her prominence; the narrative fabric is disrupted. The full-length version is the better poem. It has more unity, which results from its pictorial composition. "Sunday Morning" is not a succession of ideas, but of pictures. Stanza I is organized as a diptych—on one panel, a woman in a chair, oranges, a cockatoo, a rich, Matisse-like arrangement on an Oriental rug; on the other side, a sombre lake; silence accentuates the pictorial quality. The sense of space is enhanced by the simile "As a calm darkens," protracted by "The day is like wide water." This antithetic pattern, a picture of earthly life alternating with a scene of another world, continues in the next six stanzas. A complete resolution of the form occurs in the last stanza, for it corresponds panel for panel to the first diptych, but in reverse order. This formal chiasmic symmetry heightens our aesthetic enjoyment. The poem is framed between two visions of earth; its formal beauty depends partly on the vividness of these visions, partly on the perfect balance of its structure.

The effect of the pictorial method of composition is a tension within a balance. The atmosphere of "Sunday Morning" is anything but tense. Stevens was not in that sense a dramatic poet. There is no tenseness, but a tension—not dramatic, but spatial. It springs from the juxtaposition of antithetic blocks. The pattern of the sequence shows that the poem winds up as a complete circle. The *Poetry* version did not. And yet the final version of "Sunday Morning" has more force, perhaps a centripetal force. It achieves emotional impact within the visual daydreaming of an inconclusive meditation. It represents the triumph of a nondramatic poet over his own limitations.

The preceding remark by no means sets a claim that Stevens always composed pictorially. But, granting that his best poems are those with dramatic force, it may be that this dramatic force is best supported and actualized by their pictorial structure. A piece like "Mrs. Alfred Uruguay" does not draw its force from the rhetorical violence of its beginning ("So what said the others and the sun went down"), but rather from the spatial opposition of the two symbolic central figures. We are dealing with a poet gifted with a strong visual imagination, who presents conflicts of ideas as conflicts of forms and shapes.

Such a method of composition supposes the ability to create pictorial images, that is, representations of visual elements of reality organized pictorially. In Stevens' imagery, refined by imagist experimentation and observations of artistic devices, we cannot but thrill at the wealth of sensuous perceptions of shapes, lights, and colors. Yet we are never allowed to forget the symbolic meaning of each pictorial effect. Stevens was not, like Gautier, a painter *manqué*.

In "The Idea of Order at Key West," we are offered both the theory and the practice of "the maker's rage to order words of the sea." This is a poem about poetic creation and, by way of illustration, the poet evokes an image of a port at nightfall. The order of the description suggests the brush of a painter organizing his pictorial space. The perspective he defines with sure repetitions becomes a symbol of the victory of art over chaos. The verbs carry the magic of his act: mastering, deepening, enchanting; the nouns and adjectives are fraught with pictorial vividness: fiery poles, glassy lights, emblazoned zones.

If perspective symbolizes poetry, flatness connotes the unpoetic. Let us look at the pen-and-ink drawing entitled "The Common Life":

> That's the down-town frieze,
> Principally the church steeple,
> A black line beside a white line;
> And the stack of the electric plant,
> A black line drawn on flat air.
>
> .   .   .   .
>
> The paper is whiter
> For these black lines.
>
> .   .   .   .

MICHEL BENAMOU · 241

The paper is whiter.
The men have no shadows
And the women have only one side.

The whole poem is a single image, in which the vocabulary achieves the economy of Fernand Léger's technique. But again symbolism gives poetic meaning to plastic effects. The straight lines, the glaring contrast of black and white, the absence of depth and shadows, are metaphors for the spiritual vacuity of modern life. "Sad Strains of a Gay Waltz" and "Poem with Rhythm" afford two additional examples of this plastic symbolism, which equates shadowlessness with imaginative poverty and shadows with the life of the imagination.

Light imagery is vital to Stevens. Light is motion, change, and cheerfulness. For its evanescent appearances the poet has developed a special "vernacular of light," of which he gives us a glimpse in "Variations on a Summer Day":

> . . . words for the dazzle
> Of mica, the dithering of grass,
> The Arachne integument of dead trees,
> Are the eye grown larger, more intense.

Just as a painter will seek the challenge of light flashing on shiny objects, Stevens is lured by the glitter of crystals, diamonds, pieces of "broken glass in the grass." He seeks hard bright surfaces like bronze, tinsel, mirrors, ice, in which color is toughened by a sense of touch, a process of synaesthesia defined in the nutshell of this image: "emerald becoming emeralds."

The sharp outline and the bright surface of the forms result from the quality of light in which things are seen—a cold light for the most part, "more like snowy air," "an acid light" etching the contours of things, sharpening them with shadows. These are the "lights masculine" at work in "Of Hartford in a Purple Light," sculpturing shapes of the river, the railroad, the cathedral. But there are also "lights feminine," in which "every muscle slops away." Fewer poems belong to this late impressionistic type of imagery than to the masculine, clear-cut group. They are mostly about, or rather of, night; glitterings are toned down to glistenings, shapes merge into shades. Night is a female, soft as a woman's arm, bathed in the formlessness of green which permeates and fuses everything ("Six Significant Landscapes," stanza II; "Phosphor Reading by His Own Light"). In those images, we truly sense "a painter's light." [8] It comes to life; entering the spatial milieu created by words, called on stage by metaphors, it acts like "women whispering" or like a lion with "ruddy claws" and "frothy jaws," actualizing in poetry Henri Focillon's notion that light can become a form in itself.[9]

Stevens' gifts as a colorist shine particularly in his color matches. His palette glitters with the cheerfulness of the Impressionists. Its light tones are gaudy, with the etymological meaning of gay, never garish, for complementary associations are carefully avoided in favor of more fastidious marriages. But even images that seem purely pictorial call our attention from the poet's descriptive skill to his chromatic symbolism and his exhilarating sense of language. Let me quote two imagist tours de force from *Harmonium*:

> Last night we sat beside a pool of pink,
> Clippered with lilies scudding the bright chromes.
> ("Le Monocle de Mon Oncle," XI)

The color contrast is heightened by a clash between the subdued alliteration of plosives in the first line and the consonance of harsh "k" sounds in the second line. But the pleasure derived from this feat of virtuosity would seem a little cheap were it not for the startling nautical metaphor with its ironical overtones attuned to the context. Likewise, a typical image from "The Comedian as the Letter C" creates an acute contrast between color areas:

> The green palmettoes in crepuscular ice
> Clipped frigidly blue-black meridians,
> Morose chiaroscuro, gauntly drawn.

Just enough studio jargon for the sake of strangeness and to give a feeling for the degree of heat which painters consider important

[8] "The Poet Who Lived With His Words," a poem by Samuel F. Morse, *The Tuftonian*, Winter, 1957.
[9] "The Glass of Water," and H. Focillon, *La Vie des formes dans l'art*, p. 37.

in the arrangement of colors. But the psychological effect of the picture, its morose, gaunt, icy, crepuscular mood, extends much further than the merely visual impression. Stevens was never content with "verbal painting," if such a thing exists in poetry. He said in one of his "Adagia": "Poetry as an imaginative thing consists of more than lies on the surface" (OP, 161). Poetry lies when it tries to compete with painting. Color is in painting the real thing, in poetry a reflection of words. The true nature of an image is to become a metaphor.

Stevens' color symbolism is mostly a personal affair, based as it is on a lifelong meditation on the subjective quality of all perceptions. It starts with "Three Travellers Watch a Sunrise," and ends with "Two Illustrations That the World is What You Make of It." We shall only explore its relations with painting.

One element in the "broken color" of the Impressionist is that the eye transforms two colors into a single tone. Stevens used the device repeatedly. A lemon is "yellow-blue, yellow-green." The lilac in "Arcades of Philadelphia the Past" shows in the eye of the beholder,

> . . . in the agate eyes, red blue,
> Red purple, never quite red itself.

Pure, essential red is never seen, because it is abstract. In "Woman Looking at a Vase of Flowers" pure red is called "inhuman," and in "The Bouquet" the distinction between the particular of the eye and the abstract of the imagination clarifies the whole matter. The colors of things "are questions of the looks they get," but these colors, "seen in insight," become symbols. So the blue of the sky comes to mean the blue of the imagination. But it never ceases to denote the sky, because, essentially like a painter, Stevens always elaborates from sense data. Even when color tends toward abstraction, he never allows it to lose its sensuous quality. His last collection of verse, *The Rock*, restates an artist's love of color in this exultant flow of images:

> And a blue broke on him from the sun,
> A bullioned blue, a blue abulge,

Like daylight, with time's bellishings,
And sensuous summer stood full-height.

Such richly metaphorical visions play the same role in our enjoyment of poetry as the sensuous pulsing of color in Van Gogh's landscapes. But only the artistry of poetic language can stimulate in the reader these chromatic impressions. "Domination of Black," which Stevens at one time called his favorite poem in *Harmonium*, has no pictorial source. The only word denoting a specific color is in the title. Yet the poem releases a fantasia of colors that has the musicality of an abstract picture by Manessier or Bazaine.

Stevens' use of pictorial imagery, his plastic and chromatic symbolism, his art of composition, reveal how closely his poetry can approximate the effects of painting without lapsing into what Louis Untermeyer mistook for "verbal mosaics in which syllables are used as pigment." [10] We know now that there is as much symbolism and sense for "the edges of language" in *Harmonium* as in later works. However, the proportion of imagistic experiments in color diminishes from *Harmonium* to *The Rock*, as belonging to a style which Stevens took for granted, and also because the emphasis shifts gradually from style to feeling and thought, from description of the world to the "world as meditation." If the reader expects in the valedictory poems the kind of pictorial technique he enjoyed in the liminary pieces, he is likely to be disappointed. After *Harmonium*, we have, significantly, *Ideas of Order;* after the practice, the theory. But then Stevens, even when he theorizes on aesthetics, always remains a poet. For him the imagination identified itself with something big, blue, glittering, and sharply outlined. His ideas on poetry had a visual, sensory, rather than an abstract origin.

III

One unmistakable sign of Stevens' indebtedness to the aesthetics of modern painting is the frequency with which the words perception, object, and reality recur in his poems. Another clue inscribed in his critical vocabulary is the use of the verb "to paint" meaning

10 Louis Untermeyer, *Modern American Poetry* (New York, 1925), p. 326.

to create, and the noun "paint" for poetry. A quantity of poems illustrate the profoundest problems of artistic creation in terms of painting. Beyond mere verbal features, this alliance fostered a symbolism of shapes standing for aesthetic notions. There were two realities for Stevens—the reality of things observed and the reality of things imagined. One, the world, was in the image of a beast, a lion, a monster; the other, the poem, was an angel, "the necessary angel" of reality. Perception places the artist in contact with reality, with the beast. Sometimes, as we have seen, nature resists the imagination. Then a conflict arises between the object and the will, "a war that never ends" between the imagination and the monster of nature. When Stevens comes to grips with the monster, his "rage for order" resembles Cézanne's. In a sense, his aesthetics were Cézanne's subjective ("expressing oneself") objectivism ("realizing the object"). It is a personal meeting, an encounter with reality on terms of equality. This at least echoes the wish of "The Man With the Blue Guitar":

> That I may reduce the monster to
> Myself, and then may be myself
>
> In face of the monster, be more than part
> Of it, more than the monstrous player of
>
> One of its monstrous lutes . . .

And when he gives full attention to the object, the poet defines poetry, in the very words of Cézanne's roughhewn aesthetics, as

> An exercise in viewing the world.
> On the motive!
> ("Variations on a Summer Day")

Cézanne is the tribal god of modern painting because, as Stevens saw it, he has "helped to create a new reality, a modern reality. . . , a reality of decreation." [11] Rilke remarks that Cézanne's apples have become "indestructible in their obstinate existence." [12] They are different from edible fruit, though not less real. Their reality is poetic. They have been decreated and the painter has given them

[11] *The Necessary Angel* (New York, 1951), p. 174.
[12] *Letters* (New York, 1945), I, p. 304.

being. In modern art, at least among the votaries of Cézanne, essence is no longer divine, it is poetic, "The essential poem at the centre of things" ("A Primitive Like an Orb"). Cézanne had only one word: to realize. By this he meant very much the same thing as Stevens in his declaration of "An Ordinary Evening in New Haven":

> We seek
>
> The poem of pure reality, untouched
> By trope or deviation, straight to the word,
> Straight to the transfixing object, to the object
>
> At the exactest point at which it is itself,
> Transfixing by being purely what it is,
> A view of New Haven, say, through the certain eye,
>
> The eye made clear of uncertainty, with the sight
> Of simple seeing, without reflection. We seek
> Nothing beyond reality.

This pure reality is the monster mastered and purified by imagination.

From the encounter with the monster to the fusion with the angel of pure reality, Stevens' aesthetics has gone a long way. It bridges the gap between a painting of sheer appearances and an art which creates its own reality "in face of the monster." It reconciles the Impressionist vision and Cézanne's world within a world.

A final point remains for discussion. Even granting the enrichment of the poetic sensibility inspired by painting and the virtuosity of Stevens' transpositions from pictures, always under the deft control of poetic form, even granting this positive gain, there is a great danger that our approach may have done injustice to Stevens in the reader's mind. Through his affinities with other art lovers such as Proust, he might end up in the pigeonhole of aestheticism. Art buffers the aesthete from harsh realities. A vision of the world mediated by art is of the second degree—or even, in a Platonic perspective, of the third. But surely this cannot be the whole story about Stevens, in whom "the native element," [13] the sense of the

---

[13] Samuel F. Morse, "The Native Element," *Kenyon Review*, XX (1958), 446-465.

importance of living in an external world, counterbalanced the impulse to neutralize nature and hold it at arm's length like a picture. And the impulse to grapple with the "monster" is the aesthetic equivalent of Stevens' respect for external reality. All we can presume to do is to take stock of the art–nature duality in Stevens.

The question why Stevens and many other poets have been so dependent on the arts for their vision of the world has metaphysical implications. Pascal was critical of the reality of painting because he believed in a transcendental truth that dwarfed art to the status of all other human delusions. But we live in an age of disbelief. What makes Stevens a modern poet, *i.e.*, a poet of our time, is this modern consciousness that the arts compensate for our lost belief. Stevens was no solemn worshiper of painting and he had often enough a self-mocking word for the amateurs at Durand-Ruel's. But his practice of poetry echoes the intent faith of Baudelaire in the divine testimony of art, or rather, to avoid the term faith, Malraux's creed that art is *"la monnaie de l'absolu,"* the currency, but also the small change of the absolute. Understood as the poetic and moral principle of an order protecting us from chaos, art becomes more than a source of beautiful shapes and colors; it becomes a "supreme fiction," an inspiration tentatively analogous to the idea of god,

> For a moment final, in the way
> The thinking of art seems final when
>
> The thinking of god is smoky dew.
> ("The Man With the Blue Guitar," VI)

GEOFFREY MOORE

WALLACE STEVENS: A HERO OF
OUR TIME

1961

Wallace Stevens was not published in book form in England until 1953, when Messrs. Faber and Faber brought out a volume of fifty-seven poems selected by himself. Yet he had been publishing poems in the United States since 1914 and his first book, *Harmonium*, appeared there in 1923. Why the neglect? I suggest two reasons: first, the peculiar character of his difficulty, which is an intrinsic difficulty arising out of the nature of the poetic gesture his feelings forced him to make, and second, the extreme unfashionableness of his style and tone. In an age which demanded the bareness of the later Yeats and the early Eliot, Stevens' highly polished surfaces were unacceptable to all but the most perceptive, the most persevering or the most defiant of readers. And so, on his rare printed appearances in England before 1953 Stevens was annexed by the odd-men-out of literature: the editors of infinitesimal magazines and of fringe anthologies.

But now that he is with us, substantially, worthily published, in

·   ·   ·   ·   ·   ·   ·   ·

A lecture presented at the American Embassy in London in 1958, Mr. Moore's essay was later published in *The Great Experiment in American Literature*, edited by Carl Bode (London, William Heinemann, and New York, Frederick A. Praeger, 1961); it is reprinted by permission of the author, Mr. Bode, and Frederick A. Praeger, Inc.

a slightly changed poetic climate, there still seems a strange lack of enthusiasm for a poet of such caliber. I cannot remember having read in any piece written on this side of the Atlantic an estimate which struck me as quite fair. Even so intelligent and sympathetic a critic as G. S. Fraser has found him lacking, and I should like to quote Mr. Fraser's comment because it seems representative of prevailing critical opinion in this country:

> Yet in one's heart [says Mr. Fraser] one does not quite think he is a great poet in the sense that, say, Eliot and Yeats are "great" poets. What is it that one misses? Partly, or perhaps mainly, the whole area of life that lies between detached aesthetic perception and philosophical reflection on it; and as chief corollary to that, the urgency of ordinary human passion, the sense of commitment and the moment of final concentration. In one crude human sense, Mr. Stevens' enormous talents are being exploited a little frivolously; in all one's continuing pleasure and admiration while reading him, there is a sense all the time of a lack of the highest tension.

This is most perceptive criticism. There is certainly validity in the complaint that, at first, one does miss in Stevens "the urgency of ordinary human passion." However, his felicities are such that when one becomes accustomed to the element in which he moves much other good poetry seems slack and merely descriptive by comparison. It is not customary in criticism at this level to complain about the lack of "ordinary human passion" in, for example, the last three great novels of Henry James because James moves in an artistic milieu which is quite different from that of, say, Theodore Dreiser, who does give us "ordinary human passion" and plenty of it. It would be churlish to rail at James for this suspected inadequacy, since he amply compensates us with insights and pleasures which are on a different plane.

And so it is with Stevens. The fact that he does not write in the mode of Pound, Eliot, and the later Yeats may be a barrier to begin with, but, once surmounted, there is a rich country indeed. Mr. Eliot's manner was a barrier when his poems first appeared, but we have grown used to it. We have looked up the references in *The Waste Land*, and grown familiar with the elliptical style and the personal references. Its sharpness of notation, we say, gives us a sense of its nearness to the pulse of our time. So also can Stevens' verse if we familiarize ourselves with it in the same way. Stevens is not really flippant, or precious, or uncommitted—least of all uncommitted—any more than Eliot is a mere paster-together of quotations. The mannerisms are part of the *persona*, and what is called for is an acceptance of, and at the same time a reaching through, these mannerisms. One ends by understanding a kind of modern poetry which is, at the very least, a rewarding alternative to the "line of Eliot."

It is immediately apparent from *Harmonium* that Stevens had two susceptibilities. I feel sure that he was aware of them as such, and that, in a sense, they were necessary to him, as being part of the general act which his tentative, ironic and detached mind found necessary. Nevertheless, it is not exactly an advantage in our time to convey even a hint of archaism or aestheticism, which is what his first susceptibility—for the exotic word and phrase —in fact does. The second weakness is the occasionally frivolous tone, to which Mr. Fraser took exception, a decided disadvantage in an age in which the true voice of feeling is felt to speak through the hard clear image and the flat offhand phrase conducing to seriousness. The very ease and flow of Stevens' lines lulls the mind into believing that he is just another poet who is presenting pleasant sounds and nothing more. These things, however, are the shell. The kernel is something of another kind, a series of poetic meditations on the nature of man and his place in the universe. The reader who returns and re-returns in "wise passiveness" to the urbane impeccable stanzas of this American Dandy discovers an *alter ego*, the Large Red Man composing. I suggest, in other words, that the strength of character which allowed him to live the normal life of an insurance director in Hartford, Connecticut, and at the same time follow the dictates of his imagination, is also the ultimate strength of the poems. "Poor Stevens," we might say, "all those jokes in the golf club locker room, those bourbons on the rocks with the Elks, those chicken salad lunches with the Rotarians—

GEOFFREY MOORE · 251

how inimical they must have been to the life of poetry." But it does not seem to have been like that at all. I suspect that it was part of a pattern which Stevens thoroughly enjoyed. Behind what seem to be charming examples of Connecticut rococo there stands the solidity of a Dutch barn, a toughness and seriousness scarcely equaled among poets of our time.

The surely savored irony of his situation reveals itself in the title of his first book. The word "harmonium" links the notion of harmony, of the clear light of classical Greece with a vision of Congregational hymns being sung round a wheezy organ in the parlor. And the titles of the poems: "Le Monocle de Mon Oncle," "The Paltry Nude Starts on a Spring Voyage," "The Worms at Heaven's Gate," "Tea at the Palaz of Hoon," what are we to make of them? We are to make of them what we must or can. It is the product which counts, not the label. Some have extreme relevance, others are ironical.

If we approach with nose to the wind we may catch a wiff of Imagism, in its purest form, perhaps in "The Load of Sugar-Cane":

> The going of the glade-boat
> Is like water flowing;
>
> Like water flowing
> Through the green saw-grass,
> Under the rainbows;
>
> Under the rainbows
> That are like birds,
> Turning, bedizened,
>
> While the wind still whistles
> As kildeer do,
>
> When they rise
> At the red turban
> Of the boatman.

But in fact Imagism is a relatively minor influence. What is more striking, and characteristic, is a taste for rhetoric, and since it is this rhetoric which many readers find antipathetic, as being unserious or misplaced, I should like to quote an example of it at its most extravagant, that is, in "The Comedian as the Letter C."

Nota: man is the intelligence of his soil,
The sovereign ghost. As such, the Socrates
Of snails, musician of pears, principium
And lex. Sed quaeritur: is this same wig
Of things, this nincompated pedagogue,
Preceptor to the sea? Crispin at sea
Created, in his day, a touch of doubt.
An eye most apt in gelatines and jupes,
Berries of villages, a barber's eye,
An eye of land, of simple salad-beds,
Of honest quilts, the eye of Crispin, hung
On porpoises, instead of apricots,
And on silentious porpoises, whose snouts
Dibbled in waves that were mustachios,
Inscrutable hair in an inscrutable world.

One eats one pâté, even of salt, quotha.
It was not so much the lost terrestial,
The snug hibernal from that sea and salt,
That century of wind in a single puff.
What counted was mythology of self,
Blotched out beyond unblotching. Crispin,
The lutanist of fleas, the knave, the thane,
The ribboned stick, the bellowing breeches, cloak
Of China, cap of Spain, imperative haw
Of hum, inquisitorial botanist,
And general lexicographer of mute
And maidenly greenhorns, now beheld himself,
A skinny sailor peering in the sea-glass.
What word split up in clickering syllables
And storming under multitudinous tones
Was name for this short-shanks in all that brunt?
Crispin was washed away by magnitude.
The whole of life that still remained in him
Dwindled to one sound strumming in his ear,
Ubiquitous concussion, slap and sigh,
Polyphony beyond his baton's thrust.

One's first impulse is to cry Hamlet in a gray flannel suit, or at
least Launce or Armado in Stetsons. Yet it is not pastiche. Some
Elizabethan or Jacobean overtones are noticeable, but one has only
to compare Stevens' tone with that of, say, Edna St. Vincent Millay
to sense the quality of Stevens. "Gone in good sooth, you are," says

Miss Millay, or "Grief that is grief and properly so hight," or in that other famous sonnet:

> What's this of death, from you who will never die?
> Think you the wrist that fashioned you in clay . . .

and we know every time that Miss Millay is serious. Stevens is ironical. But it is not only that. Controlling the extravagant references, ordering the playfulness into meaning, there is a poetic intelligence of a high order, an intelligence which needed both the richness of language and the suggestion of Elizabethan bravado to bring off this serious mockery. For it is the Poet who is in question here, that slightly comic figure in an age which has turned a deaf ear and a blind eye to him. Take an instance, Stevens is saying, in which "man is the intelligence of his soil." Here Crispin is king, but an insubstantial one, a "ghost." He cultivates his garden. He is the "Socrates of snails," a little man in a known and safe world, but law unto his world. But let us ask if this "nincompated pedagogue" is also king in a different world, the sea, that is, the undomesticated universe. He is not. This "barber" might be at home with "gelatines and jupes," but in a world of porpoises rather than apricots he is lost.

Crispin has to accept the new region in which he finds himself, for "One eats one pâté, even of salt, quotha." He does not mind so much having lost his known and safe little garden world. What really bothers him is the kind of person he ought to be now—what "mythology of self" to adopt. Crispin, who was once a petty tyrant in his way, a "lutanist of fleas,"

> imperative haw
> Of hum, inquisitorial botanist,
> And general lexicographer of mute
> And maidenly greenhorns . . .

now finds that he is just "a skinny sailor." What name can we give to this "short-shanks in all that brunt"? He is nothing. He has no control of this new world. The life that remains to him seems utterly beyond his scope and understanding. It is "polyphony beyond his baton's thrust."

We are now at the end of only the first stanza of the first section, and there are six sections, occupying twenty pages in the *Collected Poems*. To summarize the rest of the poem, Crispin becomes "an introspective voyager." Made "vivid by the sea" he plunges into a new world, the world of the South, and has a vision of "elemental potencies" and "beautiful barenesses." After tossing:

> Between a Carolina of old time,
> A little juvenile, an ancient whim,
> And the visible, circumspect presentment drawn
> From what he saw across his vessel's prow.
>
> He came. The poetic hero without palms
> Or jugglery, without regalia . . .

Having realized that reality, the "veritable ding an sich," must be his subject, Crispin addresses himself to his task: "Nota: his soil is man's intelligence." This reversal of the opening line of the poem indicates Crispin's mature understanding that to the degree to which man looks clearly at and fully accepts life, to that degree is he made vital.

> That's better. That's worth crossing seas to find.
> Crispin in one cloudy phrase laid bare
> His cloudy drift and planned a colony.
> Exit the mental moonlight, exit lex,
> Rex and principium, exit the whole
> Shebang. Exeunt omnes. Here was prose
> More exquisite than any tumbling verse . . .

Paradoxically, prose is Stevens' way of referring to true poetry, poetry without pretension, in which one can have "veracious page on page, exact." He would found a colony where this great and simplest of creeds might be celebrated. But he has not reckoned with the encroachment of the "quotidian." Ordinary life in its very multifariousness, with all its pressures, puts an end to his dreams, so that, a family man and middle-aged at the end of the poem,

> The fatalist
> Stepped in and dropped the chuckling down his craw,
> Without grace or grumble.

It is a sad ending, but for all its extravagance of manner it is as realistic in theme as one could wish for. Buried in "The Comedian"'s

GEOFFREY MOORE · 255

oblique way is contending against. In his poems on belief Stevens writes as an American with the weight of the American situation on his back, whereas Mr. Eliot writes as an American "gone over" and feeling much the same excitement at the beginning, I should imagine, as the Englishman gone over to Italy. In a larger sense, of course, Stevens' inquiry into the matter of belief is that of any intelligent modern man in any part of the Western world. However, I suggest that it is given added point and force by the fact that he was an American and, like those idealistic, troubled, metaphysical, symbol-making literary forebears of his, driven by his society and the nature of his country into an extremity of questioning.

The best of the "belief" poems in *Harmonium* is "Sunday Morning." A woman, enjoying her coffee and oranges on Sunday morning instead of going to church, thinks about the Crucifixion. The pageant, the idea, seem to her dead, of the past. "Why should she give her bounty to the dead?" She would rather sense divinity in life itself, "in comforts of the sun":

> Divinity must live within herself:
> Passions of rain, or moods in falling snow;
> Grievings in loneliness, or unsubdued
> Elations when the forest blooms; gusty
> Emotions on wet roads on autumn nights;
> All pleasures and all pains, remembering
> The bough of summer and the winter branch.
> These are the measures destined for her soul.

There follows an impression of Jove who moved among us "as a muttering king,/Magnificent, would move among his hinds,"

> Until our blood, commingling, virginal,
> With heaven, brought such requital to desire
> The very hinds discerned it, in a star,

that is until Christianity came. If the earth were to seem all of paradise that we should know the sky would seem

> much friendlier then than now,
> A part of labor and a part of pain,
> And next in glory to enduring love,
> Not this dividing and indifferent blue.

Implicit here is a comparison of our view of the world as a "vale of tears" with the Greek world of gods and men. There is no joy in the thought of heaven because it is not real to us.

The things of this world are *all* that we know, in contrast to the legends of after life:

> There is not any haunt of prophecy
> Nor any old chimera of the grave,
> Neither the golden underground, nor isle
> Melodious, where spirits gat them home,
> Nor visionary south, nor cloudy palm
> Remote on heaven's hill, that has endured
> As April's green endures . . .

And yet, the woman feels—even in her contentment with the things of the world—the need of "some imperishable bliss." And the answer that Stevens gives is that Death, the all-consuming, all-important fact of Death, in a world which is here and now and only here and now, gives point to our lives and is in fact the "mother" of beauty since it makes us realize the bittersweetness of the human situation. He mocks at our vision of paradise. What is it really like? We have made paradise after our own image. Why create this platonic earth in our minds?

> Alas, that they should wear our colors there,
> The silken weavings of our afternoons,
> And pick the strings of our insipid lutes!

There follows a vision of what life might be on the earth, the beginning of which is perhaps the least successful part of the poem. I take it that it is not only figurative but slightly ironical too. But it ends well:

> They shall know well the heavenly fellowship
> Of men that perish and of summer morn.
> And whence they came and whither they shall go
> The dew upon their feet shall manifest.

The facts are true enough, Stevens suggests in the last stanza. There was a man called Jesus, but his tomb is no "porch of spirits," only a grave. We are alone on this earth. No benign spirit watches over us. We must enjoy the beauty of this world, for there is nothing else:

We live in an old chaos of the sun . . .

But still:

> Deer walk upon our mountains, and the quail
> Whistle about us their spontaneous cries;
> Sweet berries ripen in the wilderness;
> And, in the isolation of the sky,
> At evening, casual flocks of pigeons make
> Ambiguous undulations as they sink,
> Downward to darkness, on extended wings.

The problem thus presented so delicately and so beautifully is one which must touch many people born into a world in which Christianity seems more and more of a profound tragic myth and less and less of an actuality in which the mind may truly believe.

Yet one has a sense that despite the seriousness of his questioning Stevens is not being quite fair. There is a kind of Christian for whom the earth *is* full of wonders which are the more a joy because they show forth the glory of God. Hopkins was such a one. Nor for the old Puritans either, we might object, was the world entirely a vale of tears. However, Stevens is not reacting to a past or to a theoretical situation. He is reacting to what he sensed in America when he wrote that poem, and the key to it is, I believe, the outrage that he felt at the hollowness of the *"residual* pieties" in a community which had lost a vivid faith.

Between "Sunday Morning" and *Notes Toward a Supreme Fiction* there lie twenty years and a considerable amount of thought and experiment. The theme of the relation between appearance and reality is tested out in countless variations. The tone of this inquiry is well illustrated by "The Idea of Order at Key West," in which Stevens says that the order must arise from ourselves, for we alone give point to the life around us, as the jar in Tennessee gave point to the wilderness around it. The listeners know of the woman singing that

> . . . there never was a world for her
> Except the one she sang and, singing, made.

And when they turned toward the town the lights on the fishing boats gave order to that vastness, the sea.

Oh! Blessed rage for order, pale Ramon,
The maker's rage to order words of the sea,
Words of the fragrant portals, dimly-starred,
And of ourselves and of our origins,
In ghostlier demarcations, keener sounds.

This is Stevens' intimation of a sublime simplicity—order out of very fortuitousness. Through the poem we may reach order, and if that sounds a feeble gesture in the face of a world of violence and catastrophes, we should remember that for Stevens the significance of poetry was second to none. "The major poetic idea in the world," he said in a "Memorandum" to Henry Church in 1940,

> is and always has been the idea of God. One of the visible movements of the modern imagination is the movement away from the idea of God. The poetry that created the idea of God will either adapt it to our different intelligence, or create a substitute for it, or make it unnecessary. These alternatives probably mean the same thing, but the intention is not to foster a cult. The knowledge of poetry is a part of philosophy, and a part of science; the import of poetry is the import of the spirit . . .

and, in the "Adagia":

> The relation of art to life is of the first importance especially in a skeptical age since, in the absence of a belief in God, the mind turns to its own creations and examines them, not alone from the aesthetic point of view, but for what they reveal, for what they validate and invalidate, for the support that they give.

This is the burden of the final manifesto. The two books before it, *The Man With the Blue Guitar* and *Parts of a World,* seem in a sense a marking time, and perhaps more deserve the epithet of philosophizing. It is as if Stevens is trying his hand for the final performance. The same properties are there:

> I cannot bring a world quite round,
> Although I patch it as I can.
>
> I sing a hero's head, large eye
> And bearded bronze, but not a man,

GEOFFREY MOORE · 261

> Although I patch him as I can
> And reach through him almost to man.

and the salutary reminder that:

> Poetry is the subject of the poem,
> From this the poem issues and
>
> To this returns. Between the two,
> Between issue and return, there is
>
> An absence in reality . . .

However, it is not until *Notes Toward a Supreme Fiction* that we have an indisputable sense that Stevens has found both the form and language to match the dignity of his inquiry.

The form is a three-line stanza, seven stanzas to a section, ten sections to a part, three parts to the whole, these three parts being entitled "It Must Be Abstract," "It Must Change," and "It Must Give Pleasure." The lines are five-stressed but do not give the impression of blank verse because the stanzas often, although not always, partition off the thought, establish planetary systems of their own, within the universe of the sections, which themselves revolve within the galaxy of the part. It is a form which is light-years away from the clipped four-stress couplets of *The Man With the Blue Guitar*. The language is neither extravagant in the manner of *Harmonium* nor simple as in the *Blue Guitar*, but a pleasing reconciliation of the two. To start with, it is sober and comparatively direct:

> Begin, ephebe, by perceiving the idea
> Of this invention, this invented world,
> The inconceivable idea of the sun.
>
> You must become an ignorant man again
> And see the sun again with an ignorant eye
> And see it clearly in the idea of it.

But the style is sufficiently flexible to move without strain—unlike, we might note, the more artificial orchestral breaks of the *Four Quartets*—into the lyricism of:

> Bethou me, said sparrow, to the crackled blade,
> And you, and you, bethou me as you blow,
> When in my coppice you behold me be.

Ah, ké! the bloody wren, the felon jay,
Ké-ké, the jug-throated robin pouring out,
Bethou, bethou, bethou me in my glade.

The poem as a whole deals with the basic philosophical and spiritual imperatives toward which Stevens had been steadily moving. First, we must abstract the ideal of a primal, undomesticated reality, something pre-existing and not made for us. At the same time we immediately see that man's imagination both distorts reality and also allows him, paradoxically, to grasp its nature through a nonrational perception of it, a visionary sense not linked to any posited creator. Most important of all, the imagination in its attempt to "abstract" truth brings up the ideal of man, "major man" at his best—not the exceptional man, but the exceptional in every man.

In Part Two Stevens plunges into a theme he touched on in "Sunday Morning"—the idea that change, which we deplore as bringing death and destruction, is the source of the vital freshness of life and its many forms. The flow of reality is that which brings us our moments of perfection and happiness and love. Change is linked, too, with the imagination because "the bride" (that is, the beloved world, beloved life) "is never naked. A fictive covering/ Weaves always glistening from the heart and mind." An "order" must be flexible to partake of that freshness of transformation which is constantly in motion. Part Three, "It Must Give Pleasure," is in a deep sense about love, both of life and the world and of each other in this life and world. We must celebrate and praise the world by a constant and amazed delight in the unexpectedness of the moment, a more difficult rigor than to follow ceremony as in traditional beliefs. We must see things transformed—take pleasure in things for themselves. This is to love them—and it is exemplified in the way children with their fresh unprejudiced love can love ugliness (that is to say *any* kind of reality or person they can transform by their love). It is also exemplified in love between two people who "come face to face" and love the reality of each other. Imposed order, Stevens puts in at this point, is no good, only discovered order. It must be possible to hope for a knowledge of reality that will satisfy finally—"To find the real,/To be stripped of every fiction except one,/The fiction of the absolute." Things final in themselves are good and occur in vast repetitions which we enjoy, like the seasons or the repetitions of a leaf "spinning its eccentric measure." Through these repetitions, and by mastering them, we reach toward the truth and yet still we want to name that truth "familiar yet an aberration." Out of the combination of the utter reality and the fictive irrational truth within it and wedded to it can emerge what we seek. Stevens ends the poem with an invocation to the soldier (who typifies the man who is forced, as we all are, to act and suffer in this world). He says that the thinker's struggle to wed reality and imagination is reflected in the soldier's struggle to find meaning in his life. The soldier, says Stevens, needs the poet. The man of action needs the man of imagination:

> How simply the fictive hero becomes the real;
> How gladly with proper words the soldier dies,
> If he must, or lives on the bread of faithful speech.

Because of the exigencies of space, I have thought it best to provide a rough gloss of the poems I have chosen. However, with Stevens, more than with most other poets, one is constantly and uneasily aware of the inadequacy not only of the humble paraphrase but of any known critical method. His poetry exists as an aggregate of ideas and feelings, expressed with such a mutational amplitude, with such controlled jugglery of parenthetical, qualifying and extending impressions that one needs half a dozen or more streams of simultaneous commentary. Like his thoughts, Stevens' poems exist in the present moment; one has a sense while reading him that creation is proceeding before one's eyes. The whole is a continuous process, not a "talking about" but a living thing, so that in a most extraordinary and exciting way one receives through the aesthetic sense an impression of pure potency. Out of the multifariousness of the poet's impressions order emerges as a vase is drawn up from the clay on the wheel by a potter.

To provide an illustration of what I wish to say about Stevens' literary lineage I should like to quote section V of the first part of *Notes Toward a Supreme Fiction*, "It Must Be Abstract." The burden of section IV is that we must realize that "we live in a place/

That is not our own." We are not favored creatures in a world created for us, watched over by a deity who is interested in the least action of the least mortal. Far from it. We live in an alien universe, and we shall not begin to live fully until we cease to be sentimental egotists but grasp the grandeur of this idea, and of the nobility and strength in man which it can call forth. However, it is not necessary to the understanding of section V that we know section IV since, as I have pointed out, Stevens' sections circle like self-contained but dependent planets round the sun of his imagination. Section V continues:

> The lion roars at the enraging desert,
> Reddens the sand with his red-colored noise,
> Defies red emptiness to evolve his match,
>
> Master by foot and jaws and by the mane,
> Most supple challenger. The elephant
> Breeches the darkness of Ceylon with blares,
>
> The glitter-goes on surfaces of tanks,
> Shattering velvetest far-away. The bear,
> The ponderous cinnamon, snarls in his mountain
>
> At summer thunder and sleeps through winter snow.
> But you, ephebe, look from your attic window,
> Your mansard with a rented piano. You lie
>
> In silence upon your bed. You clutch the corner
> Of the pillow in your hand. You writhe and press
> A bitter utterance from your writhing, dumb,
>
> Yet voluble dumb violence. You look
> Across the roofs as sigil and as ward
> And in your centre mark them and are cowed . . .
>
> These are the heroic children whom time breeds
> Against the first idea—to lash the lion,
> Caparison elephants, teach bears to juggle.

Can we ask the "plain sense" of this section? In theory we ought not to, since to extract a plain sense from the process of "symbolic apprehending" which is Stevens' method is perhaps to convey the very wrong idea that the poem comes as a series of thoughts which are clothed in the aptest words, even possibly ornamented. It is to be doubted whether such a procedure takes place in the making of any poem, but least of all does it take place in Stevens' poetry. An intuition, a sense of the mystery is grasped through the words themselves. It is a form, as Mark Schorer once put it, of "technique as discovery" or in R. P. Blackmur's phrase of "language as gesture." "Words," says Mr. Blackmur, "bring meanings to birth and themselves contained the meaning as an imminent possibility before the pangs of junction"; or, in I. A. Richards' definition, "Words are the meeting points at which regions of experience which can never combine in sensation or intuition come together." A form of poetic communication the possibilities of which were indicated in the work of Mallarmé and Rimbaud has been absorbed into the English language tradition. However, in this case, since the writer is an American his cultural heritage is at once richer and thinner, richer in theory since he can draw on the resources of English poetry as well as American and thinner in practice because as an American he is subject to intangible but inexorable pressures from which the English poet is free.

Stevens' poetry, I believe, is part of the general movement of Romanticism which, from the work of Coleridge through that of the late-nineteenth-century French Symbolistes to the poetry of Dylan Thomas, represents a tradition running counter to the Imagistic-vernacular "true voice of feeling" posited by Sir Herbert Read. Thomas's phrase "a moving column of words" comes nearer to defining Stevens' method than it does Eliot's. There is also present—more in the early Stevens than the late—a sense of image's union with image breeding another, a Shakespearean grasp of metaphor changed by an age which produced Freud and Surrealism. Stevens' impeccable performance, his fluent and connotative meditation, should not blind us to his essentially irrational, intuitive approach, that groping toward apprehended truth which we might designate as the metaphysical-symbolic. As Stevens once said: "Poetry must resist the intelligence almost successfully," but if there is mystification in his poetry it is not mystification for its own sake but as a corollary of his grasp of the poem's function in an age of spiritual exploration.

But to return to the idea of the "plain sense" of the stanza from *Notes Toward a Supreme Fiction*. I take it—all qualifications made—that the three examples of the lion, the elephant and the bear are cited in order to illustrate the sense of identity these animals have with their surroundings. They are 'of it' in a way that civilized man can never be. We, ephebes all, strugglers to express the inexpressible, are cowed by the ineffable grace and rightness of the natural creature in his habitat, for we in our constant endeavor to impose an order on the world around us have lashed the lion, caparisoned elephants and taught bears to juggle. We Western Europeans have lost our sense of the rhythm of life, its organic order. We need to learn this over again if we are to realize the fullest possibilities of man on earth.

Our reaction might be that this particular idea is not new in the history of modern European literature. From Wordsworth to D. H. Lawrence men have said it before. However, this is only one of Stevens' several interlinking themes in *Notes Toward a Supreme Fiction*. Placed in the context of the poem and seen against the background of American literary development it has a peculiar significance. To call for an organic order, the fullest grasp of the here and now, to hymn the possibilities of man in his life on this earth, is to echo a fundamental theme of American literature in the nineteenth century. In their reaction against the Calvinist world-picture, and in the midst of abundance and apparently limitless progress and opportunity, Americans evolved Transcendentalism. Emerson the symbol-maker, exhorter, and preacher of sermons on life found an answer to his prayer in Walt Whitman and it is Whitman of whom Stevens most reminds one. Like Whitman Stevens 'presents' rather than 'talks about'; like Whitman Stevens calls for an organic order; like Whitman Stevens is a rhetorician. If at first the differences are more apparent than the resemblances it is because Stevens' nature was secretive where Whitman's was open, and because Whitman was a son of the Enlightenment, whereas Stevens is a modern who has learned from the French Symbolists. However, no less than Whitman he has Man on his mind, what Man can be and do on this earth, which is the American Dream and was prophesied like so many other things by the perceptive Tocqueville a hundred years

GEOFFREY MOORE · 267

ago. If we dig even deeper than this, however, we may distinguish a more fundamental literary mode in the light of which Stevens' work falls into place. This is the mode of allegory-become-symbolism, implicit in the Puritan attitude to life and literature. In various forms, through Hawthorne, Melville, and Whitman to James and Faulkner, allegory developed into symbolism. Stevens, responsive to European literary techniques as well as to the deep necessities of his country, worked as Poe and Whitman had done through the symbolism of language rather than, like Hawthorne and Melville, through that of the concept.

In pursuing symbolism so relentlessly Americans have, I believe, lost something which we as Englishmen can the more readily perceive since we look for it in our own verse. Mr. Fraser called it "ordinary human passion" and my reply was that one was willing to forgo this for the sake of Stevens' extraordinary felicities. I believe this to be true, but I wish to identify the lack a little more closely and to consider the reason for it. It is the absence of what I can only call a certain visceral quality and it might be tested by reading "Devouring time blunt thou the Lyons pawes," "Lycidas," "The Ode to Melancholy," and "A Refusal to Mourn," and then reading "Sunday Morning." "Sunday Morning" is magnificent, but it lacks one quality which all the English pieces have and that is a fundamental rhythm, almost a blood-beat. Conrad Aiken and Hart Crane, poets of the same type, lack it too. It is not that these American poets are bloodless. Far from it. It is I believe rather that this quality has been unconsciously suppressed because of a great and fundamental split in American society and the American consciousness, the split between Ebbets Field and Columbia Heights. In the face of the pressure of the vulgar, this kind of American literary artist, the symbolist, has done the opposite of the realistic Twains and the Salingers.

Randall Jarrell speaks of a recurrent dream. It is of a man, any man, among those Americans whom the statistics say do not read books. Jarrell asks him in the dream, "Why don't you read books?," and the man, after looking at him steadily for a long time, at length answers "Huh?" In American society there is a constant battle, none the less savage for being attenuated, between the regular guys and the eggheads, and it is savage and hysterical because in America the mass have so long and so palpably had the upper hand. In England we also have our philistines, but what one might call, altering that phrase from Lionel Trilling, the residual superiority of the educated—however they have attained their position—is felt as a fact. Or it has been until quite recently. We are approaching in England a position that the United States was committed to a long time ago, and that is why there have been recently signs of hysteria in our ranks.

These matters have fundamentally very little to do with such things as social class in the traditional sense. They have to do with kinds of people, and attitudes toward life. In *Symbolism and American Literature*, Charles Feidelson said:

> At a time when English literature was living on the capital of romanticism and increasingly given over to unambiguous narrative American literature had turned toward a new set of problems, arising out of a new awareness of symbolic method.

This peculiar American literary preoccupation—peculiar not because it is unique but because of its intensity and the forms it has taken—has arisen indirectly out of the pressures of American society. And it is a remarkable fact that a poet who developed his own unique exploratory style out of this most subtle and individual of literary modes should be concerned in the largest possible sense with the fate of Man. For all his quarrel with his society, Stevens had that society's most cherished beliefs at heart. In his work the Adamic vision underwent a metamorphosis; his hope was for a new version of the lost life, for some "harmonious skeptic" who "soon in a skeptical music/Will unite these figures of men," so that

> ... their shapes
> Will glisten again with motion, the music
> Will be motion and full of shadows.

For these reasons I consider Wallace Stevens a hero of our time. Seriously, consistently, and with great courage he tackled what he saw to be the central problem of the age. Because he did it in poetry, and poetry which is very difficult, his act has not been sufficiently recognized. But doing it this way, which was the only way he *could* do it, he was able to take speculation in a sense farther than a philosopher. I can think of no other poet the body of whose work yields so much more than the sum of the individual poems. He writes about the imagination and its transfiguring role in life, the nature of reality in all its shifting forms, the craving for order and a sense of wholeness in a life that is never completely within our grasp. His poetry begins where most poetry leaves us, in a state of heightened awareness. The play that he allowed to his natural gifts in *Harmonium* became increasingly subordinated to a controlled experiment. Through the aesthetic experience he explored the possibility of a new epistemology, pushing the boundaries of poetic communication to a new limit. There is only one other modern poet who is comparable with him in seriousness and range, who gives the reader a sense that his poetry comes out of caring terribly, and that is T. S. Eliot. Why, then, has Eliot been so assiduously followed and Stevens relatively ignored? I mentioned at the beginning two possible reasons: first, Stevens' difficulty and, second, his unfashionable manner. I suggest one other. From the choppy water of the "Hippopotamus" Eliot turned into the harbor of the *Four Quartets*. It was safe there. Outside all is unknown. But outside, perhaps, is where things are going on.

FOR FURTHER READING:

A Bibliography of Books and Articles about Wallace Stevens and Selected Reviews of His Work

I. BIBLIOGRAPHY

Morse, Samuel French, *Wallace Stevens: A Preliminary Checklist of His Published Writings: 1898–1954* (New Haven, Conn., 1954).

Tate, Allen, "Wallace Stevens," in *Sixty American Poets* (revised edition), (Washington, D.C., Library of Congress, 1954).

II. MAJOR PUBLISHED WORKS BY WALLACE STEVENS

Harmonium (New York, Alfred A. Knopf, 1923).

> *Reviews:* Edmund Wilson, *New Republic*, XXXVIII (March 9, 1924, 102–103; Louis Untermeyer, *Yale Review*, XIV (October, 1924), 156–61; Mark Van Doren, *Nation*, CXVII (October 10, 1923), 400, 402; *Bookman*, LVIII (1923), 483; "C. T. C.," *Boston Evening Transcript* (December 29, 1923), p. 5; John Gould Fletcher, *The Freeman*, VIII (December 19, 1923), 355.

Harmonium (2d ed.; New York, Alfred A. Knopf, 1931).

> *Reviews:* Morton Dauwen Zabel, *Poetry*, XXXIX (1931), 148–54; R. P. Blackmur, *Hound and Horn*, V (1932), 223–55; Horace Gregory, *New York Herald Tribune Books* (September 27, 1931), p. 28; Raymond Larsson, *Commonweal*, XV (April 6, 1932), 640–41; Percy Hutchinson, *New York Times Book Review* (August 9, 1931), p. 4; *Bookman*, LXXIV (October, 1931), 207–8.

Ideas of Order (New York, Alcestis Press, 1935).

Ideas of Order (New York, Alfred A. Knopf, 1936).

> *Reviews:* F. O. Matthiessen, *Yale Review*, XXV (1935-36), 603–7; Theodore Roethke, *New Republic*, LXXXVII (July 15, 1936), 305; Marianne Moore, *Poetry*, XLIX (1937), 268–72; Ben Belitt, *Nation*, CXLIII (December 12, 1936), 708–9; R. P. Blackmur, *Southern Review*, II (1936-37), 588–76; John

Holmes, *Virginia Quarterly Review*, XII (1936), 288–95; Stanley Burnshaw, *New Masses* (October 1, 1935), pp. 41–43; Babette Deutsch, *New York Tribune Books* (December 15, 1935), p. 18; Peter Munro Jack, *New York Times Book Review* (January 12, 1936), p. 15.

Owl's Clover (New York, Alcestis Press, 1936).
> Review: Marianne Moore, *Poetry*, XLIX (1937), 268–72.

The Man With the Blue Guitar and Other Poems (New York and London, Alfred A. Knopf, 1937).
> Reviews: William Rose Benét, *Saturday Review of Literature*, XV (January 16, 1937), 18; Benét, *North American Review*, CCXLIII (1937), 195–201; William Carlos Williams, *New Republic*, XCIII (November 17, 1937), 50; Robert Fitzgerald, *Poetry*, LI (1937), 153–57; Delmore Schwartz, *Partisan Review*, IV (February, 1938); Ben Belitt, *Nation*, CXLV (November 6, 1937), 508–9; Dorothy Van Ghent, *New Masses* (January 11, 1938), pp. 41–46; Eda Lou Walton, *New York Times Book Review* (October 24, 1937), p. 5; Ruth Lechlitner, *New York Herald Tribune Books* (November 14, 1937), p. 2; *Time*, XXX (November 1, 1937), 81–82.

"The Noble Rider and the Sound of Words," in *The Language of Poetry*, edited by Allen Tate (Princeton, N.J., Princeton University Press, 1942).
> Review: Donald Stauffer, *Kenyon Review*, IV (1942), 411–15.

Parts of a World (New York, Alfred A. Knopf, 1942).
> Reviews: Horace Gregory, *Accent*, III (1942), 57–61; F. Cudworth Flint, *Virginia Quarterly Review*, XIX (1943), 133–36; Weldon Kees, *New Republic*, CVII (September 28, 1942), 387–88; Marianne Moore, *Kenyon Review*, V (1943), 144–47; Mary Colum, *New York Times Book Review* (November 29, 1942), p. 12; Frank Jones, *Nation*, CLV (November 7, 1942), 488; Ruth Lechlitner, *New York Herald Tribune Books* (November 8, 1942), p. 26.

Notes Toward a Supreme Fiction (Cummington, Mass., Cummington Press, 1942).
> Reviews: Marianne Moore, *Kenyon Review*, V (1943), 144–47; Harvey Breit, *Poetry*, LXII (1943), 48–50.

Esthétique du Mal (Cummington, Mass., Cummington Press, 1945).

Transport to Summer (New York, Alfred A. Knopf, 1947).
> Reviews: Richard Eberhart, *Accent*, VI (1947), 251–53; Louis Martz, *Yale Review*, XXXVII (1947), 339–41; R. P. Blackmur, *Poetry*, LXXI (1948), 271–76; Victor Tejera, *Journal of Philosophy*, XLV (1948), 137–39; F. O. Matthiessen, *New*

York Times Book Review (April 20, 1947), pp. 4, 26; Robert Lowell, Nation, CLXIV (April 5, 1947), 400–2; Babette Deutsch, New York Herald Tribune Books (August 31, 1947), p. 4.

Three Academic Pieces (Cummington, Mass., Cummington Press, 1947).

A Primitive Like an Orb (New York, Banyan Press, 1948).

The Auroras of Autumn (New York, Alfred A. Knopf, 1950).

Reviews: David Daiches, Yale Review, XL (1950), 355–56; F. Cudworth Flint, Virginia Quarterly Review, XXVII (1951), 471–80; M. L. Rosenthal, New Republic, CXXIV (May 7, 1951), 26–28; William Van O'Connor, Poetry, LXXVII (November, 1950), 109–12; Joseph Bennett, Hudson Review, IV (1951), 133–43; Vivienne Koch, Sewanee Review, LIX (1951), 664–77; Lloyd Frankenberg, New York Times Book Review (September 10, 1950), p. 20; Babette Deutsch, New York Herald Tribune Books (October 29, 1950), p. 6; Time, LVI (September 25, 1950), 106, 108, 110.

The Necessary Angel: Essays on Reality and the Imagination (New York, Alfred A. Knopf, 1951).

Reviews: C. Roland Wagner, Hudson Review, V (1952), 144–48; Richard Eberhart, Accent, XII (1952), 122–25; Bernard Heringman, Kenyon Review, XIV (1952), 520–23.

The Man with The Blue Guitar (2d ed., including Ideas of Order; New York, Alfred A. Knopf, 1952).

Review: William Van O'Connor, Poetry, LXXXI (1952), 139–43.

Selected Poems (London, Faber and Faber Ltd., 1953).

Review: Times Literary Supplement (June 19, 1953), p. 397.

The Collected Poems of Wallace Stevens (New York, Alfred A. Knopf, 1954; 2d ed., 1955).

Reviews: Randall Jarrell, Yale Review, XLIV (1955), 340–53; Marius Bewley, Commonweal, LXII (September 23, 1955), 617–22; R. P. Blackmur, Kenyon Review, XVII (1955), 94–110; Hayden Carruth, Poetry, LXXXV (1955), 288–93; G. S. Fraser, Partisan Review, XXII (1955), 265–72; Samuel French Morse, New York Times Book Review (October 3, 1954), p. 3; John Ciardi, Nation, CLXXIX (October 16, 1954), 346–47; Babette Deutsch, New York Herald Tribune Books (October 3, 1954), p. 3.

Opus Posthumous, edited, and with an Introduction, by Samuel French Morse (New York, Alfred A. Knopf, 1957).

Reviews: Reed Whittemore, Yale Review, LXVII (1957), 281–88; Irving Howe, New Republic, CXXXVII (November

4, 1957), 16–19; F. Cudworth Flint, *Virginia Quarterly Review*, XXXIV (1958), 117–26; Anthony Hecht, *Hudson Review*, X (1957-58), 606–13; Rosemary Deen, *Commonweal*, LXVI (September 20, 1957), 620–21; William Carlos Williams, *New York Times Book Review* (August 22, 1957), p. 6; Babette Deutsch, *New York Herald Tribune Books* (August 1, 1957), p. 8.

Poems by Wallace Stevens, selected, and with an Introduction, by Samuel French Morse (New York, Vintage Books, 1959).

III. BOOKS ON WALLACE STEVENS

Kermode, Frank, *Wallace Stevens* (Edinburgh and London, 1960; New York, 1961).

O'Connor, William Van, *The Shaping Spirit: A Study of Wallace Stevens* (Chicago, 1950).

Pack, Robert, *Wallace Stevens; An Approach to his Poetry and Thought* (New Brunswick, N.J., 1958).

Tindall, William York, *Wallace Stevens* (Minneapolis, Minn., University of Minnesota Press, 1961).

Samuel French Morse is preparing the official critical biography of Stevens.

IV. ARTICLES, REVIEWS AND BRIEF NOTICES

Abel, Lionel, "In the Sacred Park," *Partisan Review*, XXV (1958), 86–98.

Aiken, Conrad, *Skepticisms* (New York, 1919), *passim*.

———, "The Ivory Tower—I," *New Republic*, XIX (May 10, 1919), 58–60. (*See also* Untermeyer, Louis.)

———, "Two Views of Contemporary Poetry," *Yale Review*, IX (January, 1920), 413–16.

Alvarez, A., *Standards of Excellence* (New York, 1958; published under the title of *The Shaping Spirit*, London, 1958), pp. 124–39.

Amacher, Richard E., "Stevens' 'To the One of Fictive Music,'" *Explicator*, XI (1953), Item 43.

Arms, George A. and Kuntz, Joseph M., *Poetry Explication* (New York, 1950), pp. 141–46—listing of explications of Stevens' poems.

Baker, Howard, "Add to This Rhetoric," *Harvard Advocate*, CXXVII (December, 1940), 16–18.

———, "Wallace Stevens and Other Poets," *Southern Review*, I (Autumn, 1935), 373–89.

Baym, Max I., "Three Moths and a Candle: A Study of the Impact of Pascal on Walter Pater, Henry Adams and Wallace Stevens," *Comparative Literature*, (9) II (1960), 336–48.

Belitt, Ben, in *Nation*, CXLIII (December 12, 1936), 708–9—review of *Ideas of Order*.

———, "Lion in the Lute," *Nation*, CXLV (November 6, 1937), 508–9—review of *The Man With the Blue Guitar*.

Benamou, Michel, "Jules Laforgue and Wallace Stevens," *Romanic Review*, L (1959), 107–17.

———, "Le Thème du Héros dans la Poésie de Wallace Stevens," *Etudes Anglaises*, XII (1959), 222–30.

———, "Wallace Stevens: Some Relations Between Poetry and Painting," *Comparative Literature*, XI (1959), 47–60.

Benét, William Rose, in *Saturday Review of Literature*, XV (January 16, 1937), 18—review of *The Man With the Blue Guitar, Owl's Clover*.

———, "Three Poets and a Few Opinions," *North American Review*, CCXLIII (Spring, 1937), 195–201—review of *The Man With the Blue Guitar*.

Bennett, Joseph, "Five Books, Four Poets," *Hudson Review*, IV (Spring, 1951), 133–43—review of *The Auroras of Autumn*.

Bewley, Marius, "The Poetry of Wallace Stevens," *Commonweal*, LXII (September 23, 1955), 617–22—review of *Collected Poems*.

———, "The Poetry of Wallace Stevens," *Partisan Review*, XVI (September, 1949), 895–915; reprinted in *The Complex Fate* (London, 1952), pp. 171–92.

Blackmur, R. P., "The Composition in Nine Poets," *Southern Review*, II (1936–1937), 555–76—review of *Ideas of Order*.

———, "Examples of Wallace Stevens," *The Double Agent* (New York, 1935), pp. 68–102; reprinted in *Language as Gesture* (New York, 1952), pp. 221–49.

———, "Poetry and Sensibility: Some Rules of Thumb," *Poetry*, LXXI (February, 1948), 271–76; reprinted in *Language as Gesture* under the title, "On Herbert Read and Wallace Stevens," pp. 255–59.

———, "The Substance that Prevails," *Kenyon Review*, XVII (1955), 94–110—review of *Collected Poems*.

———, "Wallace Stevens—An Abstraction Blooded," *Language as Gesture*, pp. 250–54.

Blake, Howard, "Thoughts on Modern Poetry," *Sewanee Review*, XLIII (April–June, 1935), 187–96.

Bodenheim, Maxwell, "Modern Poetry," *Dial*, LXVIII (January, 1920), 95–98.

Bogan, Louise, "*Harmonium* and the American Scene," *Trinity Review*, VIII (May, 1954), 18–20.

Bookman, LXXIV (October, 1931), 207–8—review of *Harmonium*, 1931.

Bosquet, Alain, "Deux Poètes Philosophes: Wallace Stevens et Conrad Aiken," *La Table Ronde*, No. 105 (1956), pp. 129–35.

———, "Wallace Stevens," *Nouvelle Nouvelle Revue Française*, III (October, 1955), 777–79.

Breit, Harvey, "Sanity That Is Magic," *Poetry*, LXII (April, 1943), 48–50—review of *Notes Toward a Supreme Fiction*.

Brinnin, John Malcolm, "Plato, Phoebus and the Man from Hartford," *Voices*, No. 121 (Spring, 1945), pp. 30–37.

Burnshaw, Stanley, *New Masses* (October 1, 1935), pp. 41–43—review of *Ideas of Order*.

Buttell, Robert W., "Stevens' 'Two Figures in a Dense Night,'" *Explicator* IX (1951), 45.

Cambon, Glauco, "Le 'Notes Toward a Supreme Fiction' di Wallace Stevens," *Studi Americani*, I (1955), 205–33.

Carrier, Warren, "Wallace Stevens' Pagan Vantage," *Accent*, XIII (1953), 165–68.

Carruth, Hayden, "'Without the Invention of Sorrow,'" *Poetry*, LXXXV (February, 1955), 288–93—review of *Collected Poems*.

Ciardi, John, "Dialogue With the Audience," *Saturday Review*, XLI (November 22, 1958), 10–12, 42—on reading of poetry, with Stevens' poetry as example.

———, "Wallace Stevens's 'Absolute Music,'" *Nation*, CLXXIX (October 16, 1954), 346–47—review of *Collected Poems*.

Colum, Mary M., in *New York Times Book Review* (November 29, 1942), p. 12—review of *Parts of a World*.

Culbert, Taylor, and John M. Violette, "Wallace Stevens' Emperor," *Criticism*, II (1960), 38–47.

Cunningham, J. V., "The Poetry of Wallace Stevens," *Poetry*, LXXV (1949), 149–65; revised and reprinted in *Tradition and Poetic Structure: Essays in Literary History and Criticism* (Denver, Colo., 1960), under the title "Tradition and Modernity: Wallace Stevens," pp. 106–124.

Daiches, David, "Some Recent Poetry," *Yale Review*, XL (December, 1950), 352–57—review of *The Auroras of Autumn*.

Davenport, Guy, "Spinoza's Tulips: A Commentary on 'The Comedian as the Letter C,'" *Perspective*, VII (Autumn, 1954), 147–54.

Davie, Donald, "'The Auroras of Autumn,'" *Perspective*, VII (Autumn, 1954), 125–36.

————, " 'Essential Gaudiness': The Poems of Wallace Stevens," *Twentieth Century* (London), CLIII (1953), 455–62.

Deen, Rosemary F., "Wonder and Mystery of Art," *Commonweal*, LXVI (September 20, 1957), 620–21—review of *Optus Posthumous*.

Deutsch, Babette, "Blue Burning of Fall Time," *New York Herald Tribune Books* (October 29, 1950), p. 6—review, in verse, of *The Auroras of Autumn*.

————, "Contemporary Portraits No. 2: Wallace Stevens," *Poetry London New York*, II (Winter, 1956), 42–47.

————, "The Gaudiness of Poetry," *New York Tribune Books* (December 15, 1935), p. 18—review of Ideas of Order.

————, in *New York Herald Tribune Books* (August 31, 1947), p. 4—review of *Transport to Summer*.

————, *Poetry in Our Time* (New York, 1956).

————, "Poet's Harvest: Seventy-five Years of 'Piecing the World Together.' " *New York Herald Tribune Books* (October 3, 1954), p. 3—review of *Collected Poems*.

————, "Wallace Stevens: Newly Gathered Work," *New York Herald Tribune Books* (August 1, 1957), p. 8—review of *Opus Posthumous*.

Doggett, Frank, "Abstraction and Wallace Stevens," *Criticism*, II (1960), 23–37.

————, "Stevens' 'It Must Change, VI,' " *Explicator*, XV (1957), Item 30.

————, "Stevens' 'Woman Looking at a Vase of Flowers.' " *Explicator*, XIX (1960), Item 7.

————, "Wallace Stevens' Later Poetry," *ELH: A Journal of English Literary History*, XXV (June, 1958), 137–54.

————, "Wallace Stevens' Secrecy of Words: A Note on Import in Poetry," *New England Quarterly*, XXXI (1958), 375–91.

————, "Wallace Stevens and the World We Know," *English Journal*, XLVIII (1959), 365–73.

Donoghue, Denis, *The Third Voice* (Princeton, N. J., 1959), pp. 193–94—deals briefly with Stevens' plays.

Eberhart, Richard, in *Accent*, III (Winter, 1943), 121–22—remarks on *Notes Toward a Supreme Fiction*.

————, "The Stevens Prose," *Accent*, XII (Spring, 1952), 122–25 —review of *The Necessary Angel*.

Ellmann, Richard, "Wallace Stevens' Ice Cream," *Kenyon Review*, XIX (1957), 89–105.

Fahey, William A., "Stevens' 'Le Monocle de Mon Oncle,' I," *Explicator*, XV (1956), Item 16.

Farnsworth, Robert M., "Stevens' 'So-and-So Reclining on Her Couch,'" *Explicator*, X (1952), 60.

Feldman, Steve, "Reality and the Imagination: The Poetic of Wallace Stevens' 'Necessary Angel,'" *University of Kansas City Review*, XXI (1954), 35–43.

Ferrán, Jaine, "El Poeta Wallace Stevens," *Atlántico*, No. 5 (1957), pp. 17–32.

Ferry, David R., "Stevens' 'Sea Surface Full of Clouds,'" *Explicator*, VI (June, 1948), 56.

Finch, John, "North and South in Stevens' America," *Harvard Advocate*, CXXVII (December, 1940), pp. 23–26.

Fitzgerald, Robert, "Thoughts Revolved," *Poetry*, LI (December, 1937), 153–57.

Fletcher, John Gould, "Some Contemporary American Poets," *Chapbook* (London) (May, 1920).

Flint, F. Cudworth, "Images of Secret Life," *Virginia Quarterly Review*, XIX (Winter, 1943), 133–36—review of *Parts of a World*.

———, "'Let the Snake Wait,'" *Virginia Quarterly Review*, XXVII (Summer, 1951), 471–80—review of *The Auroras of Autumn*.

———, "Poetic Accomplishment and Expectation," *Virginia Quarterly Review*, XXXIV (Winter, 1958), 117–26—review of *Opus Posthumous*.

———, "Whether of Bronze or Glass," *Trinity Review*, VIII (May, 1954), 26–27.

Ford, Charles Henri, "Verlaine in Hartford," *View*, I (1940), 1, 6 —Biographical.

Ford, Newell F., "Peter Quince's Orchestra," *Modern Language Notes*, LXXV (1960), 405–11.

Frankenberg, Lloyd, in *New York Times Book Review* (September 10, 1950), p. 20—review of *The Auroras of Autumn*.

———, "Wallace Stevens," *Pleasure Dome* (Cambridge, Mass., 1949), pp. 197–267.

Fraser, G. S. "The Aesthete and the Sensationalist," *Partisan Review*, XXII (Spring, 1955), 265–72—review of *Collected Poems*.

———, "Mind All Alone," *New Statesman*, (January 9, 1960), pp. 43–44.

Frye, Northrop, "The Realistic Oriole: A Study of Wallace Stevens," *Hudson Review*, X (Autumn, 1957), 353–70.

Gay, R. M., "Stevens' 'Le Monocle de Mon Oncle,'" *Explicator*, VI (February, 1948), 27.

Geiger, Don, "Wallace Stevens' Wealth," *Perspective*, VII (Autumn, 1954), 155–66.

Gibbs, Barbara, "A Spirit Without a Foyer," *Poetry*, XCII (1958), 52–57—review of *Opus Posthumous*.

Gollin, Richard M., "Wallace Stevens: The Poet in Society," *Colorado Quarterly*, IX (1960), 47–58.

Green, Elizabeth, "The Urbanity of Stevens," *Saturday Review*, XXXIX (August 11, 1956), 11–13.

Gregory, Horace, "An Examination of Wallace Stevens in Time of War," *Accent*, III (Autumn, 1942), 57–61—review of *Parts of a World*.

————, "The Harmonium of Wallace Stevens," *A History of American Poetry, 1900-1940* (New York, 1942), pp. 326–35.

————, "Highly Polished Poetry," *New York Tribune Books* (September 27, 1931), p. 28—review of *Harmonium* 1931.

Hartsock, Mildred E., "Stevens' 'Bantams in Pine-Woods,'" *Explicator*, XVIII (1960), Item 33.

Harvard Advocate, CXXVII (December, 1940), Wallace Stevens issue—containing articles and remarks by Allen Tate, Howard Baker, Cleanth Brooks, Harry Levin, F. O. Matthiessen, John Finch, Delmore Schwartz, Hi Simons, Marianne Moore, Theodore Spencer, William Carlos Williams, Robert Penn Warren, Morton D. Zabel *(see entries under these names)*.

Hatfield, Jerald E., "More About Legend," *Trinity Review*, VIII (May, 1954), 29–31.

Hays, Hoffman R., "Laforgue and Wallace Stevens," *Romantic Review*, XXV (1934), 242–48.

Heath, W. W., "Stevens' 'Certain Phenomena of Sound,'" *Explicator*, XII (1953), Item 16.

Hecht, Anthony, "Poets and Peasants," *Hudson Review*, X (Winter, 1957-58), 606–13—review of *Opus Posthumous*.

Heringman, Bernard, "The Critical Angel," *Kenyon Review*, XIV (Summer, 1952), 520–23—review of *The Necessary Angel*.

————, "The Poetry of Synthesis," *Perspective*, VII (Autumn, 1954), 167–74.

————, "Two Worlds and Epiphany," *Bard Review*, II (May, 1948), 156–59.

————, "Wallace Stevens: The Use of Poetry," *ELH: A Journal of English Literary History*, XVI (1949), 325–36.

Hertzberg, Max, and Stevens, Wallace, "Stevens' 'The Emperor of Ice-Cream,'" *Explicator*, VII (November, 1948), 18.

Historical Review of Berks County, XXIV, No. 4 (Fall, 1959)— Wallace Stevens number, containing contributions (mostly biographical) by Michael Lafferty and Ronald L. Sweitzer (*q.v.*).

Holmes, John, "Five American Poets," *Virginia Quarterly Review,* XII (April, 1936), 288–95—review of *Ideas of Order.*

Hough, Graham, "The Poetry of Wallace Stevens," *Critical Quarterly,* II (1960), 201–18.

Howe, Irving, "Another Way of Looking at the Blackbird," *New Republic,* CXXXVII (November 4, 1957), 16–19—review of *Opus Posthumous.*

Hudson, Deatt, "Wallace Stevens," *Twentieth Century Literature,* I (1955), 135–38.

Hutchinson, Percy, "Pure Poetry and Mr. Wallace Stevens," *New York Times Book Review* (August 9, 1931), p. 4—review of *Harmonium.*

Jack, Peter Munro, in *New York Times Book Review* (January 12, 1936), p. 15—review of *Ideas of Order.*

Jarrell, Randall, "The Collected Poems of Wallace Stevens," *Yale Review,* XLIV (1955), 340–53.

———, "Reflections on Wallace Stevens," *Partisan Review,* XVIII (1951), 335–44; reprinted in *Poetry and the Age* (New York, 1953), pp. 133–48.

Jones, Frank, "The Sorcerer as Elegist," *Nation,* CLV (November 7, 1942), 488—review of *Parts of A World.*

Kammer, A. S., "Wallace Stevens and Christopher Morley," *Furioso,* III (Winter, 1948), 50–58.

Keast, W. R., "Wallace Stevens' 'Thirteen Ways of Looking at a Blackbird,'" *Chicago Review,* VIII (Winter-Spring, 1954), 48–63.

Kees, Weldon, "Parts: But a World," *New Republic,* CVII (September 28, 1942), 387–88—review of *Parts of a World.*

Kirby, J. B., "Stevens' 'Anecdote of the Jar,'" *Explicator,* III (November, 1944), 16.

Koch, Vivienne, "The Necessary Angels of the Earth," *Sewanee Review,* LIX (1951), 664–77—review of *The Auroras of Autumn.*

Kreymborg, Alfred, "An Early Impression of Wallace Stevens," *Trinity Review,* VIII (May, 1954), 12–16.

———, *Our Singing Strength* (New York, 1929), pp. 500–4 on Stevens.

Kuntz, Joseph H.: *see* Arms, George A.

Lafferty, Michael, "Wallace Stevens: A Man of Two Worlds," *Historical Review of Berks County,* XXIV, No. 4 (Fall, 1959), 109–13, 130–32.

Laros, Fred, "Wallace Stevens Today," *Bard Review*, II (Spring, 1947), 8–15.

Larsson, Raymond, "The Beau as Poet," *Commonweal*, XV (April 6, 1932), 640–41—review of *Harmonium*.

Lash, Kenneth, and Thackaberry, Robert, "Stevens' 'The Emperor of Ice-Cream,'" *Explicator*, VI (April, 1948), 36.

Lechlitner, Ruth, "Creative Imagination," *New York Herald Tribune Books* (November 8, 1942), p. 26—review of Parts of a World.

———, "Wallace Stevens' Poetry," *New York Herald Tribune Books* (November 14, 1937), p. 2—review of *The Man With the Blue Guitar*.

Levi, Albert William, "A Note on Wallace Stevens and the Poem of Perspective," *Perspective*, VII (Autumn, 1954), 137–46.

Lowell, Robert, "Imagination and Reality," *The Nation*, CLXVI (April 5, 1947), 400–2—review of *Transport to Summer*.

Martz, Louis L., "Recent Poetry," *Yale Review*, XXXVII (December, 1947), 333–41—review of *Transport to Summer*.

———, "Wallace Stevens: The Romance of the Precise," *Yale Poetry Review*, II (August, 1946), 13–20.

———, "Wallace Stevens: The World as Meditation," *Yale Review*, XLVII (1958), 517–36.

———, "The World of Wallace Stevens," (London), V *Focus* (1950), 94–109.

Matthiessen, F. O., in *New York Times Book Review* (April 20, 1947), pp. 4, 26—review of *Transport to Summer*.

———, "Poetry," *Literary History of the United States*, edited by Robert J. Spiller, et al. (New York, 1948), II, 1354–55.

———, "Society and Solitude in Poetry," *Yale Review*, XXV (1935-36), 603–7—review of *Ideas of Order*.

Mills, Ralph J., Jr., "Wallace Stevens: The Image of the Rock," *Accent*, XVIII (1958), 75–89.

Mizener, Arthur, "Not in Cold Blood," *Kenyon Review*, XIII (1951), 218–25.

Monroe, Harriet, "A Cavalier of Beauty," *Poetry*, XXIII, No. 6 (March, 1924), 322–27.

———, "The Free-Verse Movement in America," *English Journal*, XIII (December, 1924), 691–705.

———, "He Plays with the Present," *Poetry*, XLVII (December, 1935), 153–57—review of *Ideas of Order*.

———, in *Poetry*, XVI (April, 1920), 33–35—account of performance of "Three Travellers Watch a Sunrise."

———, "Wallace Stevens," *Poets and Their Art* (New York, 1926), pp. 39–45.

Moore, Geoffrey, "Wallace Stevens: A Hero of Our Time," *The Great Experiment in American Literature*, edited by Carl Bode (London and New York, 1961), pp. 103–32.

Moore, Marianne, "A Bold Virtuoso," *Predilections* (New York, 1955), pp. 142–46.

————, "There Is a War That Never Ends," *Kenyon Review*, V (Winter, 1943), 144–47—review of *Parts of a World* and *Notes Toward a Supreme Fiction*; reprinted in *Predilections*, pp. 36–41.

————, "Unanimity and Fortitude," *Poetry*, XLIX (February, 1937), 268–72—review of *Owl's Clover* and *Ideas of Order*; reprinted in *Predilections*, pp. 32–36, under the title "Conjuries That Endure."

————, "Well Moused, Lion," *Dial*, LXXVI (January, 1924), 84–91—review of *Harmonium*.

————, "The World Imagined . . . Since We Are Poor," *Poetry New York*, No. 4 (1951)—review of *The Auroras of Autumn*.

Moorman, Charles, "Stevens' 'Six Significant Landscapes,' " *Explicator*, XVII (1958), Item 1.

Morse, Samuel French, "Agenda: A Note on Some Uncollected Poems," *Trinity Review*, VIII (May, 1954), 32–34.

————, "The Native Element," *Kenyon Review*, XX (1958), 446–65.

————, "A Note on the 'Adagia,' " *Poetry*, XC (1957), 45–46.

————, "A Poet Who Speaks the Poem as It Is," *New York Times Book Review* (October 3, 1954), p. 31—review of *Collected Poems*.

————, "Wallace Stevens: Some Ideas About the Thing Itself," *Boston University Studies in English*, II (1956), 55–64.

Munson, Gorham, "The Dandyism of Wallace Stevens," *Dial*, LXXIX (1925), 413–17; reprinted in *Destinations* (New York, 1928), pp. 75–89.

Nash, Ralph, "About 'The Emperor of Ice-Cream,' " *Perspective*, VII (Autumn, 1954), 122–24.

————, "Wallace Stevens and the Point of Change," *Perspective*, VII (Autumn, 1954), 113–21.

Nemerov, Howard, "The Poetry of Wallace Stevens," *Sewanee Review*, LXV (1957), 1–14.

New York Times (October 22, 1917), p. 13, col. 2—review of performance of "Carlos Among the Candles."

New York Tribune (October 23, 1917)—review of "Carlos Among the Candles."

Nichols, Lewis, "Talk with Mr. Stevens," *New York Times Book Review* (October 3, 1954) pp. 3, 31—biographical.

Nims, J. F., *Poetry: A Critical Supplement* (October, 1947), pp. 7–9.

O'Connor, William Van, in *Poetry*, LXXVII (November, 1950), 109–12—review of *The Auroras of Autumn*.

———, "The Politics of a Poet," *Perspective*, I (Summer, 1948), 206–9.

———, "Tension and Structure in Poetry," *Sewanee Review*, LI (Autumn, 1943), 557–60.

———, "A Vessel on the Open Sea," *Poetry*, LXXXI (November, 1952), 139–43—review of reissue of *The Man With the Blue Guitar*.

———, "Wallace Stevens and Imagined Reality," *Western Review*, XII (Spring, 1948), 156–63.

———, "Wallace Stevens on 'The Poems of Our Climate'" *University of Kansas City Review*, XV (Winter, 1948), 105–10.

Olson, Elder, "The Poetry of Wallace Stevens," *College English*, XVI (1955), 395–402.

Owen, David H. " 'The Glass of Water,' " *Perspective*, VII (Autumn, 1954), 175–83.

Pack, Robert, "The Abstracting Imagination of Wallace Stevens: Nothingness and the Hero," *Arizona Quarterly*, XI (1955), 197–209.

———, "Wallace Stevens: The Secular Mystery and the Comic Spirit," *Western Review*, XX (1955), 51–62.

Pauker, John, "A Discussion of 'Sea Surface Full of Clouds,' " *Furioso*, V (Fall, 1950), 34–46.

Pearce, Roy Harvey, "Stevens Posthumous," *International Literary Annual*, II (London, 1959), 65–89.

———, "Wallace Stevens: The Life of the Imagination," *Publications of the Modern Language Association of America*, LXVI (1951), 561–82.

Pearson, Norman Holmes, "Wallace Stevens and 'Old Higgs,' " *Trinity Review*, VIII (May, 1954), 35–36.

Perspective, VII (Autumn, 1954), Wallace Stevens issue—containing contributions by Donald Davie, Guy Davenport, Don Geiger, Bernard Heringman, Albert William Levi, Ralph Nash, and David H. Owen *(see entries under these names)*.

Powys, Llewelyn, "The Thirteenth Way," *Dial*, LXXVII (July, 1924), 45–50.

Quinn, M. Bernetta, "Wallace Stevens," *The Metamorphic Tradition in Modern Poetry* (New Brunswick, N. J., 1955), pp. 49–88.

Ramsey, Warren, "Wallace Stevens and Some French Poets," *Trinity Review*, VIII (May, 1954), 36–40.

Ransom, John Crowe, "Poets Without Laurels," *The World's Body* (New York, 1938), pp. 55–75.

Riddel, Joseph N., " 'Disguised Pronunciamento': Wallace Stevens' 'Sea Surface Full of Clouds,' " *Texas Studies in English*, XXXVII (1958), 177–86.

——, " 'Poets' Politics'—Wallace Stevens' 'Owl's Clover,' " *Modern Philology*, LVI (1958), 118–32.

Rizzardi, Alfredo, "Creazione e Distruzione del Mondo Fantastico di Wallace Stevens," *Nuova Corrente* (Genoa), I (January, 1955), 186–97.

——, "Poesia di Wallace Stevens," *Galleria* (Italy), IV (1954), 371–75.

Roethke, Theodore, *New Republic*, LXXXVII (July 15, 1936), 305—review of *Ideas of Order*.

Rosenfeld, Paul, "Wallace Stevens," *Men Seen* (New York, 1925), pp. 151–62.

Rosenthal, M. L., *The Modern Poets: A Critical Introduction* (New York, 1960), pp. 121–31.

——, "Stevens in a Minor Key," *New Republic*, CXXIV (May 7, 1951), 26–28—review of *The Auroras of Autumn*.

Schwartz, Delmore, "Instructed of Much Mortality," *Sewanee Review*, LIV (1946), 439–49.

——, "The Ultimate Plato with Picasso's Guitar," *Harvard Advocate*, CXXVII (December, 1940), 11–16.

Seiffert, M. A., "The Intellectual Tropics," *Poetry*, XXIII (December, 1923), 154–60.

Sellin, Eric, "Stevens' 'The Glass of Water,' " *Explicator*, XVII (1959), Item 28.

Silverstein, Norman, "Stevens' 'Of Hartford in a Purple Light,' " *Explicator*, XVIII (1959), Item 20.

Simons, Hi, " 'The Comedian as the Letter C': Its Sense and Its Significance," *Southern Review*, V (Winter, 1940), 453–68.

——, "The Genre of Wallace Stevens," *Sewanee Review*, LIII (Autumn, 1945), 566–79.

——, "The Humanism of Wallace Stevens," *Poetry*, LXI (November, 1942), 448–52.

——, "The Vicissitudes of a Reputation," *Harvard Advocate*, CXXVII (December, 1940), 8–10, 34–44.

——, "Wallace Stevens and Mallarmé," *Modern Philology*, XLIII (1946), 235–59.

Smith, William J., "Modern Poetry: Texture and Text," *Shenandoah*, VI (1955), 6–16.

Southworth, J. G., "Wallace Stevens," *Some Modern American Poets* (Oxford, 1950) pp. 88–106.

Spector, Robert Donald, "Stevens's 'Earthly Anecdote': Introduction to a Collection," *History of Ideas Newsletter*, V, ii (1959), 36–38.

Spencer, Theodore, "The Poetry of Wallace Stevens: An Evaluation," *Harvard Advocate*, CXXVII (December, 1940), 26–29.

Stallknecht, Newton P., "Absence in Reality: A Study in the Epistemology of The Blue Guitar," *Kenyon Review*, XXI (1959), 545–62.

Stauffer, Donald, "The *Mesures* Lectures," *Kenyon Review*, IV (1942), 411–15—review of *The Language of Poetry*, which includes Stevens' "The Noble Rider and the Sound of Words."

Stocking, F. H., "Stevens' 'Bantams in Pine-Woods,'" *Explicator*, III (April, 1945), 45.

———, "Stevens' 'The Comedian as the Letter C,'" *Explicator*, III (March, 1945), 43.

———, "Stevens' 'The Ordinary Women,'" *Explicator*, IV (October, 1945), 4.

———, "Stevens' 'Peter Quince at the Clavier,'" *Explicator*, V (May, 1947), 47.

Storm, M. J., "Stevens' 'Peter Quince at the Clavier,'" *Explicator*, XIV (1954), Item 9.

Straumann, Heinrich, "Der Mann mit der blauen Gitarre: Zum Tode des Amerikanischen Dichters Wallace Stevens (1879-1955)," *Neue Zürcher Zeitung* (August 14, 1955), unnumbered.

Sutherland, Donald, "An Observation on Wallace Stevens in Connection with Supreme Fictions," *Trinity Review*, VIII (May, 1954), 41–42.

Sweeney, John L., "The Stevens Athenaeum," *Trinity Review*, VIII (May, 1954), 42–43.

Sweitzer, Ronald L., "Wallace Stevens: Advocate of the Imagination," *Historical Review of Berks County*, XXIV, No. 4 (Fall, 1959), 117–29.

Symons, Julian, "A Short View of Wallace Stevens," *Life and Letters Today* (London), XXVI (1940), 215–24.

———, "Stevens in England," *Trinity Review*, VIII (May, 1954), 43–45.

Sypher, Wylie, "Connoisseur in Chaos: Wallace Stevens," *Partisan Review*, XIII (1946), 83–94.

Tate, Allen, "American Poetry since 1920," *Bookman*, LXVIII (January, 1929), 503–8.

Taupin, René, *L'Influence du Symbolisme Français sur la Poésie Américaine* (Paris, 1929), pp. 276–77, *passim*.

Tejera, Victor, "Wallace Stevens' 'Transport to Summer,' " *Journal of Philosophy*, XLV (February 26, 1948), 137–39.

Thackaberry, Robert: *see* Lash, Kenneth.

Time Magazine, XXX (November 1, 1937), 81–82—review of *The Man with the Blue Guitar*.

——, "Prize Pies," LVII (September 25, 1950) 106, 108, 110— review of *The Auroras of Autumn*.

Times Literary Supplement (London), (June 19, 1953), p. 397— review of *Selected Poems*.

Trinity Review (Hartford, Conn.), VIII (May, 1954), "A Celebration for Wallace Stevens"—containing tributes in verse and prose, including articles by Louise Bogan, F. Cudworth Flint, Jerald E. Hatfield, Alfred Kreymborg, Samuel French Morse, Norman Holmes Pearson, Warren Ramsey, Donald Sutherland, John L. Sweeney, Julian Symons, Peter Viereck *(see entries under these names)*, et. al.

Untermeyer, Louis, *The New Era in American Poetry* (New York, 1919), *passim*.

——, *American Poetry Since 1900* (New York, 1923), pp. 323–28.

——, "Five American Poets," *Yale Review*, XIV (October, 1924), 156–61—review of *Harmonium*.

——, "The Ivory Tower—II," *New Republic*, XIX (May 10, 1919), 60–61. (*See also* Aiken, Conrad.)

Vance, Will, "Wallace Stevens: Man Off the Street," *Saturday Review of Literature*, XXIX (March 23, 1946), 8—biographical.

Van Doren, Mark, "Poets and Wits," *Nation*, CXVII (October 10, 1923), 400, 402—review of *Harmonium*.

Van Ghent, Dorothy, *New Masses* (January 11, 1938), pp. 41–46 —review of *The Man with the Blue Guitar*.

Viereck, Peter, "Some Notes on Wallace Stevens," *Contemporary Poetry*, VII (Winter, 1948), 14–15.

——, "Some Notes on Wallace Stevens," *Trinity Review*, VIII (May, 1954), 45–46.

Violette, John M.: *see* Culbert, Taylor.

Wagner, C. Roland, "A Central Poetry," *Hudson Review*, V (Spring, 1952), 144–48—review of *The Necessary Angel*.

——, "The Idea of Nothingness in Wallace Stevens," *Accent*, XII (Spring, 1952), 111–21.

Walton, Eda Lou, in *New York Times Book Review* (October 24, 1937), p. 5—review of *The Man With the Blue Guitar*.

Watts, Harold H., "Wallace Stevens and the Rock of Summer," *Kenyon Review*, XIV (1952), 122–40.

Weiss, T., "The Nonsense of Winters' Anatomy," *Quarterly Review of Literature*, I (Spring, 1944), 212–34—defense of Stevens against Winters' criticism.

Whittemore, Reed, "Five Old Masters and Their Sensibilities" *Yale Review*, XLII (1957), 281–88—review of *Opus Posthumous*.

Williams, William Carlos, in *New Republic*, XCIII (November 17, 1937), 50—review of *The Man with the Blue Guitar*.

———, "Poet of a Steadfast Pattern," *New York Times Book Review* (August 18, 1957), p. 6—review of *Opus Posthumous*.

———, "Wallace Stevens," *Poetry*, LXXXVII (1956), pp. 234–239.

Wilson, Edmund, "Wallace Stevens and E. E. Cummings," *New Republic*, XXXVIII (March 19, 1924), 102–3—review of *Harmonium*.

Winters, Yvor, "The Hedonist's Progress," *The Anatomy of Nonsense* (Norfolk, Conn., 1943), pp. 88–119; reprinted in *In Defense of Reason* (New York, 1947), pp. 431–59. (Cf. Weiss, T.)

———, "Poetic Styles, Old and New," in *Four Poets on Poetry*, edited by Don Cameron Allen (Baltimore, 1959).

———, *Primitivism and Decadence* (New York, 1937), *passim*.

Zabel, Morton Dauwen, "The Harmonium of Wallace Stevens," *Poetry*, XXXIX (December, 1931), 148–54.

———, "Stevens and the Image of Man," *Harvard Advocate*, CXXVII (December, 1940), 19–23.

———, "Two Years of Poetry: 1937-1939," *Southern Review*, V (Winter, 1940), 568–608.

Zolla, Flémire, "Nota sur Wallace Stevens," *Letterature Moderne*, VI (1956), 213–15.